Selling
Professional
Services *to**the*
Fortune 500

GARY S. LUEFSCHUETZ

New York   Chicago   San Francisco   Lisbon   London   Madrid   Mexico City
Milan   New Delhi   San Juan   Seoul   Singapore   Sydney   Toronto

Library of Congress Cataloging-in-Publication Data

Luefschuetz, Gary S.
    Selling professional services to the Fortune 500 : how to win in the billion-dollar market of strategy consulting, technology solutions, and outsourcing services / by Gary S. Luefschuetz.
        p.   cm.
    ISBN 978-0-07-162282-0
    1. Professions—United States—Marketing.   2. Service industries—United States—Marketing.   3. Business consultants—United States.
4. Contracting out—United States.   I. Title.

    HD8038.U5L84   2010
    001—dc22
                                    2009031992

1 2 3 4 5 6 7 8 9 10 11 12   WFR/WFR   1 9 8 7 6 5 4 3 2 1 0

ISBN   978-0-07-162282-0
MHID   0-07-162282-9

Interior illustrations by Glyph International

McGraw-Hill books are available at special quantity discounts to use as premiums and sales promotions or for use in corporate training programs. To contact a representative, please e-mail us at bulksales@mcgraw-hill.com.

This book is dedicated to the memory of my father, Karl Luefschuetz. He had a true passion for life and was a respected leader and role model both personally and professionally. One of my childhood dreams was to make my father proud of me, and to this day I aspire to make that dream a reality. Unfortunately, the most important lesson he taught me was how short and precious life truly is. I only wish we had been given more time together.

Contents

Part 3 Negotiating Terms and Conditions with the Fortune 500

Part 4 Procurement and Pricing

Part 5 The Competitive Landscape

Part 6 Closing the Deal and Staying Relevant

Introduction

"In chaos comes opportunity." A colleague of mine shared this quote with me some time ago. She was not sure of its origin, but we were both quite confident that the terms "chaos" and "opportunity" certainly apply to the current state of the global economy. As I write this introduction, I reflect on the financial roller-coaster and unprecedented events we have experienced since fall 2008, many of which I never thought I would witness in my lifetime. Specifically, the Dow Jones Industrial Average lost some 2,000 points in a three-week period, including the largest single-day point drop and daily swing since the Dow was introduced in 1896, and some $8.4 trillion in paper losses have been racked up by investors in U.S. stocks (much of it in retirement accounts). As if that were not enough, unemployment in the United States has skyrocketed to over 10 percent with over 2.5 million jobs lost in 2008 (the most since 1945), gas prices have fluctuated dramatically, and the subprime mortgage crisis has in effect crippled the global economy. The subprime mortgage crisis has left many casualties in its wake, including thousands of homeowners who entered into subprime loans and were unable to meet their mortgage obligations, and a number of major and believed-to-be-impregnable financial institutions that traded in complex derivative securities tied to rapidly deteriorating real estate assets. The scary part is that the end to this E-ticket ride is still quite uncertain, and it is unclear what danger might be lurking around the next corner.

And that corner could be pretty much anywhere around the globe. While the subprime mortgage debacle was clearly U.S.-centric, the global economy continues to experience a significant level of chaos, and the impact is no more evident than in the European Union, where unemployment is greater than 9 percent, where the International Monetary

Fund predicts a 2 percent decline in the overall economy, where European Union companies have some $800 billion in debt on their balance sheets, and where the United Kingdom, Ireland, Germany, Spain, France, and Italy may likely realize negative growth in 2009.

Combine this with the fact that the credit markets have essentially frozen and that governments around the world have been forced to step in and bail out many of their largest and most iconic institutions in an effort to prevent the collapse of their financial systems, and it appears quite clear that we are witnessing a fundamental shift in the foundation of the global economy. The U.S. government has certainly taken the lead with this approach, as it has in effect taken over Freddie Mac and Fannie Mae, has orchestrated a $700 billion-plus bailout package to buy what are believed to be toxic mortgage assets, and has made substantial equity investments in major U.S. banks and automobile manufacturers in an effort to stop the bleeding and to prevent imminent—or to facilitate structured— bankruptcy. When you compound these circumstances with the fact that IPO activity has decreased significantly, that the venture funding spigot has been tightened considerably, that corporate earnings across many indus- tries and bellwether companies are weak at best, that consumer confidence is extremely low, and that retail sales have fallen significantly, you can quickly conclude that we are in the middle of what could be a rather long and protracted recession. While we might begin to see signs of recovery in the near term, this chain of events and the perfect storm it yielded will impact every aspect of the global economy for the foreseeable future.

Despite all of this chaos, there are still a few shining stars in the econ- omy that are delivering strong financial results from operations, cultivating new opportunities and building robust pipelines, refining service offerings and solutions to meet the demands of the ever-changing landscape, and delivering solutions for their clients in a timely, quality, and cost-effective manner. You might guess that the sector most immune to the economic crisis would be technology companies, given their strong cash reserves; limited borrowing; multiple revenue streams from license, maintenance, and consulting revenue; and the fact that their products are so intertwined with powering mission-critical functions within their client base.

However, this is not the case. A number of software companies, includ- ing enterprise resource planning leader SAP, have announced that their pipelines have been detrimentally impacted and that their 2009 full-year sales numbers for both software and services may fall short of guidance, given customer decisions to postpone new projects and defer investments in new applications. So who, you might ask, is best positioned to weather the storm? While no industry is going to be immune from an economic crisis, the group that appears to be best positioned is management consulting and IT services firms that provide strategy, operations management, human resources, information technology and outsourcing, and business advisory services to their Fortune 500 and education and government client base.

Consider the fact that during the week of October 6, 2008, the Dow Jones Industrial Average remarkably fell 369.88, 508.39, 189.01, 678.91, and 128 points, the worst week in its 112-year history, with its most volatile day ever. Compare that with the fact that on Wednesday of that same week, IT service provider IBM announced that it realized strong earnings with third quarter 2008 net income up some 20 percent from the year-ago third quarter and that it expected to achieve 22 percent earnings growth for the full year (they actually achieved 24 percent earnings growth over the prior year). Add to this the fact that just two weeks prior, management consulting firm Accenture reported a quarterly profit that beat analysts' expectations, record bookings of $7.67 billion in the quarter, and double-digit growth across all operating groups and geographies. Accenture Chief Executive William Green said that while financial institutions account for around 20 percent of its overall business, the recent crisis posed opportunities as well as challenges. "We're working hard in this environment—it's challenging and it's changing. Many companies are being forced to reinvent themselves, and seeking Accenture's expertise in helping companies transform into more efficient organizations." In addition to the earnings reported by both IBM and Accenture during that period, Booz & Company's CEO Shumeet Banerji commented in a *Consulting Magazine* interview in June 2008 that the company's "global commercial business has been growing at a rate of about 20 percent per year." He goes on to state that "clearly, something is working in our strategy. Do the math, if we keep that up for four years, we'll double the capacity of the business."

The strong results from operations achieved by IBM, Accenture, and Booz & Company during this highly volatile time period are partially attributable to the fact that management consulting firms and IT services providers, given their backlog of sold work, tend to lag behind the overall health of the global economy. Despite whatever detrimental impact they may have experienced, it is a very safe bet that during this economic chaos, the leaders within each of the major management consulting firms and IT services providers were focused upon tailoring their respective service offerings to address the opportunities and challenges their clients will face and upon devising a strategy to capture the revenue stream associated with them.

The market conditions that I have described are simply a snapshot of a global economy that is experiencing extreme levels of volatility. That snapshot will absolutely look quite different by the time you read the words on this page. As a consummate optimist, I can only hope that by the time you open this book the effects of the global economic crisis we are currently experiencing will have subsided and that the outlook will be much brighter. But even if that is the case, I assure you that some other form of chaos will enter the mix, and it will be critical for all management consulting firms and IT services providers to adapt to the rapidly changing environment, stay relevant to their clients, maintain their trusted advisor status, overcome any sales and delivery obstacles, and close new business opportunities, irrespective of any underlying chaos in the market.

In a December 2008 interview in *Fortune Magazine*, IBM Chairman, President, and Chief Executive Officer Sam Palmisano was asked about the global financial crisis we are currently experiencing. His response might surprise you. Rather than focusing on IBM's strategy to weather the storm, Palmisano stated, "We've been given this on a silver platter. We might as well use it as an opportunity." He goes on to say, "In the face of a meltdown, you can retrench, pull in your horns, protect the balance sheet, and preserve cash. Or you can realize that this is about humanity screaming for change." It is with this spirit that Palmisano has positioned IBM as a leader in infrastructure overhaul focused on creating intelligent networks in such critical infrastructure areas as energy, health care, air quality, and traffic congestion.

The specifics of the IBM service offerings are not important. What is important is the head-on approach that IBM has taken to find opportunities in the absolute chaos the world is currently facing in these critical areas. As Palmisano states, "These are global issues and huge opportunities. Someone has to step out and take the lead." The approach that has been undertaken by IBM and a select group of its competitors that have weathered and will continue to weather this perfect storm is emulated in a January 2009 *Fortune* interview with Jim Collins, the author of *Built to Last* and *Good to Great*. When asked how companies manage through a crisis, he likened it to his passion, mountain climbing. "As a rock climber, the one thing you learn is that those who panic die on the mountain. You don't just sit on the mountain. You either go up or go down, but don't just sit and wait to get clobbered. If you go down and survive, you can come back another day. You have to ask the question, 'what can we do not just to survive but to turn this into a defining point in history?'"

Commenting on the state of the economy in the European Union in a March 2009 *Consulting Magazine* article, Burkhard Schwenker, the CEO of strategy consulting firm Roland Berger, stated, "For the first time, we are experiencing global financial and economic crises simultaneously." Although Schwenker clearly acknowledged the impact of the financial crisis across Western Europe, he, like most strategy consultants, shifted his focus to the future. He stated, "Every crisis is also an opportunity; it forces businesses to be creative and to renew themselves. This is true for our clients as well as for our own company."

To drive this point home, I will defer to Charles Darwin, who said it best: "It is not the strongest of the species that survive, nor the most intelligent, but the one most responsive to change."

The bottom line is that firms like Booz & Company, McKinsey & Company, Bain & Company, The Boston Consulting Group, Roland Berger, Accenture, IBM, Deloitte, HP, and others will continue to seek out new opportunities and realize strong growth in the midst of this or any other crisis despite the underlying chaos the crisis may bring to the market and their respective client bases.

Their abilities to seek out opportunities and adapt to rapidly changing market conditions are critical given the significant size of the opportunities and pipeline they are chasing. Kennedy Information estimates that the global consulting market slightly exceeded $300 billion in 2008. Combine that with the Gartner Group's estimate that the worldwide outsourcing services market grew over 8 percent in 2008 to some $443 billion (forecast to reach $518 billion in 2013), and you have quite a large market with which to expand your delivery footprint, create brand awareness, develop new products and services and a corresponding reference base, and build a robust sales pipeline. The current economic climate will certainly impact consulting and outsourcing spending within the Fortune 500 buying community. However, I believe the overall reduction in spend will be minimal and that Fortune 500 companies will simply become more prudent consumers of these services across the entire delivery spectrum as they target their spend in a more laser-like fashion on engagements that will yield tactical revenue growth and increased operational efficiencies. We will dive into more of the details regarding the market and its various segments later, but the bottom line is that the market is robust and offers substantial long-term growth opportunities.

Given the size of the market, it might seem as if there is plenty of opportunity just for the asking; unfortunately, that is not necessarily the case. As previously discussed, the market for management consulting and information technology design and implementation services has realized and will continue to achieve sustained growth for the foreseeable future. In accordance with this trend, sales pipelines are robust, profitability is on the rise, average transaction sizes are increasing, discounting is prevalent but limited in size, and price increases have been a recurring theme and are looming on the horizon, irrespective of the economic chaos that has impacted most commercial industries. This was reinforced in a poll conducted by *Consulting Magazine*, reported in their March/April 2009 issue, which reflected that 52 percent of respondents were holding their rates steady, that 14 percent were increasing rates, and that the remaining 34 percent were discounting by anywhere from 5 percent to 20 percent.

However, despite this positive outlook and the myriad new opportunities it will bring, competition is nearing an all-time high. The pipeline of opportunities has brought new providers to the market that are eager to build brand awareness and a reference base, and they are willing to make investments in the form of offering deeply discounted rates and accepting contractual terms that yield an uneven allocation of risk and reward to achieve these objectives. In addition, many of the services delivered across the consulting lifecycle are viewed as commodities by aggressive client procurement organizations that heavily influence the buying process; ultimately, this results in price becoming the discriminating factor for many large and complex engagements. When you compound the number of individuals who can influence a transaction with the current trend to centralize procurement and leverage global purchasing power, the desire to streamline the supplier base with fewer "preferred" vendors, the aggressive new market entrants, and the ever-present downward pricing pressure, the landscape can certainly become quite competitive and difficult to navigate.

To effectively sell services in this environment, it is critical to build strong and trusted advisor relationships with all parties that influence the sales process. To be successful, it is important for service providers to influence the decision makers at all hierarchical levels across the organization in which their products and services are being positioned. In 2004, in conjunction with Aspatore Books (now Thomson West), I published the *Art and Science of Negotiating Professional Services Agreements*. The purpose of this book was to provide practical guidance to service providers, service receivers, subcontractors, and independent contractors to help them navigate through and negotiate human capital agreements to their advantage. Ultimately, this means finding some middle ground that yields an acceptable level of risk and reward for both parties to the transaction. The counsel offered in that book assumed that the readers had made their way through the sales cycle and were in the process of negotiating the terms and conditions that would govern the transaction.

However, making the jump from the sales process—whether it is driven through a request for proposal process, noncompetitive award, or other means—to the negotiating table can be quite challenging. I assure you that finding the way to the negotiation table within a Fortune 500 client is not always an easy path to follow; it is typically blocked with a number of substantial obstacles that must be traversed, and the current dynamics within the industry make it that much more complex.

To that end, this book will focus upon how to effectively sell professional services into Fortune 500 corporations and grab a piece of this highly lucrative market. It will not focus heavily upon sales or negotiation techniques, but rather will serve as a roadmap that will guide readers to the negotiation table and arm them with the knowledge to successfully close the deal. Specifically, this book will review:

- The overall competitive landscape for providing a full suite of services across the consulting lifecycle

- The parties that may exert authority, influence, and impact the viability of the transaction

- The buying trends that currently exist within large global organizations that spend hundreds of millions of dollars annually procuring such services

- The importance and impact that relationships have in the sales process

- The ever-increasing presence, influence, and role of corporate procurement organizations

- The complex dynamics of the negotiation process

- The strategic approach by which you can manage these stakeholders throughout the sales and delivery cycle

During the course of the past seventeen years, I have served in a variety of leadership roles within the government and commercial businesses at Accenture, Booz Allen Hamilton, Unisys, and PeopleSoft. Throughout my career, I have focused on all aspects of selling and delivering professional services with a particular emphasis in the areas of operations, pricing, capture, negotiation, contract management, procurement and strategic sourcing, quality assurance, and risk management. I have established a proven track record as a seasoned commercial negotiator with extensive experience negotiating professional services and technology agreements across the consulting lifecycle within the public sector and across all commercial industries.

During my most recent tenure at Booz Allen, my primary focus was cultivating relationships with procurement executives and executing global master services agreements through which Booz Allen Hamilton could sell its strategy and IT services to Fortune 500 entities. In my current role at Accenture, I am leading operations for a portfolio of Accenture's strategic accounts within its Health and Public Service Operating Group. I have nothing but great things to say about my tenure at Booz Allen Hamilton and Accenture. I believe they are both great companies that have exceptional brand awareness; reputations for delivering their services in a timely, quality, and cost-effective manner; trusted advisor relationships; and a strong reference base of clients in each of the industries and geographies in which they are engaged. Despite my bias, I will make every attempt to remain objective when discussing their roles and positioning in the market.

Throughout this book, I will do my best to bring my practical experience to bear and to share my thoughts and opinions regarding how strategy and IT consulting services are sold to leading companies across the financial services, healthcare, technology and communications, transportation, energy and utilities, consumer and media, and automotive industries. While the focus of this book will be on selling into Fortune 500 clients, I will touch upon selling into the public sector, given the fact that many of the large management consulting firms and IT services providers have undertaken efforts to share best practices between and deliver their service offerings across the public and private sector domain. Throughout, I don't refer to clients by name but only by the industry in which they operate, and all of the pricing, financial data, and market strategy that will be discussed in this book are drawn from publicly available information including General Services Administration Federal Supply Schedules, other publicly available pricelists and information, and SEC filings.

My ultimate objective with this book is to provide practical guidance that will allow you to:

- Gain unique insight into how the major professional services firms sell, price, and deliver their services in the market

- Learn how to effectively negotiate with aggressive corporate procurement organizations

- Develop negotiation and pricing strategies that will help your organization capture its share of the corporate consulting wallet

- Avoid having your service offerings treated like commodities

- Master the art of becoming a preferred vendor and successfully negotiating global master services agreements with multiple rate cards that distinguish premium service offerings

- Execute master services agreements that yield an acceptable level of risk and reward for both parties to the transaction

- Develop pricing structures that are commensurate with the nature of the services being provided and competitive with other vendors in the marketplace

- Know when to tell and be comfortable with telling procurement organizations "No"

- Be aware of potential pitfalls in the pricing and negotiation process

Now, let's begin by focusing on the global consulting market and delivery landscape.

Part

I

Selling Professional Services to Fortune 500 Companies

I

Understanding the Consulting Services Market and Delivery Landscape

At a macro level, the global consulting market consists of a wide variety of service offerings that span two major domains—*management* consulting and *information technology* (IT) consulting. There are many ways to segment the market beneath these two major domains. Management consulting is typically broken down into three additional focus areas: strategy, operations management, and human resources. The information technology domain can be broken down into four discrete phases: strategy and analysis, design, implementation, and operation.

In terms of understanding the market itself, it is critical to understand that there is a fairly strong line of demarcation across these two major domains, which ultimately differentiates the leading service providers, the substance of services being provided, the engagement profile that includes the leverage model (ratio of senior to junior staff), the skills and experience of the deployed staff, and the rate structure associated with delivery. While many organizations have tried to straddle the boundary and provide full consulting lifecycle services, few have achieved this objective.

I like to think of the market a little bit differently and very simplistically. I believe three major activities occur in the overall consulting lifecycle, which ranges from strategy development through implementation. Those three categories are *think, build,* and *run.*

Lifecycle Phases: Think, Build, and Run

These three categories will determine the delivery profile including the team size and engagement duration, the team composition and capabilities, the leverage model, the rate structure, and the service providers capable of delivery. In my experience, most Fortune 500 entities tend to group the *build* and *run* components together and to draw a very thick protective box around those organizations that will provide *think* services to their C-suite and extended leadership teams.

Think is pretty clear on its face; it refers to the phase of the lifecycle in which the underlying corporate, business unit, acquisition, sourcing, supply chain, IT, or other strategy is developed by working with client management to help set their agendas, solve critical business problems, and help them evaluate their most promising opportunities in the marketplace. This type of work requires rapidly understanding and resolving business issues by using a variety of business strategy, diagnostic and market, and economic analysis skills. The think portion of an engagement is relatively short in duration and is typically staffed by a small team with extensive industry and domain expertise.

Because of the importance of the think component of the lifecycle, the team itself will typically be drawn from a global roster of staff in an effort to bring the most qualified resources to bear. In addition, the think team will usually be senior in tenure and hierarchical level, will typically have MBAs or other advanced degrees, and will draw from their organization's proprietary frameworks, industry models, and robust bank of intellectual capital to develop their solution. For these reasons, "think" resources tend to command hourly rates much greater than any other resources that will be deployed during the entire consulting lifecycle.

Examples of "think" engagements would include general business strategy, manufacturing and supply chain strategy, pre and post merger analysis, geographic strategy and globalization, corporate competitor and market analysis, corporate capital and financial structure, corporate organization design and strategy, acquisition and divestment identification, sourcing strategy, IT architecture strategy, corporate performance management, and corporate partnerships, alliances, and joint ventures. Four primary competitors provide think/strategy services to Fortune 500 entities: The Boston Consulting Group (BCG), Bain & Company (Bain), Booz & Company, formerly Booz Allen Hamilton's Global Commercial Market Business (Booz), and McKinsey & Company (McKinsey).

As mentioned previously, think/strategy engagements are evidenced by rates that run from approximately $250 per hour for a recent MBA graduate to over $1,000 per hour for a senior executive/partner/director. Strategy services are very much a relationship-based sale, and there tends to be rate structure parity across the four major strategy providers.

As I mentioned previously, the primary providers of pure corporate strategy consulting services are BCG, Bain, Booz, and McKinsey. Overall, strategy services make up approximately 10 percent of the global consulting market, or roughly $30 billion in 2008. Among the four of them, I would estimate that they have previously provided or are currently providing high-end strategy services to 100 percent of the Fortune 200 and most likely 75 percent of the Fortune 500. Typically, a partner or director in one of these firms will build a relationship with and become a trusted advisor to the board of directors, CEO, or executive management team and will provide all strategy services until there is a change in leadership. Although we will dive much more deeply into the actual substance of these services, suffice it to say that corporate strategy services are typically contracted directly with the CEO on a noncompetitive basis, can be sizeable in amount, tend to be outside the purview of anyone in the procurement organization (procurement), have extensive senior executive involvement and a corresponding lower leverage model throughout delivery, are not subject to extensive price negotiation, are in some cases a line item in the annual budget, and are generally exclusively provided by one party.

The bottom line is that the strategy provider is pretty much sacrosanct when it comes to procurement process and price reasonableness. A former colleague of mine once told me that as a director for one of the major firms just identified, he had developed a longstanding trusted advisor relationship with the CEO of a financial services company where he and his team were the exclusive providers of strategy services. For a specific engagement that he was positioning with the CEO, he looked him directly in the eye and said, "The cost for the engagement will be $1 million. And that is my cost; my team is free." This is an extreme and humorous example, but it serves to epitomize the delivery of high-end strategy services, which are sold primarily on a relationship basis and are exempt from the much more rigid procurement process associated with build and run engagements.

Build and run, which are also commonly referred to as design and implementation engagements, follow the strategy/think phase of the lifecycle and are focused upon transforming strategic direction into action by developing conceptual designs, blueprinting transformative solutions, and successfully implementing them across the client organization. These engagements typically include (1) advising clients on developing a design of operations for future state capabilities and (2) determining a transformation roadmap or implementation plan to move the client to a desired future state. Typical engagements include projects involving processes, systems, project management, change management, and implementation services.

Build and run engagements are typically much longer in duration than a strategy engagement, and the range of skills required for these engagements is functionally based. As a result, teams can be quite large and can consist of staff from a variety of disciplines. These types of engagements are typically led by a project director who manages a large team of junior staff. Given the functional nature of the work, the staffing model tends to be more locally based with consultants working where they live. Because of the nature of these services, these types of engagements are typically staffed by individuals who command much lower rates than their think/strategy counterparts. The range will vary depending upon the opportunity, but a good rule of thumb is that the average hourly rate across a build or run engagement will decrease as the substance of the services being provided progresses farther to the right (closer to implementation) in the engagement lifecycle. In sharp contrast to a strategy engagement, the rate structure for a build and run engagement may range from as low as $75 an hour for entry-level resources to anywhere from an hourly rate of $300 to $500 for more senior project directors and subject matter experts.

The design and implementation domain, which accounts for the other 70 percent of the global consulting market, is much more heavily populated from a competitor set perspective and includes firms such as Accenture, Capgemini, CSC, Unisys, IBM, Booz Allen Hamilton, Deloitte, Lockheed Martin, SAIC, and many other niche providers that focus on either the commercial or public sector markets. In addition, many of the companies whose applications would be implemented in a build and run phase, such as Oracle and SAP, have built robust services organizations that are a major part of the competitive landscape as well. Examples of build and run engagements would include large-scale program management; business process redesign; change management planning and execution; IT architecture and infrastructure planning; IT supply including sourcing, vendor management, and service level agreements; the implementation and rollout of software and other technology solutions; and supply chain optimization.

Although we will discuss it in much greater detail later, a major distinguishing factor between strategy and design/implementation engagements is the level of procurement involvement in the sales process. Historically, procurement organizations within Fortune 500 entities were extremely decentralized and played a very limited role in the procurement process for consulting services. This resulted in business unit or geography leadership with complete autonomy over their consulting budget. However, over the past few years, a fundamental change has occurred in the manner by which the overwhelming majority of Fortune 500 companies procure consulting services. They have undertaken significant restructuring efforts to centralize procurement in an effort to optimize their global consulting spend and share best practices among operating entities. This trend has resulted in a tremendous amount of downward pricing pressure being placed on vendors trying to sell design and implementation services to the Fortune 500 buying community. Unlike strategy engagements, these types of services are very price sensitive, are treated as commodities by many procurement organizations, are subject to rigorous request for proposal processes and to influence by procurement officials, may be limited to a set of preferred vendors who hold a master services agreement, and tend to be much less influenced by relationships during the sales cycle.

Which Path Is Right for You?
Picking Your Sweet Spot

Given the size of the global consulting market and the wide range of delivery opportunities, it might seem like a viable option to build staff capabilities and to sell and deliver services across the think, build, and run components of the lifecycle. While this seems like a great idea, it is much easier said than done. Just like choosing a major in college, most professional services firms develop a delivery footprint and corresponding set of sweet spots within either the commercial or government market under which they will capitalize and structure their organization; hire staff with the requisite industry, domain, or functional expertise; establish brand awareness; develop a pricing model; deliver quality products and services; develop a bank of intellectual capital; and build a strong reference base.

A number of organizations have made attempts to and currently deliver a blended set of services that span the commercial and government markets as well as the strategy and design/implementation domains including Accenture, IBM, Deloitte, and Booz Allen Hamilton. Even the high-end strategy firms of McKinsey and BCG have attempted to make inroads into the public sector market, which is evidenced by their executing agreements under the General Services Administration (GSA) MOBIS (Mission Oriented Business Integrated Services) contract vehicle, which would facilitate their sale of consulting services to the U.S. federal government.

Attaining a successful blended delivery model is highly desirable, as it allows for an extremely compelling value proposition that is appealing to clients for the following reasons:

- The client can rely upon one provider for strategy development and the ensuing design and implementation of the programs, initiatives, or technology required to achieve the future desired state as articulated in the strategy plan.

- The client's ability to rely upon one provider will result in a seamless handoff between the strategy and design/implementation teams without any substantial knowledge loss typically realized during the transition.

- The client can count upon the services provider to deliver staff with industry, functional, and domain expertise that is commensurate with the nature of the services being provided and tailored to the appropriate phase in the lifecycle.

- The client will be able to negotiate a dual rate structure that is commensurate with the nature of the services being provided and priced competitively with other vendors in the marketplace.

- Given this blended services construct, the client will not be paying think/strategy rates for build/design and run/implementation work. To the extent that a master services agreement exists, a dual-rate structure based upon the nature of the services being provided will yield a clear approach that can be easily utilized by the broader buying community for similarly situated engagements in the future.

Although this approach and the value proposition it embodies is quite strong and typically very well received by Fortune 500 clients, it can be quite challenging to successfully deliver upon a blended model, as it requires a number of factors including:

- Establishing the internal business process, rigor, discipline, and structure necessary to operate and be competitive from a cost perspective in the commercial market as well as the more complex and more highly regulated public sector market to the extent you wish to cross over the public/private sector domain.

- Maintaining separate sets of workforces with different career paths and pricing structures across the public and private sector domains and the strategy, design, and implementation phases of the consulting lifecycle. The inability to maintain separate workforces with different rate structures will typically result in a complete failure of the blended model. Having a successful blended model hinges upon the ability to articulate and distinguish the respective staff that will be brought to bear throughout the engagement lifecycle. It is therefore critical to provide resources that are commensurate with the nature of the services being provided and competitive with other vendors in the marketplace.

- Allowing for the commingling of resources on a client engagement. This in and of itself can be the death of the blended delivery model. Once you break this rule, there is no turning back. As soon as strategy resources deliver design and implementation work or vice versa, the entire foundation of the blended model is undermined, the integrity of the rate structure is compromised, and it is extremely difficult, if not impossible, to repair.

- Maintaining brand awareness, a reputation for delivering in a timely, quality, and cost-effective manner, and developing a strong reference base across multiple markets and delivery domains. These can become quite challenging to achieve when competing with organizations that develop targeted solutions within a unique industry and specific phase of the consulting lifecycle. Over time, those vendors will perfect their capabilities, refine their solutions, become extremely cost-competitive, and develop a strong reference base that will make it difficult to thrive across multiple domains.

The point is that even with a large staff base, ample financial resources, a global footprint, and diverse delivery capabilities, it is difficult for one organization to straddle over the public and private sector domains or multiple phases of the consulting lifecycle. The most recent example of a large, global, and extremely successful management consulting firm that attempted to cross the public and private sector delivery and strategy, design, and implementation lifecycle domains was Booz Allen Hamilton's launch of its one-firm evolution that was publicly announced in the 2005 timeframe. In its 2005 Annual Report, CEO Ralph Shrader discussed the fundamental changes that have occurred in the global delivery landscape, namely that clients want their consulting firms to fuse ideas and strategy with functional expertise to deliver results. Despite this clear client mandate, Shrader articulated how little the market had changed. He stated, "I've observed how little most consulting businesses have changed in response to that shift in the market. Strategy firms sell strategy; technology firms advise on technology; and implementation firms implement, much as they always have. Most firms similarly draw arbitrary distinctions among different geographies." He went on to describe how Booz Allen Hamilton is different in that it is able to fuse strategy and technology and deliver measurable results for its clients, irrespective of the industry or geography in which they reside. "Booz Allen Hamilton is the one firm that corporations, governments, and nongovernmental organizations can turn to for help in solving their toughest problems. We know that today's strategic solutions are entwined with technology at the deepest level, and that no strategic transformation succeeds on paper—or in PowerPoint. Implementation is critical."

With those words, Booz Allen Hamilton formally launched its one-firm initiative under which commercial best practices and capabilities would be brought to bear downstream in the government market; conversely, the expertise developed by serving the U.S. Federal Government with design and implementation capabilities for over 90 years would be brought to bear upstream in the commercial markets with a particular focus on the intersection of the public and private sector in areas such as healthcare, security, and transportation. Booz Allen Hamilton was striving for a truly blended model that would span commercial and government domains as well as the rarely crossed strategy, design, and implementation chasm. In that same annual report, Dan Lewis, the managing director of Global Commercial Markets, goes on to state that, "We're the one firm able to serve clients globally in ways that produce results that no other competitor can emulate. Our expertise spans public and private sectors and delivers deep cross-functional services. There is no one built like us."

Booz Allen Hamilton has for 90 years and to this day been one of the most highly regarded management consulting firms in the world. Given their level of brand awareness, financial strength, reputation for delivering in a timely, quality, and cost-effective manner, and strong reference base, you would think that they, more so than anyone else, would have the foresight and leadership to achieve the blended model nirvana. So, how did they do? In May 2008, Booz Allen Hamilton announced that it was formally separating its commercial (and strategy focused) business and government (design and implementation focused) businesses. According to Shumeet Banerji, the CEO of Booz & Company, and as reported in the June edition of *Consulting Magazine*, "The split was a strategic decision based on the fact that the two businesses had become quite different over the last several years . . . and we began to wonder if they really belonged together anymore." Banerji went on to describe how the two businesses, which had for many years been operated under a single corporate umbrella, began to impose some significant restraints on their viability in the marketplace.

"Internally, we spent a lot of time attempting to harmonize across two pretty different business models." Banerji continues, "the client base of each business is vastly different, as are the resource requirements in terms of human assets, management structures, management models, and capital requirements." The article goes on to state that Booz & Company will focus its efforts on delivering strategy services to commercial clients and competing with the likes of McKinsey, Bain, and BCG.

I provide this example not to highlight Booz Allen Hamilton's inability to achieve a delivery model that was client, domain, and consulting lifecycle phase agnostic, but to highlight the difficulty in achieving a truly blended model. Despite the challenges, a number of providers have been successful in building and delivering under a blended model including Accenture, Deloitte, and IBM. Understanding the complexity of this approach and being fully cognizant of the differences between the think/strategy, build/design, and run/implementation domains is absolutely critical when developing a successful go-to-market strategy. To the extent that you can replicate a truly blended delivery model and have the requisite brand awareness, delivery capabilities, staff expertise, and reference base to do so, I strongly encourage you to pursue that approach, as it clearly aligns with the fundamental shift that has occurred in the marketplace. Alternatively, I encourage you to focus on your delivery sweet spots and to focus on those areas of the consulting lifecycle where you have strong brand awareness, quality products and services, a strong reference base, and a reputation for delivering in a timely, quality, and cost-effective manner. Neither approach is mutually exclusive, and both can yield a sustainable and financially lucrative business model through which trusted advisor relationships can be built and measurable results can be delivered.

2

Navigating the Maze: Where Do You Start?

Now that you have a better understanding of the wide-ranging delivery landscape, it is important to determine how to successfully penetrate this market. Selling professional services to Fortune 500 clients is not an easy task, especially given the competitive landscape and the fact that it consists of a very mature and savvy buying community. We will discuss strategies regarding how to approach a Fortune 500 entity to begin a dialogue regarding selling professional services, but first let's discuss some macro-level requirements for success. I have always asserted that three things are required (and you need all three) to sell any product or service within any industry. They are brand awareness, quality products and services, and referenceability. Let's discuss each of them in the realm of the professional services industry.

Brand Awareness

The first requirement for building a successful professional services business is to develop brand awareness for your organization in the marketplace around the types of services and solutions that fall within your delivery sweet spots. This can be accomplished by a number of means, but will certainly take time and vary in difficulty depending upon a number of factors including your size, history, geographic footprint, and financial resources. When it comes to brand awareness, it is critical to align your brand with the types of services you want to deliver in the market. As I mentioned, establishing strong brand awareness does not come easy. Ask anyone within the professional services industry or most senior executives within a Fortune 500 company to name the top four major strategy providers, and they should be able to very quickly shout out the names of McKinsey, Bain, The Boston Consulting Group, and Booz & Company, most likely in that order. Ask those same individuals to name the top design, implementation, and transformation providers, and they will most likely shout out Accenture, IBM, Deloitte, and Capgemini, also most likely in that order.

Developing that level of brand awareness takes time and is achieved by establishing a history of delivery excellence within major clients across multiple industries, augmented with more traditional marketing and public relations tools ranging from participating in industry events and tradeshows to sponsoring golf tournaments and other major sporting events.

The real challenge, if you choose to accept it, is crossing over the line of demarcation between strategy and design and implementation engagements. As we discussed in Chapter 1, many of the brand name firms across the consulting lifecycle are looking to expand their delivery footprint across the public and private sector domains and the strategy and design and implementation line of demarcation. The brand awareness of the leading firms will, at a minimum, give them a seat at the sales table through which they can attempt to assert their full lifecycle value proposition, but they will generally not be successful, absent a very strong trusted advisor relationship with the client or absent a strong reference base that can speak to their ability to successfully deliver similarly situated engagements.

Quality Products and Services

Second and also of paramount importance for building a successful professional services firm is developing a reputation in the market for delivering services in a *timely*, *quality*, and *cost-effective* manner. This component serves as the foundation for reinforcing your value proposition and building a strong reference base and opportunity pipeline. Depending upon the size and strategic importance of the engagement, the failure to successfully deliver across these three parameters can be a death sentence that may ultimately prevent you from winning any future engagements irrespective of the strength of your brand or reference base.

Timely, quality, and cost-effective delivery have always been extremely important, but have received unprecedented levels of scrutiny given the procurement centralization trend within the Fortune 500 over the past few years. In addition to anointing a set of preferred providers across service lines, procurement organizations are very carefully monitoring the performance of their vendors across time, quality, and cost parameters. Under the prior organizational model, which was more decentralized in structure, much more leniency was afforded to service providers that failed to successfully deliver within the time, cost, or quality parameters specified in their contract. Such failures were typically limited to a specific business unit or geography and would not have significant downstream implications in other business units or geographies, as communication among buyers was not prevalent across these boundaries.

The current model, which hinges upon centralization and quality delivery, could not be farther from that approach. We will discuss the role of procurement in much greater detail, but suffice it to say that procurement organizations are very diligently evaluating vendors across time, quality, and cost parameters for each project in which they are engaged, reviewing those results with the vendor on a recurring (typically quarterly) basis, and publishing the results across their buying community. In effect, it is no longer possible to hide out if you fail to deliver upon your value proposition, and failure comes with a high price, to the extent that a particular vendor has multiple instances of substandard delivery, their "preferred" vendor label will be taken away, and they may find themselves unable to compete for future opportunities.

Referenceability

Finally, let's talk about references. A strong reference base is an absolute requirement to build any successful business. My friends and colleagues usually tell me that I am extremely selective (OK—more like picky and very high maintenance) when it comes to choosing a service provider, but as far as I am concerned, I simply refuse to take a chance on someone who hasn't successfully delivered the same service to another consumer, unless I can see or speak to someone I trust regarding the results. I want to make sure that I am receiving the service from someone who is experienced in his or her trade and knows how to deliver results.

For me, the level of risk associated with making a bet on an unknown vendor is simply not worth the aggravation, unhappiness, and lost time and investment that will materialize if I have chosen poorly. Imagine a CIO of a Fortune 500 entity that needs to have an ERP (enterprise resource planning) solution implemented globally in the next twenty-four months. In this instance, you can imagine how important contracting with an experienced (has successfully delivered the same solution to hundreds of other customers—preferably within my industry) vendor will be, as an unsuccessful go-live resulting from missed delivery dates, failed data conversion, nonfunctioning interfaces, and cost overruns will result in the organization being severely at risk with regard to ongoing operations.

The bottom line is that to successfully sell strategy, design, and implementation services, you must have a strong reference base you can point to where you have delivered a similarly situated solution. Any references must be willing to field calls with potential sales prospects in which they will vouch for your capability and even host site visits depending upon the nature and complexity of the solution being evaluated. The best example I can provide that attests to the value of a strong reference base dates back to my early days at PeopleSoft when we were building the customer base within the education and government division.

At the time, the enterprise resource planning market was growing significantly, and almost all of the Fortune 500 and an extensive cross section of education and government entities were implementing some portion of the PeopleSoft (or a competing vendor) product suite. As we all know, implementing an enterprise resource planning product suite is complex, costly, and can have a significant detrimental impact on operations if unsuccessful. These potential consequences yielded a procurement environment in which every vendor competing for a new opportunity was required to provide a set of references where he or she had successfully (the client was live on the application, and the value proposition and return on investment [ROI] articulated in the initial proposal and business case were being achieved and realized) delivered a similar solution in a timely, quality, and cost-effective manner.

At PeopleSoft, we were acutely aware of this dynamic and made it a strategic priority to develop an ironclad reference program across all product suites and industries. The clients within the reference program would speak to potential sales prospects and host site visits during which they would discuss the benefits and return on investment they had realized through the successful implementation of the PeopleSoft product suite. PeopleSoft was founded in 1987, but the education and government division was not formally launched until 1994 and faced some unique sales challenges in that it sought to sell a newly developed and customized product (a separate code line from the rest of the PeopleSoft product suite) in a highly regulated and competitive environment.

Starting from scratch in any business is never easy, but asking sales prospects (in this case, highly visible education and government officials) to make substantial investments in relatively unproven software that would receive tremendous public scrutiny and touch every portion of their organizations is not an easy sales pitch, even for the most proven sales executive. Fortunately, we were successful in licensing and implementing the product suite to a set of early adopters and actively cultivated and heavily leveraged those relationships to serve as references for new sales prospects. That group of early adopters and the strong references they provided were critical components of the foundation that supported an education and government division that grew from zero to $500 million in a span of roughly five years.

Although the complexity, substance of the services being delivered, domain, and industry may vary, it is an absolute certainty that a strong reference base consisting of customers where you have successfully delivered a similarly situated solution is required to grow a professional services business. Any firms trying to sell to the Fortune 500 client community without a strong reference base for their respective solutions will be at a distinct competitive disadvantage, irrespective of the amount of brand awareness or reputation for quality delivery they may have in the market. So make no mistake about it: cultivating a strong reference base is an absolute necessity, and the return on any investment required to achieve this objective is simply immeasurable.

How Do You Get Started?

Let's assume that you have achieved some level of brand awareness, a reputation for delivering in a timely, quality, and cost-effective manner, and a strong reference base and want to sell strategy, design, or implementation services to a Fortune 500 client. How do you start the process to become a preferred vendor and negotiate either a stand-alone or global master services agreement through which services can be marketed and delivered?

The answer to that question will depend upon a number of factors including the:

- Size of your organization

- Level of centralization in the client's procurement function

- Degree of influence that procurement can assert over the buying process

- Nature of services—strategy/design/implementation—that you intend to sell

- Relationships you have within the client

- Internal functional organization to which you are selling

- Existence of and open-season opportunities within the preferred vendor base

- IT competitive landscape

- Rate structure

As these items may serve as significant barriers to entry, they will be recurring themes throughout the remainder of this book.

Size of Your Organization

A vendor's size should not impact its ability to sell professional services to Fortune 500 entities; however, if size dictates brand awareness, this may be a significant barrier to overcome. Of course, a number of small, local, niche, and cost-competitive service providers have established a delivery history and long-term relationships with Fortune 500 companies through which they generate a recurring revenue stream. I assure you that achieving that status required lots of heavy lifting. Large firms like Booz Allen Hamilton, McKinsey, and Accenture are of sufficient size and maintain such strong brand awareness in the market that they could most likely pitch any product or service to any of the companies in the Fortune 500. I am not suggesting that these qualities are necessary for success, but size, brand awareness, relationships, and reputation go a long way in getting to the table to discuss footprint expansion with an existing client or in penetrating a new organization.

Procurement Centralization and Influence

In addition, and as previously discussed, most of the Fortune 500 have implemented a significant amount of structure, rigor, and discipline around the procurement process and have instituted a master agreement process with a limited number of preferred vendors. The overwhelming number of firms that hold these master agreements and have the "preferred" label, for which there are a limited number of slots, tend to be the brand name service providers we have discussed.

Given this dynamic, the smaller and niche providers are at a disadvantage right out of the gate; however, they can still pursue a few viable alternatives. As we have discussed, establishing brand awareness, developing a reference base and trusted advisor relationships, and building a reputation for quality, timely, and cost-effective delivery will yield tangible results. To build capabilities, develop relationships, and enhance their brand, smaller service providers should reach out to the larger and brand-name vendors and form alliance or teaming partnerships for certain types of services or specific strategic opportunities. Providing services under the umbrella of the larger firm will, at a minimum, provide smaller firms with client exposure and allow them to begin building their brand, relationships, and reputation. With this approach, the smaller firm can incubate under the protective umbrella of the larger firm, thereby allowing it to develop a firm delivery platform from which it can establish relationships, enhance its brand, launch its marketing efforts, and eventually obtain its own "preferred" vendor label within the functional disciplines in which it excels.

A current trend that will also help small and disadvantaged (minority-, veteran-, or woman-owned) businesses build and enhance their brand awareness is a renewed focus by the Fortune 500 to ensure that their large service providers are subcontracting a targeted (and in some cases contractually stipulated) percentage of their annual transaction volume to entities of this type. When considering additions to its roster of preferred vendors, most Fortune 500 procurement organizations will require potential candidates to complete a detailed vendor questionnaire that addresses such areas as:

- Company history

- Service offerings

- Organizational structure

- Ownership configuration

- Office locations

- Staff size

- Internal system capabilities

- Background check and drug testing policies

- Standard delivery and payment terms

- Audited financial statements

- Financial viability metrics including a D&B (Dun & Bradstreet) rating

- Bank references

- Client references

- Market share data

- Executive leadership biographies

- Customer satisfaction results

- Dispute resolution and escalation process

Historically, one area that the questionnaire never addressed was the vendor's utilization of small and disadvantaged businesses during the course of delivery. However, the past few years have witnessed a renewed focus in this area, and most questionnaires now require potential preferred vendors to describe their small and disadvantaged business programs, to identify their ability to report their total spend with these types of entities on a quarterly basis, and to describe the outreach activities in which the vendor participates to identify and engage qualified companies. The failure to maintain a robust small and disadvantaged business program and achieve targeted or contractually stipulated small business spend thresholds may jeopardize the vendor's preferred vendor viability, as this issue has become a critical component of the social agenda within the Fortune 500 client community. Ultimately, this is good news for the small and disadvantaged service providers, as the larger firms will be reaching out into their respective communities to attract new participants into their programs. Conversely, and to the extent that they meet the requisite program criteria, these small firms can actively market the larger brand name firms across the strategy, design, and implementation domains to partner on specific opportunities and to become active participants in their small business outreach programs. The renewed focus in this area creates another valuable mechanism by which the smaller firms can get valuable exposure and access across the Fortune 500 client community. Through leveraging these types of programs, small businesses can build relationships, develop brand awareness, and aspire to graduate from their small business status and to maintain their own delivery footprint within the Fortune 500 client community.

Service Offerings and Relationships

Another critical variable that will impact your ability to attain preferred vendor status is the nature of the services that you wish to sell. I will not dwell on this, as we have already discussed the implications and complexities of selling a full consulting lifecycle suite of services to the Fortune 500 client community. I will say that it is extremely difficult to walk into the corporate headquarters of a Fortune 500 company, ask for the procurement department, and attempt to sell corporate strategy services, unless you have a relationship with the CEO or other member of the executive leadership team. In my opinion, McKinsey is truly in a class by itself when it comes to selling these types of services. A lot of consulting firms have McKinsey-envy and are foolish enough to think they can devise a strategy that will result in McKinsey being unseated from their corporate strategy perch within a particular client. While the other major strategy providers including Bain, BCG, and Booz have their fair share of work in this area, McKinsey is the clear leader, with the largest footprint across the Fortune 500 client base. Attempting to unseat any of the major strategy providers will be extremely difficult unless the client makes a decision to engage another vendor, or a change in executive leadership occurs. While there may be opportunities to provide strategy services within very specific disciplines or areas of expertise, the vast majority of the strategy wallet will be reserved for McKinsey and its brethren.

Design and implementation services are a completely different animal and offer much more opportunity for success. As we have discussed, the overwhelming majority, some 75 percent of the corporate consulting wallet, is allocated for design and implementation services. It therefore might be prudent to leave the strategy work on the table for McKinsey and others and to focus on the services being purchased across this phase of the consulting lifecycle. Do the math—a small piece of this wallet will significantly trump the revenue you can achieve through delivering corporate strategy work, and it is much easier to capture. I am a big proponent of carefully picking your battles—why expend scarce business development resources trying to unsuccessfully compete with McKinsey, Bain, or BCG when so many opportunities exist elsewhere? When it comes to design and implementation services, numerous service providers span the entire IT lifecycle, and it is in this area where procurement organizations become heavily engaged, where price is a dominant evaluation factor, where having a large appetite for risk may assist in footprint expansion, and where having a strong reference base is critical for success.

When it comes to selling IT services to Fortune 500 clients, you better come armed with quality products and services, brand awareness, references, and live customers. Fortune 500 clients want assurances that you have successfully completed a similarly situated project in a timely, quality, and cost-effective manner. Firms such as IBM, Accenture, and Deloitte have an extensive industry-specific reference base and an abundance of live customers that establish their credibility and give them a distinct competitive advantage in the market. In addition, they are capable of providing an end-to-end solution across the full IT lifecycle. When it comes to quality and repeatable solutions, it is critical to have a well-defined and structured methodology for each type of engagement you wish to sell across the IT lifecycle—from strategy and analysis through implementation and ongoing operations. Each of the firms I just mentioned has proven implementation and delivery methodologies that are repeatable in nature, that are transferable across industry boundaries, and that can be tailored based upon the scope and complexity of the solution. Having such a proven methodology and delivery track record, these firms can implement technology solutions on a fixed-price or incentive fee basis, can agree to more aggressive delivery terms and conditions, and can price in an extremely competitive manner.

Finally, we can't forget brand awareness; to successfully sell these types of services, you must be recognized by the buying community as a viable and experienced provider of the services in question. If you lack brand awareness, you will never even make it into the request for proposal pipeline for these opportunities.

IT Lifecycle and Competitive Landscape

Before we go any further, it is important to discuss the overall IT lifecycle; this will provide you with a better understanding of the potential entry points for services delivery and yield a better understanding of the competitive landscape. I have previously referred to any services beyond corporate strategy as design and implementation. What I would like to do now is expand that definition one additional layer. I think of the IT lifecycle in four major phases; they are (from left to right) strategy and analysis, design, implementation, and operation. Each area consists of a different set of core services, a different rate structure, and potentially, a different competitor set. Understanding where you want to sell within the lifecycle is critical, as it will drive your overarching go-to-market strategy. Let's discuss each component of the lifecycle.

The strategy and analysis component of the IT lifecycle, as its name suggests, consists of developing the IT and technology strategy that will drive the future success of the client. This work sits very close to the line of demarcation between strategy and design/implementation, as many of the traditional strategy providers consider work within this portion of the IT lifecycle to be within their delivery sweet spot. It is therefore not uncommon to see the strategy providers compete for this type of work under a rate structure that is commensurate with the more generic corporate strategy services they deliver. Where they run into challenges is when they are competing with firms like Accenture, IBM, and Deloitte, and other large systems integrators that are capable of providing a full IT lifecycle solution and will typically provide the strategy and assessment component of the engagement at drastically reduced prices in exchange for the downstream and very highly lucrative implementation engagement of the technology or software solution to follow. At a macro level, this phase of the lifecycle consists of the following types of engagements:

- IT business strategy
- Sourcing strategy
- Business continuity planning
- Technology strategy
- Systems/requirements analysis
- Project objectives and scope

- QA and risk management
- IT governance
- Competitive analysis/ benchmarking
- ROI and cost/benefit analysis
- Infrastructure and security strategy
- Project planning

As I previously stated, the strategy firms have tried to migrate slightly downstream to capture these types of opportunities, but have experienced challenges given their limited reference base, lack of experienced staff with functional and product expertise, lack of alliances with the technology product companies, and the aggressive pricing structures being put forth by the full lifecycle providers.

The second phase of the IT lifecycle is the design phase. Keep in mind that the farther to the right that we migrate from the strategy phase of the consulting lifecycle, the more we enter the realm and delivery sweet spots of Accenture, IBM, Deloitte, and the other large system integration firms. From this point in the lifecycle and beyond, small boutique providers that have developed a set of core competencies around a particular industry, technology, or product suite will also be prevalent. Many of the boutique providers are similar to Accenture, IBM, and others in that they maintain an extensive reference base of live customers, maintain staff with extensive industry and functional expertise, and have developed implementation methodologies, packaged services, and a variety of other quality and repeatable solutions across specific industries, technologies, and product suites.

Another area where the smaller and niche firms differentiate themselves is the amount of risk they are willing to undertake in delivery. The smaller firms, despite their strong delivery capabilities, may lack brand awareness, so they have to make up for that gap through other means, which tend to be aggressive price and delivery terms. These firms are actively looking to expand their delivery footprint and reference base and desperately want to capture a share of the Fortune 500 consulting wallet. When you combine this desire with the fact that they do not have the financial stability and brand strength of the larger firms, they are typically willing (or forced) to pursue extreme measures, which include proposing heavily discounted rates and agreeing to rigid delivery terms and conditions that fall outside the typical risk profile, economic model, and comfort zone of the larger and more diversified firms. This approach is quite appealing to aggressive procurement organizations, as they are looking for low-cost providers willing to execute their standard terms and conditions (which are very heavily skewed in their favor) with no modifications.

Another formidable competitor that you will encounter from the design phase forward is the large product companies that have built extensive services organizations capable of implementing their product suites. Examples would include SAP Global Services and Oracle Consulting. The product company services organizations, while not newcomers to the market, have extensively grown their delivery organizations in the past ten years. A good reference point would be the evolution of PeopleSoft Global Services over this timeframe.

When I first joined PeopleSoft in 1997, its focus was licensing its human resources, financial, and supply chain product suites across all major industries; while the firm did have a boutique services arm in PeopleSoft Consulting, the bulk of the design and implementation work was being handed-off to and delivered by the Big 5 consulting firms, all of which were strong alliance partners. In late 1999, PeopleSoft and the other large product vendors at the time—namely Siebel, Oracle, and SAP—began to experience significant challenges generating new license revenue, as large companies were postponing any major investments in ERP software given that Y2K was looming on the horizon; there was tremendous uncertainty as to the ramifications of Y2K on the stability of their IT environments.

At this time, PeopleSoft undertook a new strategic course under which it would evolve from a software license company to a full services solution provider; it would license the product suite to its customers, implement the product suite on a fixed price or incentive fee basis, and train its user community through its expansion of PeopleSoft University. It was at this time that the product companies began to assume their position as full services solution providers, and they have grown those capabilities and solidified that standing ever since. While there has been a tremendous amount of consolidation in the market in recent years, both Oracle and SAP maintain robust consulting organizations that are formidable competitors in the market.

The general rule is that the farther we go to the right in the IT lifecycle, the more competitors and price sensitivity we are likely to encounter. Within the design phase of the lifecycle, these types of engagements are typical:

- Business process design
- Data design
- Compliance design
- Infrastructure design
- Gap analysis

- Vendor selection process
- Security architecture design
- Organizational design
- Training design
- Testing plans

As you can see from this list, the farther you move to the right in the IT lifecycle, the more specialized the level of services becomes. The reason why the full lifecycle firms are so successful is that they can bring the right level of resources to bear at the right price points across the lifecycle, which minimizes delivery risk and knowledge loss during transition throughout the various phases of the engagement lifecycle.

The next phase in the lifecycle is the all-important implementation phase. As in the design phase, a significant number of providers are focused on providing implementation services to Fortune 500 clients. Sample services within this phase include the following:

- Security testing
- Change management
- Business process building and testing
- Quality assurance
- Technology implementation

- Application building and testing
- Data conversion and interfaces
- User acceptance and training
- IT standardization
- Integration management

The implementation phase is where the rubber finally meets the road. You can strategize, plan, design, and theorize about the solution, but it is in the implementation phase where brand awareness and reputations are developed and where references are built. If you are unable to successfully implement the solution, you can't deliver upon your value proposition, and the client can't realize a return on its investment. The failure to execute properly within this phase can severely impede the ability of any vendor to expand its delivery footprint across the Fortune 500 buying community.

The final phase of the IT lifecycle is the operation phase. There is a significant amount of competition with regard to selling services within this phase of the lifecycle to Fortune 500 entities. As with the implementation phase, a number of providers are delivering services to Fortune 500 clients in this area. As a result, services in this area are extremely cost-competitive and aggressively negotiated by Fortune 500 procurement organizations. A representative listing of the types of services covered in this area includes the following:

- Applications management
- Audit/assessment/re-sourcing
- Best practices
- Network administration
- Performance benchmarks
- Help desk

- Cost management
- Outsourcing
- Ongoing training
- Vendor management
- Service level agreements
- Call centers

Rate Structure

We have now discussed the types of services that you might want to sell and the competitive challenges you might encounter across the strategy and IT phases of the consulting lifecycle. When picking your delivery sweet spots and deciding upon a lifecycle entry point, it is important to consider a number of other factors, including the rate structure, the amount of centralization in the client's procurement function, the level of influence that procurement can assert over the buying process, the internal functional organization to which you are selling, the relationships you have within the client, the existence of and open season opportunities within the preferred vendor base, and the competition you may encounter in the sales process.

We will spend a lot of time talking about rates, overly aggressive procurement organizations, and master services agreements, but suffice it to say that procurement organizations have been and continue to be extensively involved in the IT services buying process across the Fortune 500 client community. Their primary focuses are the rate structure and the terms and conditions under which services are being provided. Procurement organizations are measured by and want to be recognized for optimizing third-party consulting spend; they pursue these objectives by putting extreme downward pricing pressure on their vendors to attain favorable pricing, particularly in those areas where they believe the services being provided are commodity-like in nature.

The general rule is that the farther you move to the right in the IT lifecycle, the more likely the services being provided will be viewed as commodity-like in nature and will be more subject to extensive cost scrutiny. As we all know, once something is classified as a commodity, the most compelling factor in the buying process is the price. As we have also discussed, Fortune 500 procurement organizations are driving the migration to multiyear global master services agreements with a select group of preferred vendors. Procurement is not too heavily focused on corporate strategy, as these services are a small part of the overall consulting wallet, are typically contracted for by the CEO or some other C-suite executive, and tend to be outside the realm of their rate reduction efforts.

You might ask why this all matters. I have had the opportunity to spend countless hours negotiating master services agreements with procurement executives within Fortune 500 clients across all industries, and a failure to understand the overall delivery landscape and competitive environment will result in very limited success in penetrating this client base. Unlike selling door-to-door, opportunities with Fortune 500 procurement organizations are limited; it is critical to be able to concisely articulate your value proposition and to come armed with the reference base and brand awareness to back up your claims. I assure you there is nothing more uncomfortable than sitting in front of a Fortune 500 client, either procurement or otherwise, and being told that you missed the mark on your proposal or don't have the requisite brand awareness, reference base, and delivery capabilities to be labeled as a preferred vendor across the various categories by which they segregate their consulting spend. Procurement doesn't pull any punches. Over the past few years, I have had the unfortunate privilege of receiving feedback similar to the following during a variety of proposal debriefing or general feedback sessions:

- The team articulated in your proposal was too strategy focused and lacked the specific industry and product suite knowledge and expertise required for this opportunity.

- The proposal that you submitted was simply too generic and not specialized to our operating environment.

- Your team lacked the industry and technology-specific references that were necessary to establish your credibility for delivering services of this type.

- Your prices are simply too high for this type of work and not competitive with other vendors in the market.

- You have failed to listen to our requirements and are trying to give us what we really don't want or need.

- The fact that you are not known for delivering this type of work combined with the limited reference set you provided had a significant detrimental impact on your evaluation.

- The evaluation team is concerned that you lack the routine methodology and preexisting bank of intellectual capital to deliver this type of solution.

- We didn't think you did this type of work and therefore did not include you in the RFP distribution.

- The evaluation team made this purchase decision based upon our perception of the safety and reliability of the winning vendor as signaled by its reputation and experience for similarly situated industry-specific engagements.

- The winning team had extensive references and qualified staff with deep industry and product suite experience.

- Given your performance on a prior engagement, the evaluation team had concerns about your ability to deliver this solution.

As you can readily ascertain from this feedback, I cannot stress enough the importance of brand awareness; a reputation for quality products and services that you can deliver in a timely, quality, and cost-effective manner; and a strong reference base for similarly situated engagements. Successfully selling professional services to Fortune 500 companies requires navigating through a complex maze, and second chances with procurement organizations or proposal evaluation teams may never materialize. To help minimize these circumstances and to prevent you from taking a wrong turn, I provide the following rules of the road:

1. Carefully pick your entry point and delivery sweet spots in the consulting lifecycle; proceed with caution if you intend to cross over the strategy, design, and implementation phases or public and private sector domains.

2. Know the competitor set within the respective area of the lifecycle in which you intend to focus. Specifically, develop an understanding of their value proposition, pricing structure, industry focus, and where they maintain deeply entrenched client relationships.

3. Know the industry in which you intend to focus. Specifically, bring staff to bear that have industry-specific expertise and can speak the client's language.

4. Bring references or go home. Unless you can provide references where you have delivered a similarly situated solution, don't expect an easy road to success.

5. Avoid being commoditized. Carefully articulate your value proposition and the distinct advantages that differentiate you from the competition. Once procurement or anyone within the buying community perceives the services you are providing to be commodities, they will focus very heavily on price and migrate to the low-cost provider.

6. If you lack brand awareness, size, or a reference base, learn to crawl before you walk. Consider developing or leveraging a relationship with a larger or more entrenched industry-focused provider through teaming, alliance, or joint royalty and marketing agreements.

7. If you intend to deliver services at different points across the consulting lifecycle and across the public and private sector domain, it is absolutely critical to differentiate the engagement parameters, staff type and capabilities, and pricing structure associated within each domain. If you only remember one rule, it should be this: never undermine the integrity of your rate structure (providing premium services for commodity prices), and never commingle staff across the various phases (allowing premium service staff to deliver commodity services) of the lifecycle in which you focus.

8. Propose a rate structure that is commensurate with the nature of the services being provided and competitive with the other vendors in the marketplace. If you fail to achieve this objective, you will not succeed. Remember, strategy rates will be benchmarked against McKinsey, Bain, Booz, and BCG, and design and implementation rates will typically be benchmarked against Accenture, IBM, and Deloitte.

9. It is very difficult and costly to attempt to unseat a firmly entrenched competitor that is delivering in a timely, quality, and cost-effective manner. It may be more prudent to direct your sales efforts toward other functional areas, geographies, or components of the consulting wallet when faced with this dynamic.

10. Build strong relationships with Fortune 500 procurement organizations, as they heavily influence the buying community and can be a distinguishing factor between success and failure. It is their perception of brand awareness, delivery capabilities, and reputation for quality that will drive your standing within their buying community.

3

The Risk and Reward Dilemma

The primary objective when negotiating with a Fortune 500 client is to execute an agreement that yields an acceptable level of risk and reward for both parties to the transaction. The key to achieving that objective is simple and straightforward: always remember to temper your approach—specifically how you price, how you negotiate, and how you propose—*based upon the amount of risk inherent in delivery*. This mantra is paramount when negotiating price and delivery terms and conditions with Fortune 500 clients. I guarantee that this simple rule will serve you well in your efforts to capture, negotiate terms and conditions for, and deliver professional services to Fortune 500 companies. While this might seem like a logical, balanced, and intuitive approach, it is not always followed.

Let's assume you have carefully chosen your delivery sweet spots, successfully articulated your value proposition, established strong relationships within the client organization, including procurement, and have finally made your way to the table to negotiate terms and conditions, a rate structure, and hopefully a global master services agreement. Next, the procurement organization will hand you a set of standard terms and conditions that will most likely be very heavily skewed in the client's favor across each of the substantive delivery terms including warranty, limitation on liability, indemnity, payment, acceptance, and ownership of work product.

The burning question is, how much risk are you willing to undertake as a service provider to win new business and to grow your footprint across the client organization?

Before you answer that question, we should talk about the key drivers of risk, how risk should be approached in the negotiation process, the various contract types you may encounter when contracting with Fortune 500 companies, and the key factors that should be evaluated when gauging the amount of risk inherent in delivery.

When negotiating with Fortune 500 entities for the delivery of strategy and IT services, a key objective for both parties is to minimize any risk and legal exposure that could materialize under the terms and conditions of the agreement. If we assume that all strategy, design, and implementation engagements can be defined within a specific project scope, then it is possible to define project risk and the methods by which it is expressed. In its simplest form, *project risk* is the degree of exposure to negative events, and their probable consequences impacting on project objectives, expressed in terms of *scope, time/schedule, quality*, and *cost*. In every engagement, it is these four factors that impact the delivery process and the terms and conditions under which delivery will occur. We will discuss some key terms and conditions later, but let's first review each of these key risk drivers.

Scope

The primary reason projects fail is *scope creep*, or deviations from the agreed upon scope contained in the statement of work. According to the Standish Group, only 35 percent of IT projects are completed successfully; one of the primary reasons that they identify for this dynamic is a failure by both management consultants and software providers to properly define scope. *Scope* refers to the actual tasks and deliverables that will be completed during the period of performance. Project scope is typically articulated in a statement of work that is attached to the terms and conditions that will govern the agreement. The extent to which the statement of work will be narrowly tailored or more general in nature will usually depend on the nature of the services being provided and the contract type under which the services will be delivered. A general rule is that the more fixed an agreement is in terms of time, price, and results, the more narrowly tailored the statement of work will be. Consider two examples. Let's assume that I am interested in having a leading management consulting firm ("consultant") conduct some strategic planning activities for my financial services company. The contract type agreed to by the parties will not only significantly impact the look, feel, and level of specificity contained within the statement of work, but will also set the expectations of both parties to the transaction.

Option A: If I communicate to the partner leading the engagement that I want to purchase some time from him and his team over the next few months to assist in developing a strategic plan and in identifying potential programs and initiatives that will facilitate footprint expansion, the statement of work for this effort will most likely be written in a very generic manner, with little or no specificity in terms of actual deliverables and milestone dates. During our discussions, we also agree upon some weekly rates for different levels of staff and that we will have a bimonthly meeting to review any costs incurred to date and the future direction of the engagement. The focus of this engagement is procuring consultant's time to work on general strategy activities, which may consist of interviewing employees, analyzing market conditions, reviewing competitor information, identifying potential acquisition or divestiture candidates, reviewing pricing structures, evaluating service offerings, and attending product development meetings, just to name a few.

The general concept behind this type of open-ended engagement is that the number of staff deployed and the specific activities in which the consultant is engaged will fluctuate greatly over time, and the client can agree to make adjustments to the budget as necessary. Given these engagement parameters, the actual scope of work is not too clearly defined or narrowly tailored, and deviations from scope are not too significant. The key success driver here is based upon the level of effort and number of hours worked by the consultant, not on achieving a specific objective or delivering a specific deliverable.

Option B: Under this option, I communicate to the consultant that I am looking for a formal five-year strategic planning document, which I will review with my executive leadership team at an upcoming meeting. The document contains a detailed financial analysis, valuation, and strategic review for each of the various lines of business within the company and provides specific recommendations that must be taken for each in terms of headcount, alliances, sales strategy, pricing structure, potential acquisition candidates, and research and development investments to achieve out-year business objectives and growth aspirations. In addition, I require that this report be completed within three months, and I will pay a fixed fee of $500,000 upon its completion, delivery in accordance with my requirements, and acceptance.

Clearly, these terms are quite different from those articulated in the first option. Here, the consultant will be focused solely on conducting the necessary analysis and gathering the necessary data to complete the report within the specified timeline, and its project and staffing plans will be tailored accordingly. Given the specific delivery requirements, the statement of work will be very narrowly tailored and will clearly define the sections to be contained in the report, the metrics that will be presented in the financial analysis, the method to be used for valuation, the level of support and documentation that may be required from company staff, the methods that will be utilized for data gathering, the requirement for preparing a draft report for review and comment, and the hopefully objective, measurable, and verifiable acceptance criteria that have been agreed to by the parties. In addition, there will most likely be a detailed change order process that must be strictly followed if the scope of work should change during the period of performance. The key success drivers here are the abilities of the consultant to complete a specific deliverable within the time and cost constraints identified at the time of contract execution.

An important point about scope is that it definitely drives the allocation of risk inherent in the engagement. In the first option, the risk for both the consultant and the financial services company is quite low. The consultant is not under any time constraint to deliver any specific deliverables, and the client can have tremendous flexibility to modify the scope of services being delivered and the cost associated with delivery. Conversely, the second option yields much more delivery risk for the consultant, as it has agreed to deliver the report on-time, in accordance with the specifications stipulated in the statement of work, and within the fixed budgetary ceiling. It also yields significant risk for my financial services company in that my out-year strategy needs to be finalized so that it can be reviewed and implemented by its executive leadership team, and any delays in delivery may severely impact their ability to succeed in the marketplace. Ultimately, the risk inherent in each of these engagements will be the primary driver in the negotiation of the contractual terms and conditions that will govern service delivery and the allocation of risk and reward between the parties. When faced with either engagement type, simply remember to temper your stance based upon the amount of risk inherent in delivery.

Time and Schedule

Time and schedule refers to the specificity of the timeline under which the services will be delivered. The varying levels of time specificity are also clear when evaluating the strategic planning effort referenced earlier. In the first scenario, the consultant would most likely develop a flexible work plan and would provide the company with some high-level estimates regarding the completion of certain tasks based upon the direction and budget agreed to by the parties. Grossly misjudging the completion date is not too significant under this scenario because the client is procuring the consultant's time and because there are no specific deliverables that must be completed. In fact, because the metric by which the consultant is measured is time worked, he or she may be motivated to broaden the scope of the engagement and to generate additional billable hours on the engagement.

Under the second engagement scenario, time is clearly of the essence. A typical deliverable-based contract will specify firm milestone delivery dates for each deliverable identified in the statement of work. Failure to meet those targets may impact the project plan and will certainly not be viewed favorably by the client, especially given the critical nature of the services being provided. In addition, cost overruns or penalties to which the consultant may be subject for untimely delivery may significantly impact the profitability of the engagement. It is therefore critical that the roles and responsibilities of the consultant and the level of cooperation required from client personnel are clearly articulated in the agreement. Similar to project scope, it is clear that the timeline specificity of an engagement will be an important factor in the negotiation of governing terms and conditions and the allocation of risk and reward.

Quality

Quality delivery is also a critical factor in every engagement, and it plays an instrumental role in the negotiation process. Ideally, and as a matter of good faith, we should assume that all firms, irrespective of where their sweet spots fall across the consulting lifecycle, strive to deliver their service offerings in a quality manner. But as we all know, in unfortunately many instances, quality standards suffer and project deliverables are proffered that fail to meet the acceptance criteria contained in the statement of work. Under either of the two delivery scenarios articulated previously, the agreement will contain terms and conditions relating to the quality of the services being delivered that will be expressed in the warranty provisions of the agreement and will vary depending upon the contract type, scope, and timing specificity.

Under Option A, the client is buying time and the consultant would most likely warrant that the services will be performed in a professional and diligent manner in accordance with recognized industry standards. This is generally not a difficult standard to achieve, as it tends to be subjective in nature. In Option B, a specific deliverable will be produced in conjunction with the engagement, and it must be delivered in accordance with the acceptance criteria contained in the statement of work. Under this scenario, it would not be uncommon for the consultant to offer, and for the client to demand, a warranty period for any work product created under the agreement. In this case, the financial services firm would have a contractually stipulated period during which it would be required to accept the strategic plan document or identify any areas of nonconformance.

If the deliverable does not conform to the acceptance criteria contained in the statement of work, then the consultant will typically be required to repair or replace that deliverable, at its own cost, so that it is in conformity with the acceptance criteria contained in the statement of work. Under the engagement parameters associated with Option B, producing quality deliverables is mission critical for the consultant; failure to do so will impact not only the profitability of the engagement, but also the relationship with and referenceability of the client as well as the reputation of consultant in the marketplace. Quality is absolutely a key factor in the negotiation process. Like they say at Ford, "Quality is Job One." Agreeing upon warranty provisions and acceptance criteria that are reasonable for both parties to the transaction is a critical part of the negotiation process and should be treated accordingly.

Price

Price is also a particularly important factor in determining the risk associated with any professional services agreement, irrespective of where it may fall across the consulting lifecycle. It is, in many instances, the most heavily scrutinized issue in the negotiation process. The final negotiated price will be a direct reflection of the allocation of risk and reward between the parties to the transaction.

Let's return to the strategic plan engagement outlined previously. In Option A, the consultant is not subject to a significant amount of risk in conjunction with this engagement. It provided my financial services firm with both a set of rates for the various staff levels that would be deployed and a high-level estimate as to the effort and cost the consultant thought it would take to complete the strategic planning effort. The consultant may even consider offering a flat or volume-based discount to the client. Under this contract scenario, and assuming the rates are set appropriately, it is difficult to operate in an unprofitable manner. Of course, this does assume that the consulting firm can effectively manage its cost base. In its simplest form, the general rule for an engagement of this type is that more hours worked results in more revenue and profit margin generated by the consulting firm. Under an open-ended time and materials engagement of this type, the consultant is not subject to any deadlines or penalties if it incurs costs in excess of its original estimate, if it must deploy additional staff, or if the project plan is extended beyond original expectations. Given the open-ended nature of the agreement, charges would continue to accrue until the consultant completed its tasking or the client terminated the engagement.

Under Option B, the fixed nature of the work, the fairly aggressive delivery timeline, and the risk inherent in delivery will most likely result in the consultant holding firm on its price and not offering any additional discount (flat, volume-based, or otherwise) to the client. Given the fixed nature of the agreement—a specific report in a specific timeline for a specific price—the consultant bears all of the risk associated with delivery. The vendor must complete the strategic planning exercise in a manner that conforms to the acceptance criteria contained in the statement of work for a fixed price of $500,000, irrespective of the actual cost incurred by the consultant. The bottom line is that failure to properly scope and estimate the price associated with delivery can have significant financial implications. Price will definitely impact the terms and conditions that are agreed upon by the parties, and it is directly related to the allocation of risk and reward between the parties. When it comes to risk allocation, I like to follow the general principle that if I make a decision to assume additional delivery risk, I should be compensated accordingly.

Risk in the Negotiation Process

Now that we have discussed the four primary drivers of risk, it is important to discuss how risk should be addressed in the negotiation process. Before beginning to dissect the terms and conditions of specific contracts, it is important to have a formal approach and process by which risk will be managed. Maintaining a structured approach to risk management is a critical component of the negotiation process. Having a formal risk management approach will not eliminate the risk associated with a particular engagement; rather it will provide the framework through which overall engagement risk, expressed in the form of technical, financial, legal, quality, and business risk, is identified so that it can be balanced across the risk/reward continuum and managed and mitigated throughout the negotiation and delivery process (see Figure 3.1).

Risk can be managed in a number of ways. Although it's clearly not an optimal solution, many organizations take a completely reactive

Figure 3.1 Identifying and balancing risks and rewards

approach to risk management. They execute contractual agreements under which they are exposed to an uneven allocation of risk and reward. While the business reason for absorbing additional risk may be compelling, it is not a license to ignore the negotiation process, cross your fingers, and hope that nothing goes wrong during delivery. Under this laissez-faire approach to risk management, the organization will simply wait until a problem arises before any corrective action is undertaken. Likening the situation to the risk of "being shot," three possible actions may result under this approach:

- The organization may move out of the way to avoid the bullet by allocating additional investment or resources to solve the problem.

- The organization may deflect the bullet by blaming someone else for the problem.

- The organization may seek to repair the damage done by the bullet by commencing legal action or filing a warranty claim to resolve the problem.

While this approach may temporarily stop the bleeding, it is nothing more than a loosely fitting bandage for the situation. Even if the bullet leaves a minor flesh wound or results in minimal damage, it will eventually resurface and cause irreparable harm. In fact, a crisis-management approach of this type is one that clearly should be avoided. A more desirable approach to risk management is one in which the organization anticipates risk, plans for contingencies, and negotiates terms and conditions that balance the sharing of risk and reward inherent in the transaction. This approach will allow the organization to more effectively dodge bullets and will hopefully put them in a position under which they can avoid staring down the face of the gun barrel.

No one likes being shot, and a disciplined and structured approach to risk management seems like it would be a natural component of the internal control structure within most large organizations. However, it is not uncommon for risk management to take a back seat, leaving many organizations without any substantive and formal approach to managing risk. The bottom line with regard to any risk—technical, business, legal, financial, quality, or otherwise—is that it should only be undertaken if the potential reward and chance of winning exceed the cost of an unsuccessful decision and ultimate loss. To help reach this determination, the following questions should be asked:

- Why should the risk be taken?

- What will be gained?

- What could be lost?

- What are the chances and consequences of success and failure?

- Is the potential reward worth the risk?

- Has accepting a risk of this type been successful in the past?

- What is the reward, in both qualitative and quantitative terms, if this risk is undertaken?

These questions should be answered with a focus on the reward for a given level of risk. Ultimately, the only reason to accept any given level of risk is the potential reward that it might offer. Such rewards might include:

- Winning a new client or capturing a new business opportunity

- Gaining market share or assuming a leadership role in a specific market

- Enhancing sales, revenue, or margin

- Expanding into new industries or geographies

- Advancing the market penetration of a product or service offering

- Achieving high levels of customer satisfaction and building a reference base

- Developing a quality and repeatable solution that can be leveraged in a variety of client situations

- Developing intellectual capital that can be utilized in future engagements

- Achieving some distinct competitive advantage

- Enhancing brand awareness

Once the contracting party has identified the rationale for and potential reward it may realize by assuming a particular risk, a decision must be rendered with regard to proceeding with the risk level in question or pursuing alternatives. As a general rule, the risk should not be taken in any of the following instances:

- You cannot afford to lose.

- The exposure to the outcome is too great.

- The project is not worth the risk.

- The odds are not in the project's favor.

- The benefits are not identified.

- There appear to be numerous acceptable alternatives.

- The risk does not achieve a desired objective.

- The expected value from the baseline assumptions is negative.

- A contingency plan is not in place should the results be less than originally forecasted.

The guiding principle I suggest you strictly adhere to is that a contracting party should never absorb a particular risk if it is not best able to control the events that may lead to its occurrence. If at the time of contracting, the risk allocation is such that one party may cause the risk that is then sustained by the other party, a dispute will most certainly occur. The questions listed earlier fit into a structured risk management approach that contains four major phases. By following an approach of this type, the key risk drivers in any professional services transaction will be identified, escalated to the appropriate hierarchical level, and addressed accordingly. The structured risk management approach I suggest you follow consists of four components: *identification*, *assessment and prioritization*, *response*, and *documentation*. This four-phased approach can be as formal as necessary given the markets and industries in which you operate, the products and services you bring to bear in the marketplace, your delivery sweet spots, and the size and complexity of your global delivery model. The key is simply that you are cognizant of the risks associated with delivery and have an approach by which they are addressed during the negotiation and delivery process.

Step 1: Identification

During the identification process, each party should identify all of the possible risks that may impact the overall success of the project. The identification of these issues will require a detailed review of the technical, financial, legal, quality, and business risk inherent in the transaction. Similarly situated transactions from prior periods should be reviewed to identify unforeseen risks that occurred during the delivery process.

Step 2: Assessment and Prioritization

Once the potential risks have been identified, they must be individually assessed to determine their ranking in terms of type, impact, and probability. The assessment phase may be informal and consist mainly of the subjective evaluation of the identified risks in question. If necessary, the assessment process may consist of a more detailed, quantitative measurement of a particular risk item. This phase should include input from all stakeholders in the transaction.

A number of analytical techniques may be used to assess risk. In that many of these methods are mathematically complex, a simplified model can be utilized that focuses on three key variables. They are as follows:

- **Risk event**—The consequences to the project if the risk event were to occur

- **Risk probability**—The likelihood that the event will occur

- **Amount at stake**—The severity of the consequences if the risk event should occur

By assigning a value to these variables, a ranking can be established for each risk event expressed as follows:

Risk event status = Risk probability × Amount at stake

While this model is not the most mathematically sophisticated, it allows for the quick measurement of the probability magnitude of a particular risk event. Once a ranking has been assigned to each risk event, it can be plotted in a graphical format across four quadrants, as seen in Figure 3.2.

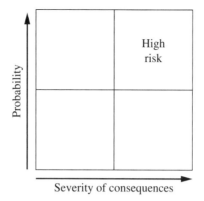

Figure 3.2   Plotting risk events

Obviously, those events with a high probability and high severity ranking require prompt attention.

Step 3: Response

The response phase of the structured risk management approach is the most critical. Within this phase, the respective parties must develop an action plan to address each of the identified risks. Depending upon the magnitude of the identified risks, the team responsible for developing the action plan should be cross-functional in scope and seek input from all relevant stakeholders. The action plan developed by the response team may range from absorbing the risk with no further action required, to deflecting the risk to a third party, to developing an appropriate contingency plan that can be followed to control and mitigate the risk event if it should occur. For each risk identified, the response team may pursue a variety of options including:

- Ignore the risk.

- Recognize the risk but take no formal action—absorb the risk as a matter of policy.

- Avoid the risk by taking the appropriate measures.

- Reduce the risk by following an alternative approach.

- Share the risk with others via a joint venture or enhanced partnership.

- Transfer the risk to others via contract or insurance.

- Retain and absorb the risk via appropriate financial allowances.

- Address the risk through a combination of the preceding options.

Step 4: Documentation

No risk strategy is complete without a formal documentation process. The purpose of the documentation phase is to build a repository of data that will facilitate the evaluation of risk in the future. Maintaining a repository of the risks identified, the response utilized, and the success of the approach will be a significant asset when evaluating the risk criteria associated with similarly situated downstream opportunities. The decision-making process will definitely be enhanced by maintaining a knowledge management repository of this type. Ultimately, the strategic intelligence gathered during the first three phases of this approach is useless unless it is properly documented and accessible to the organization.

Ultimately, maintaining a structured approach to risk management is a critical component of the negotiation and delivery process. Strictly adhering to such an approach should facilitate timely, quality, and cost-effective delivery. As we have previously discussed, the current contracting environment for strategy, design, and implementation services is extremely competitive. To that end, recent trends indicate that the Fortune 500 buying community is aggressively pursuing contracts that are fixed in terms of time, price, and scope in an effort to minimize the level of risk inherent in delivery. Potential vendors must be cognizant of this trend, as it will certainly impact their approach from a pricing and negotiation perspective. When presented with what can be unfavorable demands from a potential client, I strongly encourage you to follow an approach similar to what is outlined in this chapter. At a minimum, and absent a formal policy, be cognizant of the risks associated with delivery, accept only those risks where you are able control the events that may lead to its occurrence, develop an appropriate contingency and response should the risks materialize, and temper your pricing and negotiation stance accordingly.

Risk by Contract Type

Another significant factor that will impact the risk profile associated with an opportunity is the contract type under which the services will be delivered. When evaluating the appropriate contract type, a number of factors must be considered including:

- The range of risk inherent in the delivery of the services

- The ability to identify objective, measurable, and verifiable performance criteria

- The complexity of the requirements articulated in the statement of work

- The lack or abundance of other similar service providers in the market

- The ability to develop a narrowly tailored statement of work and the likelihood of changes during the course of service delivery

- The types of deliverables—paper based versus functioning hardware and software—required under the statement of work

- The types of resources that will be utilized during the course of service delivery

- The financial viability of the engagement

- The duration of the engagement

- The potential for loss

Let's discuss the four major contract types that are the most common across all phases of the consulting lifecycle. They are as follows.

Fixed Price

A fixed price contract mandates the delivery of work product or set of services for a fixed price regardless of the total costs incurred by the delivery party. Assuming there are no deviations in scope, the delivery party will not be able to recover any costs incurred in excess of the agreed upon fixed price for the engagement. A fixed price agreement will contain a very narrowly tailored statement of work that will explicitly define the deliverables to be completed during the course of the engagement, the timeline by which certain milestones must be achieved, any other parameters of the agreement that are fixed in nature, and a fixed price for delivery.

Buyers typically prefer fixed price agreements because they bear no risk from a price perspective. In addition, buyers like the idea of having a fixed timeline and listing of key deliverables that will be produced. However, fixed price agreements are not always appropriate if the scope of services to be completed is difficult to clearly define. They also can be challenging to administer if the scope of services to be completed is susceptible to change.

A general rule is that vendors typically like to steer away from fixed price agreements, because the vendors bear all of the risk associated with delivery; however, that is not the case in those instances where they have developed a quality and repeatable solution that can be successfully delivered in a profitable manner across multiple clients. Developing quality and repeatable solutions is the equivalent of consulting nirvana, as the vendor has, through consistent delivery, perfected the intellectual capital, risks, resources, and capabilities required for successful delivery. With this knowledge, the vendor is able to establish a fixed price that will yield high profit margins.

Beyond the governing terms and conditions of the overarching contract, the most important part of any fixed price agreement is the statement of work. The statement of work must be narrowly tailored, free of ambiguity, and able to stand on its own. In addition, it is critical to have a clearly defined change order process if changes to the scope should arise during the course of the engagement. The statement of work will define both the scope and the nature of the specific deliverables that will be completed under the engagement. The majority of disputes that arise under fixed price agreements are related to ambiguity or uncertainty within, or deviations from, the agreed upon statement of work. Typical management consulting engagements that are delivered on a fixed price basis might include:

- Implementing a software product

- Delivering a training course or workshop on a recurring basis

- Developing a specific report, analysis, or plan

Time and Materials

Under a time and materials contract, the service provider will receive payment for all services rendered in accordance with a set of fixed hourly or daily labor category rates. Unlike a fixed price agreement with a clearly defined statement of work, time-and-materials agreements are much more open-ended. Instead of focusing on a set of milestones, they are geared toward the delivery of services over some period. What differentiates time and material agreements is that the deliverable being purchased is the actual time itself. Under this type of agreement, a total budget is established against which the hours delivered are charged. Once the budget is depleted, the client can allocate additional funds to the effort, or the project may be terminated.

Most time-and-materials agreements are open-ended in terms of scope; however, it is not uncommon to see a time and materials not-to-exceed agreement. Here, the service provider will be reimbursed for a given number of hours at agreed upon rates with a price ceiling. Once the not-to-exceed ceiling is reached, the service provider will typically bear all costs associated with completing the engagement. This type of time-and-materials agreement is much more fixed price in nature, in that a set of deliverables must typically be completed within the not-to-exceed budgetary ceiling. Typical human capital services that are delivered on a time-and-materials basis might include:

- Providing ongoing information technology support services

- Managing a 24-hour help desk or call center operation

- Completing a financial or IT audit

Cost Reimbursable

A cost reimbursable contract allows the service provider reimbursement for all allowable costs incurred up to a predefined funding ceiling. This type of agreement is often utilized when delivering management consulting services to governmental entities. The types of services delivered under a cost-type agreement are similar to those of a time-and-materials engagement;

they tend to be more generic in scope, and the statement of work will not be as narrowly tailored as under a fixed price agreement. Under this type of contract, identifying the actual hourly cost rate (salary/2080 hours) for each individual engaged in the delivery of services is required. Once that cost rate is determined, it is burdened with a fringe, overhead, general and administrative, and fee component. The fee may be either fixed in nature or variable based upon the vendor's ability to achieve a set of performance criteria.

Under this type of agreement, the vendor will, at a minimum, recover its cost plus some profit depending upon the terms contained in the contract. The profit margins realized under a cost reimbursable engagement are typically less than what would be realized on either a fixed price or time-and-materials agreement. As with a time and materials not-to-exceed agreement, a cost reimbursable contract will have a budgetary ceiling against which the fully loaded hourly labor rates will be charged. To administer a cost reimbursable contract, the service provider must maintain a capable cost accounting system and maintain detailed cost records that may be subject to audit. Typical services that are delivered under a cost reimbursable basis might include:

- General management support services

- Software development

- Project management services

- Network support or other administrative services

Incentive or Award Fee

Obviously, the contract type will significantly impact the risk allocation on any engagement. As we have discussed, vastly different preferences have developed within Fortune 500 procurement organizations and their vendor community as to their contract type of choice. Generally, vendors favor time-and-materials and cost-reimbursable engagements, while clients prefer fixed price contracts. A solution to help bridge the gap between the low-risk cost reimbursable and high-risk fixed price contracts is the *incentive* or *award fee* contract.

These hybrids may contain components of both fixed price and time-and-materials contracts and serve to balance the competing interests of the parties. A contract of this type will allow the vendor to receive an award or incentive if the engagement is completed within a contractually stipulated time, cost, or quality parameter or other success metric. Similarly, if the consulting firm fails to meet that target objective, it will be penalized accordingly. The typical Fortune 500 procurement organization prefers this type of agreement because the vendor has "skin in the game" and will be rewarded accordingly for timely, quality, and cost-effective delivery. Although there may be a preference for this type of hybrid engagement, it is a viable option only in those instances in which a set of objective, measurable, and verifiable performance criteria can be identified by which the success of the engagement can be gauged.

An award fee contract typically involves placing a portion of the fee in an award pool that is paid out to the service provider in accordance with a set of predefined performance objectives. The customer project management or steering committee usually determines the actual award amount to be received by the vendor. Typically, the vendor will be able to recover some portion of its fees during the course of service delivery; the award fee amount will be determined by the client in accordance with a predefined range that varies based upon performance. Under a typical award fee agreement, the service provider would be guaranteed some minimum incentive fee. For example, if the award fee ranges from 5 percent to 15 percent, the service provider would be guaranteed a minimum fee of 5 percent; any additional fee would be based upon the performance criteria contained within the contract.

The structure for an incentive fee contract might include identifying a target number of hours and related cost that will be required to complete the engagement in question. If the consulting firm completes the engagement at the target number of hours, it will be entitled to the entire fee. If the engagement is completed for fewer hours, the firm will be entitled to its fees accrued to date as well as a share in the cost savings in a pre-negotiated amount. If the engagement is completed for more hours than the original target, the consulting firm will be entitled to recover its entire fee, but it will be reduced by its share of the excess cost in a pre-negotiated amount as well. An incentive fee engagement might also allow for a bonus or penalty payment if the provider cannot deliver a particular deliverable within a specified timeline. Typical services that are delivered under award fee and incentive fee contracts include:

- Large scale construction and public works projects

- Complex software product suite implementations

- Engagements focused on cost savings and efficiency improvements

Table 3.1 provides a high-level summary of the characteristics associated with the various contract types we have discussed, expressed across a number of variables including the range of risk associated with delivery, the statement of work elements, the deliverable types, the potential for changes in scope, the loss potential, and the typical fee structure. As they are hybrids, award and incentive fee agreements may contain components of each contract type.

A variation of the incentive-based contract that is becoming more prevalent in the market is the *performance-based* contract. Under this type of contract, a performance benchmark, cost savings, or other efficiency metric will be identified that the service provider must meet in order to be compensated for its efforts. For example, assume that the vendor is going to implement a financial management application for its client.

Table 3.1 Characteristics of Different Contract Types

VARIABLE	COST REIMBURSABLE	TIME AND MATERIALS OPEN-ENDED	FIXED PRICE AND T&M NOT-TO-EXCEED
Range of risk	Low—customer bears all risk	Medium—risk shared evenly	High—contractor bears all risk
Statement of work elements	General—project based	General types of work	Specific
Deliverable types	Level of effort	Hours by labor category	Specific result or end product
Scope change	Flexible	Flexible within labor categories	Not flexible
Loss potential	Low	Low to medium	High
Typical fee	Low	Medium	High

Typically, the consultant and client would agree upon one of the contract types listed previously; the consultant would commence the implementation effort and would invoice the client accordingly for its services. Conversely, under a performance-based contract, the consultant would agree to implement the product and absorb all of the costs associated with delivery; its payment would be based solely upon the total cost savings that the client would realize during an agreed-upon term. Of course, an engagement structured in this manner requires that a detailed baseline analysis of the client's current financial management costs be undertaken and agreed to by the parties.

Once the project is completed, the vendor's compensation would be based solely upon the difference between the baseline costs and the post-implementation cost profile. This would include all cost savings realized through the implementation of the software including efficiencies in headcount, capital expense, and business process. Another example would be if the consultant were to approach the client and agree to renegotiate all of their supplier agreements in exchange for a percentage of the savings they would realize on an annual basis. Like an incentive-based agreement, a performance-based contract is desirable from the client's perspective in that the consultant has a significant vested interest in the success of the project. Ultimately, the consultant will be compensated only if a specific cost savings, performance benchmark, or other efficiency is achieved through performance.

How Can Risk Be Measured in the Negotiation Process?

Now that we have discussed the key drivers of risk, a structured approach to addressing risk in the negotiation process, and the various contract types you may encounter when contracting with Fortune 500 companies, let's discuss some of the key risk factors that should be evaluated when gauging the amount of risk inherent in delivery. When undertaking this process, I tend to focus very carefully upon the nature of the services to be provided. If I am delivering a strategy engagement with paper-based deliverables, my risk tolerance will be much greater than if I am implementing a complex software product that interfaces with a number of legacy systems and is mission critical to the client's ongoing business operations. When negotiating a master services agreement, it is critical to remember that the term of the agreement will typically run for many years; therefore, if you have any intention of delivering more complex services at a later time, make sure to negotiate terms that will yield an acceptable level of risk and reward for any out-year work being contemplated.

When gauging the amount of risk inherent in delivery, I recommend an approach in which you identify a set of risk criteria that will impact your ability to deliver in a timely, quality, and cost-effective manner. I suggest grouping these criteria across four major categories (background, management, scope, and contract/price/timeline), assigning a weight to each of the four categories, and then developing a risk score for each criterion that can range from 1 for low risk to 5 for very high risk. By developing a weighted average risk score across the four categories, you can determine how to temper your negotiation and pricing stance in a manner that will yield an acceptable level of risk and reward over the life of the agreement. Examples of the risk criteria, categories, and weighting I would recommend reviewing before entering into a professional services agreement with a Fortune 500 entity include the following:

BACKGROUND (5%)

- Average annual client revenue
- Client relationship and positioning
- Historical relationship with client
- Client industry
- Size of client entity
- Competitive landscape

CONTRACT/PRICE/TIMELINE (25%)

- Project timeline
- Contract type
- Terms and conditions
- Pricing
- Payment terms
- Financial viability of client

SCOPE (40%)

- Geographic scope

- Project scope

- Deliverable types

- Functional domain

- Degree of process change in solution

- Services type

- Complexity of IT architecture

MANAGEMENT (30%)

- Client commitment to project

- Level of project sponsor

- Formal change-management strategy

- Technical expertise of client team

- Client decision-making ability

- Level of subcontractor/ partner involvement

- Current client footprint

- Strength of reference base and staff

- Past performance for similar engagements

- Bank of intellectual capital

The development of a risk score for an opportunity can be done on a formal or informal basis depending upon the organization's tolerance for risk. A scoring grid can be developed that classifies opportunities as low, medium, or high risk. Based upon the risk level associated with the opportunity, decisions can be reached regarding capture strategy, pricing strategy, negotiation strategy, internal reviews and approvals, and the level of quality assurance reviews and risk management practices that should be conducted and followed during the course of delivery.

In this chapter, I have provided you with a framework by which you can determine how to approach the negotiation process when delivering services at any point across the consulting lifecycle. I can tell you from extensive experience that procurement and legal organizations across the Fortune 500 client community are quite demanding with regard to the terms and conditions they expect to execute with their preferred providers. In addition, and in exchange for the "preferred" vendor label, they expect a discounted rate structure that is commensurate with the nature of the services being provided and competitive with other vendors in the marketplace.

Every organization has a different level of aversion toward risk that may fluctuate based upon the opportunity being evaluated. For each opportunity, that level of risk tolerance can best be gauged by carefully evaluating the factors previously identified across the background, scope, management, and contract/price/timeline categories. An additional factor that must be considered when evaluating new opportunities across the consulting lifecycle is that a number of service providers—especially those relatively small in size with less to lose—will agree to extremely risky and unfavorable terms and conditions and offer significant price discounts in exchange for building a delivery footprint across the Fortune 500 client community. *When evaluating risk and considering new business opportunities, my counsel is as follows: carefully pick your delivery sweet spots, develop quality and repeatable solutions, and most importantly, temper your pricing and negotiation stance based upon the amount of risk inherent in delivery.*

4

Ensuring Client Longevity

So, you've carefully chosen your delivery sweet spots, successfully built relationships within procurement and the executive leadership within your client base, and have commenced service delivery. The next question to be addressed is how to ensure longevity and footprint expansion within the client. When it comes to longevity, I believe the recipe is quite simple—combine timely, quality, and cost-effective delivery with trusted advisor relationships with key executives across the client organization, and you will guarantee longevity for many years to come.

When it comes to gauging delivery quality, the growing trend within Fortune 500 entities is to implement a fairly structured approach by which delivery success is evaluated across time, quality, and cost parameters. This approach will allow for a 360-degree review of each specific engagement, with the client evaluating the external consultant and vice versa. A weighted average overall performance score can be calculated for the engagement and evaluated against a detailed scoring grid. By taking a 360-degree approach to measuring the quality, timeliness, and cost-effectiveness of delivery, procurement organizations are able to evaluate and gauge the effectiveness of both external consultants as well as their internal project teams, based upon a consistent set of objective, measurable, and verifiable criteria. A sample set of criteria would be as follows.

Client Measurement of the Consultant

The following are sample criteria that would be utilized by the client to measure the quality and effectiveness of the consultant:

- **Quality of consultant team**—Did the consultant team bring the requisite level of experience as well as industry and functional expertise?

- **Consultant value delivered**—Did the consulting firm exceed the value proposition articulated in their proposal or in the original project objectives? Did it bring industry-leading solutions and leverage their tools, techniques, methodologies, and bank of intellectual capital? Was there an effective knowledge transfer embedded into the client base?

- **Consultant service levels**—Did the consultant exceed client service-level expectations in terms of proactively resolving issues, delivering quality proposals, and managing the change control process and overall delivery process throughout the engagement lifecycle?

- **Timeliness of delivery**—Were milestones met and deliverables provided in a manner consistent with the requirements articulated in the statement of work?

- **Cost-effectiveness of delivery**—Were actual costs less than budget? Did the consultant focus upon controlling and reducing costs where possible? Were invoices submitted in a timely and accurate manner?

Consultant Measurement of the Client

The following are sample criteria that would be utilized by the consultant to measure the capabilities of the client team and the delivery environment:

- **Quality of the client team**—Did the client staff have the requisite experience? Were they available and dedicated to the project, and did they provide input where appropriate?

- **Client project management capabilities**—Was the project fully defined in a narrowly tailored statement of work? Was the scope managed well, and was the change control process clearly defined and followed?

- **Client support/delivery environment**—Did the client meet consultant data requests in a timely manner? Did the client-provided facilities meet consultant expectations and facilitate service delivery?

- **Client timeliness and decision making**—Was the project commenced as agreed upon in the statement of work and overarching project plan? Did the client escalate decisions as necessary to facilitate timely delivery?

- **Payment**—Did the client pay for services in accordance with the terms agreed upon in the contract?

Clearly understanding an evaluation model of this type and its underlying performance metrics is important in that it will be the primary measuring stick that will be utilized by procurement to gauge delivery quality. As we discussed in the previous chapters, procurement is taking a much more aggressive role in evaluating the quality of the vendor base and removing those vendors that do not meet the requisite quality standards.

Another area where high performance ratings will help is with new buyers from the client community that seek counsel from procurement regarding potential vendors that can meet the delivery requirements articulated in their respective statement of work. Never underestimate the amount of work that can potentially flow from this encounter, given that new buyers are the project leads and decision makers for as much as 50 percent of the new opportunities being brought into the procurement process within many Fortune 500 companies. If you are successful in achieving high scores on these evaluations, you will be making significant strides in ensuring longevity across the client buying community.

The other critical component that is required for achieving client longevity is building and sustaining long-term and trusted advisor relationships within the client community. Ask any management consulting executive what type of relationship they aspire to achieve with their clients, and they will all undoubtedly spout out the words "trusted advisor." This is not a status that can be achieved through one, two, or even ten engagements, but requires building a long-term and collaborative partnership with a client under which you help them solve their short-term problems and achieve the broader mission, vision, and strategic agenda they have articulated for their organization. Such trusted advisor relationships do not come easily, but when combined with a history of timely, quality, and cost-effective delivery, will yield a group of strategic accounts in which you will remain engaged for the long term.

Having trusted advisor relationships and a history of quality delivery will play a significant role in the area of footprint expansion across different functional areas and phases of the consulting lifecycle. As we have discussed, brand awareness and a strong reference base are critical when attempting to sell services within a Fortune 500 client. However, one thing will mitigate the overwhelming reliance that a typical buyer places in these two areas: the coveted "trusted advisor" relationship.

Most Fortune 500 buyers—at all hierarchical levels—would agree that they would prefer to have a very limited set of vendors that could meet all of their full lifecycle consulting needs, as long as they could deliver in a quality manner at competitive price points that are commensurate with the nature of the services being provided. Under this approach, their consultants would become trusted advisors and partners that would deliver a complete solution, strategy, design, and implementation across the entire consulting lifecycle. Given that strategy is so deeply connected with the underlying technology that is required for execution, this approach would minimize the knowledge loss that is unfortunately realized when the strategy provider exits, and the designers and implementers arrive. Despite knowing that clients would prefer a model of this type, most management consulting firms have not changed their delivery models.

Under the current environment, the strategy firms focus on strategy, and the design and implementation firms focus on architecting solutions and their subsequent implementation. While many of these firms, particularly the strategy consultancies, have tried to extend their delivery capabilities downstream beyond the strategy and design boundary, few have been successful, as they lack the brand awareness, reference base, price competitiveness, and quality and repeatable solutions required to build a pipeline of opportunities.

You might ask how trusted advisor status will assist with footprint expansion across the strategy, design, and implementation domains. The answer is simple: once you have achieved trusted advisor status with your clients and developed a reputation for quality delivery, the concrete line of demarcation between these two domains will begin to crumble at the edges. Ultimately, Fortune 500 clients make purchase decisions based on safety, reliability, predictability, vendor reputation, and industry-specific experience.

Once you have established a trusted relationship with clients, they are much more likely to minimize their reliance and their focus on brand awareness for delivering a specific type of service and may even lessen their focus on price sensitivity, assuming their trusted advisor can establish that they have properly skilled staff and can successfully deliver upon the work being contemplated. It is because of their trusted advisor status that many of the large strategy providers have been able to successfully move downstream and deliver services beyond their typical strategy domain. It is the same dynamic that has allowed some of the more traditional downstream providers to move farther upstream in the consulting lifecycle and to expand their delivery footprint into the previously impenetrable strategy domain. Just remember that the key to either of these doors is achieving trusted advisor status with your clients. Even though you may possess the requisite skill set and delivery capabilities, failing to achieve trusted advisor status will keep the doors locked and the strategy, design, and implementation lines of demarcation firmly cemented in place.

Ensuring longevity and footprint expansion within a Fortune 500 client is based solely upon building trusted advisor relationships and developing a reputation for delivering in a timely, quality, and cost-effective manner. It is that simple and that complex. My counsel is to focus on delivery basics and to build strong relationships, and long-term success will follow. I liken my recommended approach to the counsel I gave my nephew who has just started playing football. The games are not too exciting, as every play tends to be a rushing play—either student body left or right. But I tell him to remain focused on basic blocking and tackling, and before he knows it, his team will be running a complex West Coast offensive scheme and traversing down the field with ease. As on the gridiron, trusted advisor relationships with Fortune 500 clients don't simply materialize overnight. The key is to focus on timely, quality, and cost-effective delivery, and the pipeline of opportunities, reference base, relationships, footprint expansion, and longevity will result.

5

How Are Services Really Sold?

Let's assume that you have established brand awareness, a strong reference base, and even a history of quality and timely delivery with middle market customers. Is it possible to try and break into a Fortune 500 account and be successful? This begs the following very important question: is it possible to penetrate a Fortune 500 prospect with limited preexisting relationships and to effectively sell consulting services with limited brand awareness, a reference base with smaller clients, and a history of quality delivery? I strongly believe the answer to this question depends primarily upon the nature of the services being provided, and this can best be described under what I refer to as the *relationship/best value continuum*.

Think of the entire consulting lifecycle. When it comes to high-level strategy services, relationships will always carry the day and trump best value time after time. Remember my former colleague who told the CEO that the cost for the engagement was $1 million, and that was his cost, and that his team was free? While that approach might be viable in the C-suite with a longstanding client who has a good sense of humor and with whom you have a trusted advisor relationship, its application is extremely limited. As you progress farther to the right across the consulting lifecycle and leave the strategy realm, best value becomes much more important; vendors become more prevalent, services are more commodity-like in nature, and procurement becomes much more heavily engaged in the buying process. If you were to try the $1 million line for a nonstrategy engagement, you

61

would most likely be seeing the pavement outside the client's headquarters in a very expeditious manner.

Strategy Consulting and Trusted Advisor Relationships

As we previously discussed, successfully selling high-level strategy consulting services to a Fortune 500 entity will require building a trusted advisor relationship with its C-suite leadership. These relationships do not develop overnight and once established will typically not be broken unless there is a change of leadership or control within the company. This means that the likelihood of a new vendor entering a Fortune 500 company and selling strategy services to their C-level executives or unseating their current strategy provider is slim to none. This is not to say that the vendor lacks the requisite ability and foresight to help shape the strategic agenda of the company; rather, the trusted advisor relationship and bond that has been established between the strategy provider and the C-level leadership is simply too strong to break. This is even the case when the party attempting to do the unseating is one of the other four brand name strategy providers.

This trusted advisor relationship between the C-suite and their preferred strategy provider is even surprisingly reinforced by procurement organizations which, as we know, are constantly striving for price reductions and finding best value from the vendor community. I have been a party to countless numbers of discussions in which senior-level procurement representatives have told me explicitly that corporate strategy services are only provided by a specific vendor, that the vendor is immune from any rigid pricing negotiation with procurement, and that no other agreements will be executed that contemplate work that crosses into the corporate strategy domain.

Based upon these experiences, I would assert that when it comes to selling strategy services to Fortune 500 entities, longstanding trusted advisor relationships will drive success and endure until a change in leadership or control should occur. I would therefore suggest that potential strategy vendors focus their efforts on selling one or multiple levels beneath the C-suite, or attempt to partner or establish some form of alliance with the entrenched strategy provider. Selling a few hierarchical levels below the C-suite is not a bad proposition; as we have discussed, the bulk of the typical Fortune 500 strategy wallet is targeted for consulting services that will be delivered beyond the boundary of the C-suite. The people who are actually doing the buying tend to be one or more levels removed from this level in the hierarchy anyway. If you have or can develop a trusted advisor relationship with the C-suite leadership within a Fortune 500 company, I urge you to leverage that relationship to its fullest extent—to deliver corporate strategy services and expand your delivery footprint downstream if you are so inclined.

To the extent that you lack such a relationship, target your business development efforts toward functional leadership that may be a few layers removed from the C-suite. They have both strategic and tactical agendas to pursue, have an ample budget, and are likely to engage external consultants to help them achieve their objectives.

Why spend a lot of time focused upon entering a segment of the consulting lifecycle that is driven by long-term and trusted advisor relationships, that is pretty much impossible to penetrate unless you are a member of an elite group of providers, and that makes up the smallest portion of the total global consulting spend of any Fortune 500 company? My answer to that question is don't waste your time. As I previously mentioned, when it comes to strategy services, I believe that all roads lead to McKinsey and its corporate strategy brethren. Remember the Michael Jordan commercials in the 1990s that said everyone wants to be like Mike? When it comes to corporate strategy, everyone wants to be like McKinsey. So I would tell a new vendor to let Booz, McKinsey, Bain, and BCG compete and fight for this work while you focus on that portion of the consulting wallet where the real buying takes place.

Selling Beyond Strategy

That being said, let's focus on how services are being sold outside the corporate strategy realm. If you think about the relationship/best value continuum, best value will become more important the farther you move to the right in the consulting lifecycle. Don't get me wrong; relationships within the organization will most certainly help in selling design and implementation services as well, but their relative weight becomes diminished as the services become more commodity-like in nature.

Let's look at an example that highlights this issue. Assume that you have a great relationship with the IT leadership in a leading telecommunications provider, and they are contemplating the award for the implementation of a customer relationship management application. You have a reputation for delivering in a timely, quality, and cost-effective manner, and your brand awareness and reference base is quite strong. You are one of two competitors that have made it to the down-select process for this program. Both vendors have similarly situated technical solutions, delivery timelines, and relatively equal capabilities in terms of staff and industry expertise. However, the other vendor is 20 percent lower on price. The burning questions are how much is the relationship actually worth, and how much price sensitivity will there be when it comes down to the final evaluation process?

While 20 percent may not be a big deal on a $100,000 engagement, a global CRM implementation of this type may span multiple years, is mission-critical to the organization, and will most likely require a significant investment. I strongly believe in the value of relationships and the influence they have in the sales cycle. To that end, I believe most clients will choose the vendor with whom they feel most comfortable and with whom they have a strong relationship. But at what point does the price variance become too high to justify an award that will cost 20 percent more during the implementation lifecycle? If the lower-cost vendor has a less technically viable solution and there are questions about their ability to deliver, then maybe 20 percent is not a big deal and not worth the risk associated with failure. But that is not the case here, as these vendors are quite similarly situated in terms of capability and likelihood of success. So, what is the value of the relationship? How strong of a technical solution, reference base, and reputation for quality delivery does it take to justify an award to a higher-priced vendor? Is it 5 percent? Is it 10 percent?

There is no firm answer here, but I do have a reference point to share that comes from the public sector. The Federal Acquisition Regulations (FAR) govern the procurement of goods and services by the U.S. federal government (and provide for a "best value" approach in the selection process. Best value is defined in Section 2.101 of the FAR as "the expected outcome of an acquisition that, in the government's estimation, provides the greatest overall benefit in response to the requirement." While the FAR guidelines do not state a specific guideline that would allow for an award other than to the lowest price offeror, there seems to be an unwritten rule that a 5 percent gap in price is an acceptable variance that would justify making an award to a higher-priced vendor based upon best value. Under this scenario, the government is required to carefully document how the perceived benefits of the higher priced proposal shall merit the additional cost. Given the current economic climate, Fortune 500 entities are very heavily focused on cost-cutting efforts, and I would believe that a 5 percent to 10 percent gap at most would be the benchmark in a typical Fortune 500 award process.

There will always be exceptions to this general rule, but the bottom line is that services outside of the corporate strategy realm are becoming extremely competitive, and new and capable low-cost vendors are cropping up that may lack strong relationships, but that have strong delivery capability and very attractive price points. It is therefore critical to carefully pick your delivery sweet spots prior to approaching a Fortune 500 entity and to make sure that you can deliver in a manner that is both commensurate with the nature of the services being provided and competitive with the other vendors in the market. I am not in any way downplaying the role of strong relationships, but the inherent value of these relationships will certainly be mitigated as you move farther to the right in the consulting lifecycle and as commoditization and price sensitivity become much more important in the decision-making process.

Buying Trends and the Preferred Vendor Selection Process

6

Just How Big Is That Wallet?

Kennedy Information estimates that the global consulting market slightly exceeded $300 billion in 2008. Combine that with the Gartner Group's estimate that worldwide outsourcing spending grew over 8 percent in 2008 to some $443 billion (forecast to reach $518 billion in 2013), and you have quite a thick wallet and countless opportunities through which you can expand your delivery footprint, create brand awareness, develop a reference base, and build a robust pipeline. The consulting lifecycle is quite broad, and the depth and breadth of potential opportunities range from conducting a strategic analysis of potential acquisition or divesti- ture candidates, to leading the multiyear implementation of a human resources, financial management, or customer relationship management product suite.

It would be foolish for me to suggest that the current economic climate will not detrimentally impact consulting spend across the entire lifecycle for the foreseeable future. Growth rates will certainly slow and total spend my not rebound to 2008 levels for some time. Most Fortune 500 companies will be looking for opportunities to do things better, faster, and cheaper, and one of the areas that will most likely get some additional scrutiny is the use of third-party consultants. This advice was even proposed, believe it or not, by McKinsey & Company in a recent *McKinsey Quarterly* in which they suggested that Wall Street firms could realize savings by reducing their utilization of consultants. I suspect that many companies may heed the advice of McKinsey and will reduce their budgets for both strategy and design and implementation services given the current economic climate.

But I believe the overall reduction in spend will be minimal and that Fortune 500 companies will simply become more prudent consumers of consulting services across the entire delivery spectrum. They will be more focused on the quality of the services being delivered and will become much more diligent in the procurement process. They will also target consulting spend in a more laser-like fashion on engagements that will yield tactical revenue growth and increased operational efficiencies. In addition to focusing on reducing costs within and gaining more efficiency in business operations, Fortune 500 buyers at all hierarchical levels, with the able assistance of their procurement organizations, will become more aggressive in the negotiation process and will focus much more heavily on performance-based agreements under which both the buyer and service provider will mutually agree upon a set of objective, measurable, and verifiable criteria that will become the measuring stick by which the consultant's ultimate fee will be determined. Such pay-for-performance fee structures are not uncommon and have been around for many years, but still are not utilized nearly as much as their time and materials and fixed price brethren. The current allocation of roughly 40 percent time and materials, 50 percent fixed price, and 10 percent incentive- and performance-based agreements will shift, and pay will become much more closely linked to performance. The bottom line is that clients will still procure consulting services across the entire delivery spectrum, but will demand that their consultants have skin in the game and deliver measurable and sustainable results.

What About Public-Sector Opportunities?

Another wallet that many of the large consulting firms have tapped is that of the global public sector. All of the large firms including McKinsey, Bain & Company, The Boston Consulting Group, Booz Allen Hamilton, Accenture, IBM, Deloitte, and others have built very successful practices around delivering strategy, design, and implementation engagements to governmental entities around the world. The large consultancies have realized that there is a middle ground—an intersection—between their public and private sector lines of business and that they can transport their best practices and knowledge base across this historically impassable divide. This opportunity has definitely been facilitated by the fact that there has been a convergence with regard to the issues and concerns that both public and private sector leaders face, particularly in the areas of security, healthcare, and transportation.

The level of brand awareness that has been achieved by the large consulting firms in the public sector was certainly evident in the most recent U.S. Presidential election. A November 2007 *Time* magazine article, "Can McKinsey & Co. Fix the Government?" referred to Mitt Romney's statement in the *Wall Street Journal* article that if he were elected president, he would "probably hire McKinsey & Company to tell him how to reorganize the government." He went on to state that he wasn't kidding, and that it might be another management consulting firm such as Bain or The Boston Consulting Group. The article goes on to state how firms like McKinsey are restructuring educational systems, reforming cabinet agencies, advising on natural disasters, and bringing their commercial practices to bear across the public sector. Within the United States, the current political climate is all about change and reinventing the role of government irrespective of partisan beliefs. The *Time* article also referenced a *Times of London* column in which McKinsey's then managing director, Ian Davis, addressed the notion of government as a business. In that article, he stated, "This is not a partisan issue but an issue beyond political stance."

Selling management consulting services to the public sector is much more complex than selling in the commercial markets, given the level of public scrutiny and regulatory compliance. Despite the rigid regulatory environment and compliance issues associated within the public sector, the major firms have been willing to navigate these issues and pursue opportunities within this market.

I hope you now have a clearer picture of the breadth of the consulting lifecycle, the size of the global consulting market, and the vast opportunities available across the public and private sector domains. The current environment, while focused on cost reduction, tactical revenue generation, and operational efficiency, still presents viable opportunities across the consulting lifecycle. While some programs may be temporarily postponed and third-party spend may be reduced, 2009 financial results from the largest strategy and IT firms suggest that procurement activity is still robust across the consulting lifecycle in the areas of corporate strategy, operations management, human resource management, financial management, and business advisory services. The bottom line is that the wallet is still quite thick, even if it is reduced in the short term. So pick your delivery sweet spots, build relationships, and let the quality, timeliness, and cost-effectiveness of your delivery capability serve as your calling card.

7

Maximize Your Share of the Wallet and Avoid Being Labeled as a Commodity

We know the wallet is quite large and that opportunities abound across the public and private sector domains. The next question, therefore, becomes how to maximize your portion of that wallet in the market and delivery domain in which you want to specialize. We have already discussed that this can be a complex answer, as it requires relationships, references, brand awareness, and a history of quality and timely delivery. It also requires avoiding being viewed as a commodity by a prospective client. I would assert that the word *commodity* is one that is feared by consulting leaders around the globe. While there will always be a market for commodity-based services, successfully selling to Fortune 500 companies will require an enhanced value proposition that will yield quality solutions and drive tangible results and growth opportunities. Failure to achieve this position will result in an endless number of meetings with procurement representatives in which they demand lower prices and threaten to migrate their consulting spend to a lower-cost provider.

Avoiding the Commodity Label

I assure you that the latter experience is quite uncomfortable. I cannot tell you how many times I have been sitting on the other side of the table from a procurement executive who labeled as commodities the services I was trying to sell and focused the entire negotiation on price reductions that would result in parity with an existing preferred vendor. Moving them off this position is not easy and requires engaging the business leadership and articulating the proposition that the services being provided do not stand in isolation, but are part of a broader delivery agenda that will help the client solve a mission-critical business problem; empower its customers, suppliers, and employees with technology; create new opportunities in the market; and help ensure their longevity in the market.

Although this sounds good, successfully asserting this position is not easy, as the commodity-focused approach has become very strongly engrained in the minds of procurement executives and buyers in recent years. A May 2008 *Consulting Magazine* article addresses how this commodity-focused approach came into existence within the IT consulting domain. In that article, writer Eric Krell identifies two very different profiles of IT consultants that have developed over the past 15 years. The first profile is the IT consultant who "at one time would examine a new strategy, one enabled by some sort of technology change, and then design a way to make the strategy work in reality." These consultants clearly fit the preferred profile, as they are able to understand the desired future state and to undertake and implement the programs, initiatives, and technology required for success. However, another IT consultant profile came into the mix in the 1990s, when implementing a PeopleSoft, SAP, Siebel, or Oracle product solution was the flavor of the decade. As Krell suggests, this ERP revolution fostered a generation of IT consultants focused on "slapping in" a system rather than addressing business challenges and designing solutions to solve them. In my time at PeopleSoft from late 1996 through 2002, I can certainly attest to the fact that the "get the customer live" mantra was certainly well-engrained across the organization.

This approach certainly has had a major impact on the current competitive landscape, as many firms kept business consulting and technology consulting as separate and distinct service offerings, which flies completely counter to what Fortune 500 clients expect and demand from their trusted advisors and partners. In his article, Krell quotes Stephen Pratt, the CEO and managing director of Infosys Consulting, who commented that "It's difficult to find the star athletes who combine real technology savvy and real business savvy." Pratt goes on to describe how segregating these two service lines for so many years has "helped foment professional friction between prima donna MBAs and propeller heads." He goes on to state that some firms have "built up super blueblood cultures that can't tolerate people with technical skills. Some technology consulting firms have built up an arrogant stance that we do the real work and the MBAs are the blue-sky guys who don't know anything." Based upon my experience, Pratt is spot-on in his assessment, and it is this dynamic that has created a lot of infighting and challenges for firms that are trying to span the full consulting lifecycle. As we previously discussed, a number of firms are trying to move either up or down stream in the consulting lifecycle, and key measures of their success will be the level of collaboration and integration they can achieve across their business and technology consulting lines of business, and how they articulate their value proposition across the business and technology consulting continuum.

As I read this article, the whole notion of being commoditized came full circle for me, especially when dealing with overly aggressive procurement organizations within Fortune 500 entities. Procurement organizations within Fortune 500 organizations have become much more centralized and influential in the buying process. Procurement is much more aligned with the second IT consultant profile just articulated in that they are more focused on accomplishing discrete engagements within a low-cost rate structure and are not necessarily focused on the overarching business strategy their organization is trying to achieve. While you can attempt to utilize business relationships to exert some pressure on procurement to try and think outside of this box, they will most likely have limited success, as the farther you move into the IT world, the more control and influence procurement wields.

No-Man's Land

The possible impact of having your service offerings labeled as commodities adds an additional layer of complexity to the sales process. If you focus on delivering an isolated technology solution within a certain niche in the

IT lifecycle, you will most definitely be viewed as a commodity by procurement organizations and will be constantly benchmarked against the low-cost provider in the market. This is in effect being in "no-man's land," as there will always be a new entrant in the market that is willing to deliver services under a rate structure that is simply not financially viable for the larger service providers, given their cost base and overhead structure. So, unless you are willing to be in a constant state of renegotiation with regard to your rate structure and enjoy margin erosion, I would avoid this dynamic at all costs. Or as I always like to say, you might as well just head to the golf course and focus your sales efforts elsewhere.

To avoid the commodity label, it is critical to find the right spot on the business and technology consulting continuum. To the maximum extent possible, develop a full service solution that crosses over the full lifecycle, and negotiate a master services agreement that will allow for multiple rate cards that are commensurate with the nature of the services being provided. If you are not a full solution provider, make sure you understand the client's strategic agenda and carefully articulate how your service offerings, even if they are just a small piece of the overall solution, will assist them in achieving their strategic objectives. Finally, distinguish yourself from the other vendors in the marketplace and carefully articulate your value proposition. Failing to achieve that objective, irrespective of strong brand awareness and reference base, will result in your services being labeled as a commodity and will detrimentally impact your long-term viability across the Fortune 500 client community.

8

Your Sales Lifeline: The Master Services Agreement and Preferred Vendor Status

Historically, selling services to Fortune 500 entities was fairly straightforward. A services provider would identify a potential consulting opportunity, pitch its service offering to the prospective client, agree upon the scope of work and corresponding price, execute a contract, and commence service delivery. Procurement organizations were extremely decentralized, functional and geographic leaders had complete autonomy over their external consulting budgets, and service providers were routinely engaged at different points within the corporate hierarchy and across multiple business units within the organization. Given this level of procurement decentralization, coordination around third-party consulting spend was nominal at best, and multiple agreements, many with conflicting pricing structures and delivery terms and conditions, would prevail at any one time. Because of the significant size of third-party consulting spend within many Fortune 500 companies, in some cases in excess of $100 million annually, this process was clearly inefficient and yielded an extremely suboptimized procurement and performance management process.

Corporate Procurement Centralization

To combat this trend, Fortune 500 companies across all industries and geographies have undertaken completely centralizing and streamlining their procurement processes, particularly in the area of third-party consulting spend. To that end, they have instituted a much more sophisticated buying methodology and have migrated toward a very centralized procurement process under which global master services agreements are executed with a select group of preferred vendors. Through this process, the Fortune 500 strive to optimize their global consulting spend and to share best practices among operating entities, to streamline their vendor base by identifying a set of preferred vendors authorized to deliver across a set of discrete service lines, to aggressively negotiate terms and conditions and price structures in exchange for bestowing the "preferred" label, to require vendors to have skin in the game, to evaluate the vendor community in terms of rates, performance, and competencies, and to heavily influence the procurement process by actively promoting those firms that they believe deliver best value.

As we have discussed, relationships still carry a lot of weight when contracting for professional services with Fortune 500 companies, especially at the most senior levels. While relationships will not be completely ignored by procurement for any type of work across the consulting lifecycle, the reality of the current delivery environment is that effectively selling services and establishing a footprint within the Fortune 500 community requires building relationships with procurement executives, attaining the "preferred" vendor label, and executing master services agreements that contain the rate structure and terms and conditions that will govern delivery on a global basis. If you are only selling high-level corporate strategy services to C-suite executives and don't have aspirations beyond that delivery footprint, then you can certainly opt out of what is usually a mandatory process for all preferred vendors. However, unless your firm name is McKinsey & Company (and the trend is changing for them as well), I would not recommend pursuing this course of action.

As we have discussed, establishing a long-term trusted advisor relationship within a Fortune 500 client is critical to establishing longevity, and footprint expansion and maintaining a lengthy list of master services agreements will certainly help facilitate meeting that objective. The utilization of the master agreement and preferred vendor process is not a fad and is not in limited use. I have contracted with roughly half of the Fortune 500 and can assure you that the leading companies across all industries including financial services, healthcare, energy and utilities, telecommunications, automotive, transportation, consumer and media, and technology all have broadly adopted the utilization of master services agreements that drive the delivery of consulting services on a global basis.

The Master Agreement Process

Let's talk a little bit about how the master agreement process works. It typically starts with a request for proposal in which potential preferred vendors are asked to respond to a very detailed solicitation and questionnaire, which will be utilized by procurement to gauge their viability as a preferred vendor within a single or across multiple service lines. Typical service lines may include corporate strategy, human resources, operations management, finance, and information technology. The solicitation will require the potential vendors to provide extensive information in the following areas:

- Company overview
- Financial statements
- Corporate history
- Organizational structure
- Staff composition, size, and location
- Quality assurance process
- Customer satisfaction metrics
- Small business program
- Diversity programs
- Primary service offerings

- Terms and conditions of delivery
- References
- Payment terms
- Service performance measures
- Travel and expense policies
- Executive officers
- Bank references
- Ownership configuration
- Office locations
- Competitive differentiators

- Dispute resolution process
- Operational infrastructure
- Corporate values and ethics
- Background screening process
- Performance measures
- Pricing structure

- Largest clients
- Discount structure
- Tax and compliance programs
- Delivery capabilities

Once the proposals have been submitted, the corporate procurement department will review the submissions and down-select those vendors that will advance to the next step in the master agreement process. The next phase of the process will typically involve face-to-face meetings with procurement to have a more in-depth discussion regarding capabilities across the various service lines as well as to discuss and negotiate a rate structure. In parallel with this process, the attorneys for each organization will negotiate the requisite terms and conditions that will govern delivery. Both of these processes can take significant time, as rate structures for global delivery across multiple service lines can become quite complex and heated; procurement tends to be quite aggressive in attaining the most favorable rate structure possible in exchange for the preferred vendor label.

In addition, the terms and conditions negotiations between the attorneys can be quite cumbersome, as every Fortune 500 client has its own set of standard delivery terms and conditions that typically serve as the starting point for these negotiations. As you can imagine, the terms and conditions are very heavily skewed in favor of the client and require fairly extensive negotiation. In the next part of the book, we will discuss the key delivery terms and conditions and how the negotiation process hopefully results in an agreement that yields an acceptable level of risk and reward for both parties to the transaction. Once the negotiation process is complete from both a rate structure, and terms and conditions perspective, the master agreement is executed, and the vendor can focus on business development and service delivery. Of course, an ongoing relationship with procurement will continue, and there will typically be a stringent quality assurance process to evaluate vendor performance across time, quality, and cost parameters for every opportunity in which they are engaged.

When discussing the current Fortune 500 procurement landscape, I have witnessed many sales and delivery executives become quite concerned with the migration to the master agreement process, as they see it as an inhibitor to the sales process. I take the opposite approach and strongly support executing a master services agreement with every client with whom you are currently engaged and have growth aspirations. A few years back, I remember seeing an internal communication from one of the senior leaders of a major consulting firm that dated back to the early 1980s. In the communication, the senior executive commented that he had become aware that clients had been asking for contracts above and beyond the standard proposals that were routinely submitted. His message was to strongly discourage entering into formal contracts, as he felt they increased the difficulty of doing business and most importantly, demeaned the professional stature of the firm.

While this might have been the case in the early 1980s, it couldn't be farther from the truth today, as all of the major consultancies have embraced (some willingly, some by force) the master agreement process, maybe with the exception of a few of the strategy providers, as a standard part of doing business with the Fortune 500 client base. Although the strategy firms have been reluctant to embrace this change, I can assure you, based upon recent conversations, that they are rethinking their strategy and approach in this area. While the master agreement process can be rigorous and cumbersome, it can be helpful for a consulting firm looking to expand into the Fortune 500 as it facilitates new client acquisition, existing client retention, and footprint expansion. From an acquisition perspective, the master agreement process is fairly structured and rigid, but is generally open to all firms that want to attain the preferred vendor label within a respective service line. While they may not make it to the down-select or award process, it does allow for an entry path into a client base where there are fairly significant barriers to entry.

From a retention perspective, once a consulting firm has successfully executed a master services agreement, it has what can serve as a global hunting license for new opportunities across the organization. In addition, procurement organizations routinely measure the performance of their preferred suppliers across time, quality, and cost parameters. Achieving high scores in these evaluations will ensure longevity with the client base and enhance their relationship with procurement that may positively impact future buying decisions. From a footprint expansion perspective, having a master agreement in place may help facilitate expansion into other service delivery areas across the consulting lifecycle, as it contributes to building brand awareness, an internal reference base, and a reputation for quality delivery across the organization. Master agreements are not merely a commercial best practice; the U.S. federal government has long utilized a master agreement-like process through its General Services Administration Federal Supply Schedule program that allows all cabinet agencies to access a broad vendor base of products and services under an expedited sales cycle.

But master agreements also have some disadvantages associated with them. Because Fortune 500 firms, and particularly Fortune 500 procurement organizations, view the master agreement as a valuable asset, they expect very favorable pricing in exchange for executing the agreement and awarding preferred vendor status. As we have previously discussed, this downward pricing pressure may be prevalent throughout the term of the agreement, even if a multiyear rate structure and corresponding escalation factor are built into the agreement. In addition, being a preferred vendor comes with a lot of scrutiny in the delivery process; the performance management process is such that any challenges with regard to the quality or timeliness of delivery are escalated very quickly and must be promptly addressed by the vendor. Remember that the "preferred" label is not permanent. Through the quality review process, Fortune 500 procurement organizations routinely recruit new vendors and retire underperforming vendors from the program. Other disadvantages include having to compete for more work, as Fortune 500 companies may issue mini-RFPs to a set of preferred vendors to create additional competition for new opportunities, as well as potentially having to respond to RFPs that are wired for other preferred vendors but run through the process to comply with procurement policies.

The final disadvantage is that preferred vendors are typically given a master agreement that authorizes them to deliver and that contains a rate structure commensurate with a discrete set of service lines. Crossing over into other functional disciplines (human resources, operations management, finance, IT) will require establishing some credibility for delivery in those areas and negotiating a rate structure that is competitive with the other preferred vendors in that space.

For any vendor wishing to enter the Fortune 500 professional services market, I suggest carefully evaluating the level of centralization within the client's procurement organization as well as the level of sophistication around the master services agreement process. These two dynamics should help drive your overall business development strategy. The potential range of sophistication crosses the spectrum from a purely administrative use of master agreements (20 percent) to a comprehensive use (60 percent) that is promulgated by procurement. A number of hybrid models (20 percent) fall out somewhere between these two boundaries. The different approaches and their respective characteristics are as follows:

ADMINISTRATIVE UTILIZATION OF MASTER SERVICES AGREEMENTS

- Delivery terms and conditions only—no rate structure

- No competition or RFP requirements for buyers

- Decentralized procurement organization with limited influence over the buying community

- No preferred vendors across discrete service lines

- Decentralized decision-making process around vendor selection and service delivery

COMPREHENSIVE USE OF MASTER SERVICES AGREEMENTS

- Delivery terms and conditions as well as pricing structure and rate cards

- Rigid competition and RFP process

- Centralized procurement organization that heavily influences the buying decision

- Preferred vendor base across discrete service lines

- More centralized decision-making process around vendor selection and service delivery

- Structured vendor performance management process across cost, time, and quality parameters

Never forget the importance of procurement. We will discuss procurement later, but suffice it to say that it is critical to build upon existing relationships and to establish new relationships with client procurement executives. Whether it is for an individual transaction or a master agreement, these executives exert significant influence over their buying community and can serve as an internal champion for your respective delivery capabilities. Never forget that in large organizations, new buyers are frequently coming into procurement with statements of work, looking for guidance as to which potential vendors the request for proposal solicitation should be submitted. If you speak with most services sales and delivery executives, they are not big fans of Fortune 500 procurement organizations; however, I take the complete opposite approach, and it has served me quite well. I strongly believe that procurement can be your friend and ally and can serve as an extension of your sales force; they can assist with building a pipeline, including your firm in the request for proposal flow, promoting your service offerings within their buying community, and driving your value proposition down into their organization. I speak from experience in this regard, as during my tenures at Booz Allen Hamilton and PeopleSoft, I developed strong relationships with key procurement executives within the client base that facilitated the execution of valuable global master services agreements, assisted with new opportunity capture and footprint expansion, and yielded a strong return on investment.

Part
3

Negotiating Terms and Conditions with the Fortune 500

9

An Introduction to Negotiation

The ability to successfully negotiate delivery terms and conditions is critical for any professional services firm that seeks to establish a global footprint within the Fortune 500 client base. However, achieving this objective is not always easy. Almost every Fortune 500 company with which I have been engaged maintains their own set of standard delivery terms and conditions that tend to be extremely unfavorable to the service provider. Given the enterprise wide impact of the services being provided and the extensive risk inherent in delivery, many organizations, through their standard terms and conditions, seek to deflect all possible delivery risk and the consequences related thereto squarely onto the shoulders of their management consulting, systems integrator, or outsourcing services provider. While negotiating changes to their standard terms and conditions is certainly possible and almost always occurs, it will extend the sales cycle, create tension among the two parties, and may detrimentally impact a relationship that has yet to officially commence.

You would think that the terms and conditions that will govern delivery would establish the foundation for building a long-term and trusted advisor relationship between the two parties, would raise the probability of success, would create opportunities for collaboration and incentives, and would ultimately yield an acceptable level of risk and reward for both parties to the transaction. In practice, that is far from the truth, as the terms and conditions negotiation typically sets the stage and creates the framework for how the parties will address and allocate the consequences of failure. I was always amazed how the initial discussions with a corporate procurement organization regarding the execution of a master services agreement would go so well. I would typically come to the initial meeting with various leaders from my firm who would be responsible for service delivery, and the conversation would focus upon how the depth and breadth of our delivery capabilities would help the client achieve their mission and vision, advance their strategic agenda, and realize a significant return on their investment. In return, we would build a robust pipeline of opportunities, enhance our reference base, expand our delivery footprint, and hopefully begin developing a long-term trusted advisor relationship.

Coming out of these initial meetings, I was always quite confident that the rate structure and terms and conditions negotiation would go smoothly, as the focus seemed to be on collaboration and value creation, not on low price and risk deflection. Unfortunately, my optimism always faded quickly, as the participants in the follow-up conversations were limited to procurement staff and legal counsel, and it was quite clear that the courting process had concluded, and it was time to hash out the terms and conditions of the prenuptial agreement. Once this process commenced, it would typically become quite emotionally charged and could, depending upon the reasonableness of the parties and their desire to strictly adhere to a corporate standard, continue on for some time before reaching closure.

If you question the contention that most contracts support the allocation of failure rather than promoting collaboration, consider an annual study conducted by the International Association for Contract and Commercial Management in which they solicit feedback from more than 500 international companies regarding which terms and conditions they negotiate most frequently. Since 2002, when they began conducting this study, the results have remained relatively unchanged with regard to the top ten most frequently negotiated (and most likely to result in blood pressure elevation) terms. While there has been some slight movement over the years, the most consistently negotiated terms and conditions, from the perspective of both buyer and seller, are as follows:

1. Limitation on liability

2. Indemnity

3. Intellectual property

4. Price

5. Termination

6. Warranty

7. Confidential information/data protection

8. Delivery/acceptance

9. Payment

10. Liquidated damages

While there are certainly differences depending upon the buyer and seller, geographic region, and applicable law, it appears clear that most Fortune 500 companies—at least their procurement and legal organizations—view the terms and conditions contained in the services contract as the mechanism by which blame will be allocated when a delivery failure should arise. Maybe this approach is acceptable given the scope and complexity of engagements and the significant risk associated with their potential failure. However, there is clearly a dichotomy between the message being communicated by C-level executives regarding collaboration, partnering for success, and the ease of doing business with their respective entities, and the methods and tactics being promulgated by their procurement and legal organizations in the execution of these agreements. The complexity of the current delivery environment necessitates that these ten key terms will always reside at the top of the list, but I would hope to see some slight movement in favor of those terms that promote collaboration and the likelihood of success.

Keeping Your Competitive Arousal in Check

As an attorney, I have no problem in making the assertion that most attorneys tend to be extremely competitive and are trained to see conflicts in terms of right and wrong. So you can only imagine the level of intensity and competitiveness that results when two attorneys from opposing sides attempt to negotiate delivery terms and conditions. Even more so than their procurement colleagues, they are laser-focused on the allocation of blame and the consequences of failure that may occur during service delivery. Given their perceived role as the defenders of their respective organizations, they very quickly take a position from which they are unwilling to yield.

In almost every master services agreement negotiation in which I have been engaged, the Fortune 500 client will provide their standard terms and conditions for review and comment by the services provider. Either a contracts representative or an attorney for the consulting firm will review the terms and conditions, redline them extensively, and send them back to the client. Upon receipt, the client will review the changes, delete most of them using another color in the Track Changes function in Microsoft Word, and the process will usually continue for multiple iterations until a call or meeting is scheduled to formally negotiate any outstanding issues. If you have ever been a party to one of these calls or meetings, battle lines are drawn quite quickly, and it is not too long before an impasse is reached, as neither party is willing to retrench from their position. Now I do not want to indict all attorneys as members of the deal prevention force, as many of them are able to find a reasonable middle ground that will yield an acceptable level of risk and reward given the nature of services being provided. But they are clearly the exception to the rule.

Those attorneys who can see the vast expanse between right and wrong, and understand the commercial aspects of the pending transaction should be sought out for these types of negotiations. Consider a survey that was conducted by the Advanced Commercial Mediation Institute in which commercial mediators were asked if the disputing parties were more focused on winning or in obtaining a good deal. The responses revealed that the disputing parties were much more likely to focus on winning when their attorneys were heavily involved and influential at the beginning of the dispute. In a *Harvard Business Review* article from May 2008, Deepak Malhotra, Gillian Ku, and J. Keith Murnighan suggest that this type of decision making is driven by an "adrenaline fueled emotional state" called competitive arousal.

Probably we can all think of a time when we were victims of our competitive arousal and made a decision in the heat of battle that in retrospect, looks quite foolish. Sometimes, we want to win at all costs, even if the decision-making process lacks any sound judgment and is solely based upon competitive arousal. I encounter this dynamic all the time, as I collect Basketball Hall of Fame sports memorabilia and frequently participate in auctions run by many of the large auction houses. Once I find an item I like, it is very difficult for me to stop bidding, even if I have well exceeded any budget I may have established before the auction began and even if I know the price has reached a value beyond the going market rate for the item. It is this "heat of battle" type of bidding that is completely driven by my competitive arousal, in which I am unwilling to lose to some nameless and faceless bidder who, like me, is sitting at his computer at 3:00 a.m. unwilling to yield. Unfortunately, it is this same "win at all cost" mentality that can creep into the negotiation process for delivery terms and conditions and cause significant damage.

To mitigate this dynamic, it is critical that the business leadership understand the legal issues, so they can retain control of the negotiation and only bring the attorneys to the table when absolutely necessary. Similarly, once they have been invited to the party, the attorneys need to understand the nature of the services being contemplated in the transaction and the amount of risk inherent in delivery. By following this approach, the level of competitive arousal can be kept in check, and reaching agreement on key terms and conditions can be achieved.

Approaching the Negotiation Process

So, let's assume that we have our competitive arousal in check, our attorneys are in the bullpen, and we are now about to commence the negotiation process. The key question to be asked is: How do you reach an agreement that will yield an acceptable level of risk and reward for both parties to the transaction? My answer to this question has been constant for many years and has served me well in the marketplace. Frankly, it is not overly complex:

1. Temper your approach based upon the amount of risk inherent in delivery.

2. Temper your approach based upon the geographic region in which you are engaged.

3. Temper your approach based upon the individual sitting across from you at the negotiation table.

In the past week, I have added one additional principle to the list (which I haven't changed in 15 years, so this was a big deal). The addition came from a speech given by former Senate majority leader George Mitchell, who was recently named as a special envoy to the Middle East. After being introduced into this most critical and challenging role, Senator Mitchell stated that "conflicts are created, conducted, and sustained by human beings and can be resolved by human beings." This statement, while obvious on its face, made me pause and think about some of the most challenging negotiations I have ever experienced in my professional career and how I could have resolved them much more effectively by being cognizant of this simple rule. Now I am in no way comparing negotiating professional services terms and conditions to negotiating peace in the Middle East, but it is something we should all think about when drawing the battle lines around potential "deal-breaker" provisions.

Many contracts and legal professionals are unable to follow these principles, as they are too focused on adhering to some predefined standard template, or they are simply unable to adapt their position for certain types of opportunities. Many large professional services firms also strive to achieve some corporate standard in the negotiation process and fail to temper their quality assurance, risk management, and approval thresholds based upon the amount of risk inherent in delivery; they treat all transactions the same, which results in a very inefficient risk management process. You can read lots of books and attend plenty of training on successful negotiation techniques and tactics, but I assure you that if you accept the fact that no two professional services transactions are the same and follow these four simple principles, you will make great strides in the art of negotiation.

What exactly does it mean to temper your negotiation stance based upon the amount of risk inherent in delivery? As we have previously discussed, a number of factors should be considered in determining the amount of risk inherent in delivery. A thorough understanding of these risk criteria will assist in the classification of the risk profile associated with an opportunity, and that in turn will drive the stance to be taken in the negotiation process. The risk criteria that should be considered are as follows:

BACKGROUND

- Average annual client revenue
- Client relationship and positioning
- Historical relationship with client
- Client industry
- Size of client entity
- Competitive landscape

SCOPE

- Geographic scope
- Project scope
- Deliverable types
- Functional domain
- Degree of process change
- Services type
- Complexity of IT architecture

MANAGEMENT

- Client commitment to project
- Level of project sponsor
- Formal change management strategy
- Technical expertise of client team
- Client decision-making ability
- Level of subcontractor/ partner involvement
- Current client footprint
- Strength of reference base and staff
- Past performance for similar engagements
- Bank of intellectual capital

CONTRACT/PRICE/TIMELINE

- Project timeline
- Contract type
- Terms and conditions
- Pricing
- Payment terms in solution
- Financial viability of client

At a macro level, I would recommend looking at the type of services that will be provided and the nature of the deliverables that will ultimately be tendered to the client. Let's consider a short-term strategy engagement for which the output to the client will be a series of paper-based deliverables submitted during the period of performance. Typically, such documents are delivered or presented to the client, who will then take the report or analysis completed by the consultant and pursue the requisite course of action. To the extent that the deliverable is not satisfactory to the client or that there are concerns regarding the findings, they will most likely raise those issues with the consultant, who will typically address any concerns, conduct any additional interviews, research, or due diligence if necessary, reevaluate their conclusions, and retender the document for review. Clearly, paper-based deliverables do not function and do not have working parts, so the potential liability associated with these types of deliverables is much less than delivering a software application that must meet fifty different performance benchmarks and serve as the nucleus for a mission-critical IT system that must function on a daily basis. Strategy consultants are typically undertaking these engagements on a best-efforts basis, and their findings and recommendations are based upon their preexisting work product, prevailing market conditions, and any proprietary information provided by the client on its business and the issue in question. My point is simply that if the engagement is purely strategy focused, the stance toward negotiating the key terms and conditions referenced previously can be relaxed in line with the nature of the services being provided.

Conversely, consider a design, implementation, or outsourcing engagement in which the deliverable being submitted by the consultant consists of an information system that has many functioning parts and that will serve as the foundation for a mission-critical human resource or financial management business process. These types of engagements typically run for lengthy periods, require a significant resource commitment by both the consultant and the client, tend to be very large and complex in scope, and must meet stringent acceptance criteria, function properly, and operate properly during some contractually defined warranty period. For these types of engagements, a much more stringent stance on the key terms and conditions is warranted, as the risk inherent in delivery is so much greater. I have been responsible for negotiating countless numbers of strategy and technology consulting engagements during my career, and as you can imagine, it is always the deliverables with moving parts and performance benchmarks that result in client dissatisfaction and potential litigation.

When looking at engagements in isolation, it is easy to classify the substance of the services being delivered—strategy versus implementation—and the amount of potential risk inherent in delivery. But what if you are negotiating a master services agreement under which a broad variety of consulting services is being contemplated during the period of performance? In this instance, it is prudent to err on the side of conservatism and assume that delivery will be complex in nature and to negotiate accordingly. That being said, let's review the terms and conditions that get the blood pressure of the attorneys and procurement folks elevated during the negotiation process. I will walk through the terms and conditions that are most consistently negotiated, identify the meaning of each provision, and discuss the negotiation stance that should be considered given the nature of the services being provided and the risk inherent in delivery.

In accordance with the second principle, it is important to temper your approach based upon the geographic region in which you are engaged. What works well in New York or San Francisco doesn't necessarily work well in the United Kingdom, Germany, Japan, or the Middle East. Before jumping into the negotiation process in a foreign country, it is important to understand not only the local laws but also the impact that culture may have in the negotiation process. Is the style quiet and less flamboyant, requiring some level of deference like you might find in Japan, or louder and more aggressive, like you might find in France or the United Kingdom? I am not a cultural expert but have negotiated terms and conditions in a number of countries and can absolutely tell you to conduct adequate due diligence and to seek the advice of local colleagues before simply jumping into the process. Once you are there, remember to temper your approach accordingly, both in terms of style and prevailing law.

Finally, remember to temper your style and approach based upon the individual sitting across from you at the negotiation table. While you can study countless books on negotiation tactics, I urge you to make every attempt to understand the style, personality, motivation, and interests of the individual with whom you will be negotiating; ultimately, your success will hinge upon your ability to work with him or her to reach an agreement that yields an acceptable level of risk and reward for both parties to the transaction. To that end, I would like to introduce you to what I refer to as the "Harley Principle." I have been riding Harley Davidson motorcycles for the past ten years, and it is a great passion of mine. I have a VROD and a Screaming Eagle Springer, and simply love the feeling of rolling down the road with the wind in my face on a beautiful summer day. If I enter the office of a procurement executive or attorney with whom I will be negotiating and see anything Harley Davidson or motorcycle related, I always inquire, and the conversation quickly shifts to a passion that we both share.

Finding this common interest allows us to identify with each other in a manner beyond the pricing, terms and conditions, and adversarial negotiation process that we are about to undertake. While I am not suggesting that a common passion for Harley Davidson motorcycles will result in an easy negotiation process, it allows me to identify with the individual with whom I am engaged. Though I have no scientific evidence, I can absolutely tell you that my negotiations with motorcycle enthusiasts over the years have been quite successful. So make an effort to identify with the party with whom you will be negotiating beyond the terms and conditions in the agreement; it definitely makes a difference. That being said, let's dive into the following chapters and discuss some key terms and conditions.

10

Limitation on Liability

Let's start with a discussion around what is the most consistently negoti-ated term, as it defines the allocation of risk among the parties to the transaction: limitation on liability. The limitation on liability provision is extremely important, as it identifies the potential exposure to which the services provider (or both parties if the clause is mutual in scope) will be subject in the event they are found to be in breach of contract as determined through the applicable judicial or dispute resolution process.

The actual liability cap may be expressed in a number such that it is limited to the amount of fees paid by the client under the agreement or over some period, limited to some multiple of the fees paid under the agree-ment, or limited to some specified dollar amount. Limiting the cap to the amount of fees paid under the agreement seems to be clear on its face, but may become more complex under a master agreement, as multiple engage-ments will typically be performed over the life of the contract. In these instances, the service provider will typically pursue a liability limitation that is limited to the amount of fees paid under the engagement from which the breach or claim arose.

In addition, the limitation on liability provision may contain a num-ber of what are referred to as *carve-outs*, or areas from which any liability resulting from a breach of contract would not be subject to the liability cap agreed upon by the parties. The carve-outs typically focus on those areas where a breach could cause substantial harm to the opposing party, such as a breach of confidentiality or where a party engages in behavior that is negligent or that is willful misconduct. The limitation on liability provision will also typically explicitly state that neither party to the agreement will be liable to the other for any incidental or consequential damages that may occur but are not directly related to the delivery of services.

Is There a Right Answer?

Over the years, I have had many sales and delivery executives ask me for strategic counsel with regard to liability caps on strategy, design, and implementation engagements. Unfortunately, I am forced to tell them that there is no right answer with regard to the amount of liability that a services provider should agree to or that the receiving party should strive to achieve. As every engagement and client relationship is different, the agreed upon liability terms will vary depending upon the services being provided and the negotiating leverage and savvy of the two parties to the transaction.

Irrespective of the types of services being provided, it is pretty much a given that the client will always negotiate heavily for a broad limitation on liability, in some cases as much as three to five times the amount of fees paid under the agreement. In addition, the client will typically identify a number of carve-outs under which the consultant's liability would be unlimited. For a consultant, the best answer I can provide is to carefully review the level of risk inherent in delivery, the complexity of the engagement, the deliverables or output being provided to the client, the anticipated profitability of the engagement, the strategic importance of the opportunity, the overall risk profile it is striving to achieve across its active engagement base, and the ability to deliver in a timely and quality manner. This review should be conducted by gauging the strength of the relationship with the client and their historical level of litigiousness versus working in partnership and through non-adjudicative means to solve problems and achieve resolution on issues that arise during the course of delivery. Specifically, it is critical to evaluate the potential likelihood that the client will assert any downstream claims that the actions of the consultant or the products and services they provided resulted in any direct damages for which the client will seek recovery.

Irrespective of the level of risk tolerance of the services provider, I would strongly discourage executing agreements in which you are subject to unlimited liability, irrespective of the conclusions reached through the risk analysis. While most large professional services may be a party to engagements in which their liability is unlimited, this approach should only be followed in unique and extreme circumstances where the risk inherent in delivery is minimal, where the solution is clearly within your delivery sweet spot, and it cannot be avoided.

Sample Limitation on Liability Provisions

That being said, let's take a look at a few sample limitation on liability provisions and their potential implications to the services provider (Consultant) and services receiver (Client). The first limitation on liability clause is as seen here:

> **Unless further limited elsewhere in this agreement, neither Consultant, its suppliers, nor its subcontractors shall be liable for damages, whether arising in contract, tort or otherwise, in excess of the greater of: (a) $250,000 us; or, (b) the applicable price for the product or service (as per the applicable statement of work) directly related to the damage. In no event shall Consultant corporation, its suppliers, or its subcontractors be liable for any special, incidental, indirect, consequential, or punitive damages including, without limitation, any damages resulting from loss of use, loss of data, loss of profits, loss of savings, or loss of business arising out of or in connection with this agreement or the performance of the services, whether or not Consultant has been advised of the possibility of such damages. The parties agree to the allocation of liability set forth in this section. Client acknowledges that without its agreement to the limitations contained herein, the price charged for the services would be higher.**

This clause clearly favors the consultant, as it limits its liability for damages, in contract, tort, or otherwise, to the greater of $250,000 or the amount paid for the product or services under the applicable statement of work *from which the claim arose.* In addition to limiting its liability for direct damages, consultant is also disclaiming any liability for any special, incidental, indirect, consequential, or punitive damages that may result through the delivery of its services. If the client were to accept this language, the consultant would be liable for the greater of $250,000 or the amount of the statement of work from which the claim for damages arose for any breach of the services agreement, including copyright infringement, the improper handling or release of confidential information, warranty claims, and even negligent behavior or willful misconduct. This provision may be appropriate for a consultant to introduce in those instances where the consultant is delivering a service for which no reasonable alternatives exist, where the services are critical to the client's business, and where the client is willing to accept the risk associated with delivery. This would be the type of limitation on liability provision that would be contained in a standard agreement provided by the services arm of the major enterprise resource planning vendors in the 1990s, as their market position and unique delivery capabilities gave them great leverage in the negotiation process.

However, the negotiation leverage needle has shifted back toward the middle of the spectrum in recent years, as Fortune 500 companies have a number of vendors delivering strategy, design, and implementation services that are aggressively competing for a piece of their wallets. To that end, every Fortune 500 client with whom I have been engaged will typically provide potential vendors with their standard set of terms and conditions for review and comment as a part of the master agreement process. As we have discussed, these terms and conditions are frequently negotiated and go through multiple iterations, and the limitation on liability provision certainly receives significant scrutiny. A more typical limitation on liability provision contained in a standard set of terms and conditions would be as seen here:

> **Each party's maximum liability to the other for any action arising under this agreement, regardless of the form of action and whether in tort or contract, shall be limited to one and one-half**

(1 $^1/_2$) times the total amount of services fees paid by customer during the term of this master agreement. The foregoing limitation shall not apply to any liability arising out of any claim based on (1) a breach of the confidentiality provisions hereunder; (2) negligent actions or inactions or willful misconduct; (3) claims subject to the indemnification provisions contained in this agreement; and (4) claims subject to the warranty provisions contained in this agreement. In no event shall either party be liable to the other for indirect, special, incidental, or consequential damages of any kind, including without limitation, lost data or lost profits, however arising, even if the injured party has been advised of the possibility of such damages. The parties agree to the allocation of risk as set forth herein.

This provision results in a more balanced allocation of risk between the consultant and the client, as it specifies a liability cap that is more directly proportionate to the total value of the services that will be delivered under the agreement. In addition to being applicable to both parties to the agreement, it also carves out a number of areas that would not be subject to the liability cap, including breaches of confidentiality, negligent or willful misconduct, indemnification, and warranty. With this provision, the parties would most certainly negotiate the fee multiple and the potential carve-outs that would not be subject to any liability cap during the period of performance.

The best guidance I can provide in this area is to carefully review the liability limitation and carve-outs and to determine if, along with the other critical terms and conditions contained in the agreement, it yields an even allocation of risk and reward for both parties to the transaction. In addition, be cognizant that this provision has been the most consistently negotiated for each year in which the IACCM (International Association for Contract and Commercial Management) has conducted its survey. To that end, don't treat it lightly, as it can have significant ramifications for the financial health of the specific engagement being contemplated as well as the broader financial health of your organization.

11

Indemnification

Closely related to the limitation on liability provision is the issue of indemnity. As we discussed previously, the indemnity provisions of a services agreement are in many instances identified as carve-outs to the limitation on liability provision and therefore could subject the indemnifying party to unlimited liability as a result of their potential actions during the course of services delivery. It is therefore critical that the indemnity provisions of a contract be reviewed and tailored accordingly.

Indemnity simply refers to the act of making a party "whole" for any damages or losses it has incurred or will incur as a result of the actions or conduct of the party that caused the harm. The general idea is that a party should not be held liable where that party in no way contributed to the underlying infringing action. The typical issue being negotiated under an indemnity provision is the standard of conduct, which may range from any (good, bad, or otherwise) conduct related to the delivery of services to grossly negligent or intentionally wrongful acts or omissions, which will trigger the provisions contained in the indemnity clause of the contract. The indemnity provisions contained in a master services agreement will typically be mutual to both parties and will cover two different areas—patent and copyright indemnity and general indemnity.

Patent and Copyright Indemnification

A typical patent and copyright indemnity provision would be as seen here:

Consultant will defend and indemnify Client against claims that any Consultant Product or Service infringes a patent or copyright or misappropriates trade secrets protected under applicable law, provided Client (a) gives Consultant prompt written notice of the claim, (b) permits Consultant to defend or settle the claim, and (c) provides all reasonable assistance in defending or settling the claim.

For any Consultant Corporation Product or Service subject to a claim, Consultant may, in its reasonable judgment, as its sole obligation, and at its option and expense: (a) obtain the right of continued use of the Product or Service for the Client, or, (b) replace or modify the Product or Service to avoid the claim. If neither alternative is available on commercially reasonable terms, then, at Consultant's request, Client will stop its use of the Product and Client will return the Product to Consultant. Upon return of the Product, Consultant will give Client a credit for the price paid to Consultant, less a reasonable offset for use and obsolescence. This Section describes Consultant's entire liability and Client's only remedies for patent or copyright infringement and trade secret misappropriation.

Consultant will not defend or indemnify Client if the claim (a) is based upon information furnished by the Client, (b) results from Client's design, alteration, or misuse of any Product, or (c) results from use of any Product in combination with any other (non-Consultant) Products, or (d) relates to another vendor's Product alone.

The foregoing provisions of this section state the entire liability and obligations of Consultant, and the exclusive remedy of the Client, with respect to any actual or alleged infringement of any intellectual property rights arising out of or in connection with the performance of the services and the use of the work product.

Before we discuss the specifics of this indemnity provision, let's review an example as to why a patent and copyright indemnification provision is so important, especially in a consulting engagement in which the output being provided to the client consists of paper-based deliverables or other design documentation. Consider a strategy engagement under which the consulting firm provides its Fortune 500 client with a series of paper-based deliverables as outlined in a mutually agreed upon statement of work. Client, having paid the consultant for its services, and being pleased with its work, decides to utilize the deliverables and accompanying information to carry out its respective business strategy. Shortly thereafter, the client's primary competitor in the market, Archrival, files a copyright infringement suit against the client, claiming that it has ownership of the data contained in the deliverables, that client is not authorized to utilize the data in the deliverables for its commercial gain, and that it is violating Archrival's copyright by doing so. Ultimately, the client is subject to a binding legal judgment of $1 million to Archrival and settles the claim accordingly. Under the concept of patent and copyright indemnity, the consulting firm that provided the infringing materials agrees to make the client whole for its losses given that it initially provided its client with deliverables containing data that infringed upon the valid copyright of a third party.

In the scenario I described, the consulting firm would indemnify its client for the $1 million judgment and either replace or modify the infringing components of the deliverable, refund the fees paid by the client for the infringing deliverable, or secure a license for the client to use the deliverable to achieve its strategy. Given the amount of data transferred from the consulting firm to the client in a typical engagement, it is paramount that the client has reasonable assurance that the work product being provided by the consultant does not infringe upon the patent or copyright of any third party.

In the sample provision I just identified, the consultant asserts that it has ownership of the work product being provided under the agreement and that the work product has not been misappropriated from any third party. To the extent that assertion proves to be false or that a claim is brought against the client asserting a patent or copyright infringement, this provision will determine the remedy of the client and the obligations of the consultant with regard to the infringing materials. Through this provision, the consultant is making an affirmative claim that its work product is unique and that it will secure an appropriate remedy for the client should the deliverables provided under the contract be deemed to infringe upon the rights of a third party. However, the consultant clearly exempts itself from any indemnification burden to the extent that the tainted work product results from information the client gave to consultant, if the client modified the consultant's work product, or if the infringement results from utilizing the consultant's work product in conjunction with another party's work product. In addition, the consultant clearly seeks to limit its liability for a violation of this provision by limiting the remedies the client may pursue under these circumstances. In addition, the consultant retains complete discretion with regard to settling the infringement claim and potentially securing the continued use of the work product by the client.

Most Fortune 500 entities with which I have been engaged will insist that a patent and copyright indemnification be included within the master agreement. Clearly, the client should not be held accountable for patent or copyright infringement or trade secret misappropriation by their consultants and particularly by their management consultants that are partners in crafting business and technology strategy and developing and implementing critical information systems. In practice, most clients will not agree to a limited remedy and will not give the consultant complete autonomy in determining how it will cure the infringing work product that is subject to the third-party claim, as providing sole discretion to the consultant may not yield a viable solution or full compensation for any potential loss the client may realize as a result of the infringing work product.

For example, let's assume that the consultant delivers a software product to the client that contains some code that will become the subject of a patent infringement claim. Unaware of this issue at the time of delivery, the client implements the product on a global basis, as it satisfies a critical piece of functionality necessary to run its financial system. The costs associated with the implementation are extensive, as there is a significant change management effort associated with the new product. Organizations are streamlined, headcount is eliminated, data is converted, interfaces to legacy systems are built, and all major financial business processes are changed as a result of the key functionality delivered through the new product suite. Six months after go-live, an infringement claim is filed against the client for violating a patent held surrounding the code embedded within the product suite. Upon receiving notice of the claim, the client immediately notifies the consultant, who assumes responsibility for defending the claim and, under the language contained in the sample indemnity provision shown earlier, for providing the client with whatever remedy the consultant deems appropriate under the terms of the contract. After a few months of litigation, the patent claim is deemed to be valid by a court of competent jurisdiction, and the consultant is subject to an injunction from using the software code within its product and to a large financial settlement, which it promptly satisfies. Given this result, the client is now unable to continue utilizing the product suite around which it has restructured its financial operations.

Despite its best efforts, the consultant is unable to obtain a license for the client to continue its use of the infringing product, and no viable replacement exists in the market. To comply with the legal judgment, the consultant demands that the client return the infringing product and provides a full refund to the client for the license fee and the implementation. Under the terms of the sample provision I identified earlier, the consultant would clearly be within its rights to proceed in this manner, and the client would have no further recourse. While this example is somewhat extraordinary, it clearly magnifies why the client should negotiate nonexclusive remedies as well as the level of discretion maintained by the consultant in determining how it will cure any infringing work product.

You would normally assume that a patent and copyright indemnity provision would be mutual in scope and applicable to any data or specifications provided by the client to the consultant, but this is not always the case. I have actually been a party to a negotiation with a Fortune 500 client in the financial services industry in which the client refused to agree to a provision that stated that any information provided to the consultant would be free from infringement, complete, accurate, and prompt, and it was unwilling to negotiate this issue irrespective of the cost and time associated with having to validate anything exchanged during the course of service delivery. Fortunately, this was a unique instance and it is much more common that a provision of this type will be mutual in scope. To the extent that a mutual patent and copyright indemnity provision could be agreed upon, it will require the client to indemnify the consultant to the extent that the client provides the consultant with any materials or specifications that are embedded within the output provided by the consultant back to the client during the course of service delivery. A sample provision would be as seen here:

> **The Client shall indemnify and hold Consultant harmless against any claims that those portions of any work product that contain the Client's confidential information, software code, or ideas, including, without limitation, any portion of work product that is developed pursuant to Client's specifications infringe any copyright, provided that Client (a) is given prompt written notice of the claim, (b) has the sole authority to defend or settle such claim, and (c) is given information and reasonable assistance by Consultant in defending or settling the claim.**

In a typical services agreement, the consultant relies upon the client's leadership and functional experts to share their institutional knowledge and expertise around client process and systems to facilitate service delivery. A critical part of this process requires the sharing of client information with the consultant that will assist in the development of their respective solution. The free flow of data among the parties is paramount, given the complexity of the services being provided and the interconnectivity that is required in many engagements to achieve timely, quality, and cost-effective delivery. It is therefore critical that the client, just like the consultant, make sure it has ownership to all data and related information provided to the consultant during the course of the engagement. Given that the consultant will rely upon and incorporate this data into its deliverables, it is critical that the client adhere to this provision.

General Indemnification

Let's shift our focus to the concept of general indemnity. Unlike patent and copyright indemnity, the general indemnity provision will allow the indemnified party to recover for any losses it may incur as a result of the actions of the other party to the transaction. The negotiation of general indemnification provisions is typically centered around the standard of conduct that will trigger the indemnification obligation of the parties to the transaction as well as the mutuality of the indemnification provision. Fortune 500 clients will typically want a very broad indemnification clause in which they are indemnified by their consultants for any losses, liabilities, or damages they may incur arising out of any claim, suit, or proceeding resulting from the consultant's delivery of services.

Conversely, the consultant will strive to attain an indemnification provision in which it is only obligated to indemnify the client for any losses they may incur arising out of any claim, suit, or proceeding brought by a third party based upon bodily injury or damage to tangible personal property that results from the negligent actions or willful misconduct of the consultant. As we discussed in the limitation on liability section, Fortune 500 clients will seek to carve out the indemnification provisions from the limitation on liability cap identified in the contract, resulting in unlimited liability for the consultant with regard to any potential indemnification obligations under the contract.

Given this dynamic, a typical Fortune 500 company standard master agreement will include a very broad one-way general indemnification provision as seen here:

> **Consultant will defend, indemnify, and hold harmless Client and its Affiliates, and their respective directors, officers, employees, agents, attorneys, assigns, and successors-in-interest from and against any and all liabilities, damages, losses, claims, demands, assessments, actions, causes of action, costs (including attorneys' fees and expenses) and any of them, arising out of or resulting from any of the following:**
>
> **(A) Personal injury or death or damage to property, including theft, on account of the performance of work or services by Consultant or Consultant's employees or subcontractors**
>
> **(B) Any claim or demand asserted against Client that results from an act or omission of Consultant, its employees, agents, or subcontractors**

As we discussed previously, a broad indemnification provision of this type will result in the consultant indemnifying the client for any claim or demand asserted against the client stemming from any act or omission of the consultant during the course of delivery. To the extent that the indemnification provision is a carve-out from the limitation on liability, the consultant would face significant exposure (in effect unlimited liability) by agreeing to this provision. To the extent it was not carved out, the consultant's indemnification obligation would be limited to the maximum amount specified in the limitation on liability provision. As a result, both parties will most likely negotiate an indemnification provision that is mutual in scope, that is subject to a narrow standard of conduct, and that may be carved out of the limitation on liability provisions. A provision that accomplishes these objectives would be as seen here:

> **Each party (Indemnifying Party) shall defend, indemnify, and hold harmless the other party (Indemnified Party), its affiliates and their respective officers, directors, employees, and agents and their respective successors and assigns from and against any and all claims, losses, liabilities, damages, and expenses (including, interest, penalties, and costs, including reasonable attorney's fees) (collectively, "Losses"), arising out of or in connection with a claim, suit, or proceeding brought by a third party based upon bodily injury (including death) or damage to tangible personal property to the extent caused by the negligence or willful misconduct of the indemnifying party, its employees, or agents, while performing its obligations pursuant to this agreement. This indemnification obligation is contingent upon the Indemnified Party's providing the Indemnifying Party with prompt written notice of such claim, information, all reasonable assistance in the defense of such action, and the sole authority to defend or settle such claim.**

This provision yields a much more even allocation of risk and reward, as it is mutual in scope and limits the indemnification obligation of the indemnifying party to those instances where the indemnified party is subject to losses arising out of any claim brought by a third party that is caused by the negligence or willful misconduct of the indemnifying party that results in bodily injury or damage to tangible personal property. It may be carved out, as it is not unreasonable for each party's liability to be unlimited with regard to bodily injury or property damage that results from its negligence or willful misconduct.

To the extent the client is demanding an indemnification obligation that extends beyond bodily injury or damage to tangible personal property, the parties may agree to an additional provision that would not be carved out (so the indemnifying party's obligation would be limited), but that would extend to losses arising from any claim (not limited to bodily injury or damage to tangible personal property) that resulted from their negligence or willful misconduct. Such a provision would be as follows:

> **Subject to the limitation on liability provision in this agreement, the Parties shall defend, indemnify, and hold each other harmless against and from all Losses arising out of or in connection with a claim, suit, or proceeding brought by a third party to the extent proximately caused by the negligence or willful misconduct of the indemnifying party or its agents acting within the scope of the performance of Services under the Agreement. This indemnification obligation is contingent upon the Indemnified Party's providing the Indemnifying Party with prompt written notice of such claim, information, all reasonable assistance in the defense of such action, and the sole authority to defend or settle such claim.**

My counsel with regard to indemnification provisions is to carefully review the standard of conduct that will trigger the indemnification provision, the scope of the claims related to the breach of that standard, and whether or not the obligation is carved out of the limitation on liability provision. Under the more narrow indemnification provision articulated earlier, serious bodily injury or damage to personal property must occur and result from negligent behavior or willful misconduct in order for the indemnification obligation to be triggered. To the extent that the scope of claims is broadened, the parties would most likely negotiate the standard of conduct required to trigger the obligation as well as any carve-out provisions.

Consider the following extreme example: Two of consultant's employees, Jack and Jill, make a wager to see if Jack can drop a piece of computer equipment out the window on the fifth floor into a small pond below. When Jack drops the equipment out the window, it veers off course, hits a parked car in the lot, and causes a large explosion. As a result of the explosion, a number of the client's customers, suppliers, and employees are injured, and there is extensive damage to personal property. Following this incident, multiple lawsuits are filed against the client by the injured parties for the damages they sustained in the explosion. Given the clearly negligent behavior of the consultant's employees and the bodily injury and damage to tangible personal property, their indemnification obligation would clearly be triggered under this scenario.

But what if the consultant's conduct is not so extreme and the indemnification provision is not limited to personal injury and property damage. Assume that Jack and Jill are in the middle of a human resource management product suite implementation for their client. To implement the product suite, Jack and Jill require access to the client's data center, which contains all employee and customer records, including sensitive personally identifiable information. Given the aggressive implementation timeline, Jack and Jill must work around the clock in the data center, which is a secured access facility that requires a card key and biometric identifier for entry. While working alone in the data center late one evening, Jack and Jill decide they need to go outside for a smoke break and leave the entry doors to the data center wide open. Once outside for their smoke break, they decide to quickly run across the street to the 7-Eleven to get some snacks, as they have not eaten all day. Upon returning, they realize that during their absence, someone entered the data center and removed a number of hard drives containing sensitive customer and financial information. As a result of the hard drive theft, thousands of the client's customers bring claims against the client for the damages they have incurred as a result of the unauthorized release of their financial information.

Again, this may be an extreme example, but the claims are clearly a result of the negligent behavior of consultant's employees, even though their actions do not appear to have caused bodily injury or damage to tangible personal property. Depending upon the scope of claims limitation, the indemnity obligation may not be triggered. Given the potential number of client claims associated with this incident, the losses incurred by the client could be quite significant. So I urge you to carefully review the standard of conduct that will trigger the indemnification provision, the scope of the claims related to the breach of that standard, and whether or not the obligation is carved out of the limitation on liability provision, as it may significantly impact the level of risk associated with the master agreement.

12

Intellectual Property and Ownership of Work Product

Irrespective of where it falls in the consulting lifecycle, every professional services engagement results in some type of deliverable being provided by the consultant to the client during the period of performance. Every deliverable that is prepared will consist of at least one of the following: content that is first produced under the engagement, content that consists of client-owned preexisting work product and confidential information, and preexisting work product that is owned by the consultant. The challenge in the master services agreement negotiation process is determining who retains ownership of the deliverables and their respective content after delivery has occurred. The spectrum of possibilities is quite broad, with the consultant and client heavily entrenched at either pole.

Naturally, most Fortune 500 clients will attempt to assert ownership over all work products delivered during the course of the engagement. Conversely, most professional services firms want to retain ownership of their preexisting work product, including their concepts, approaches, methodologies, models, tools, generic industry information, and any relevant knowledge and experience they possessed prior to, or that was acquired by them, during the performance under the agreement. Through the negotiation process, the needle will most likely come to rest somewhere in the middle of the spectrum, with the client owning all deliverables that are first

113

produced during the engagement, the consultant retaining ownership to all of its preexisting work product intertwined therein, and the client receiving a perpetual and nonexclusive license to use the preexisting work product for its internal business purposes only.

While this sounds like a happy medium, it can actually be quite complicated to put into operation given the fact that deliverables can be lengthy and can contain preexisting work product as well as content first produced during the course of the engagement. Every consulting firm relies very heavily upon its preexisting bank of intellectual capital, as it is an absolute requirement if it is able to successfully deliver quality and repeatable solutions to its clients. To that end, the consultant will go to great lengths to preserve its ownership rights and to keep them out of the hands of its competitors. This protective approach also provides an advantage to clients, as they receive the benefit of the knowledge and experience gained by the consultant in all of its preceding engagements. Through retaining ownership, the consultant can bring that bank of intellectual capital to bear when delivering similarly situated solutions across its client community. As we have discussed, quality and repeatable solutions are leading indicators of timely and cost-effective delivery.

How Are Intellectual Property Clauses Enforced?

Ensuring that work product exchanged during the course of service delivery is properly utilized can be quite challenging, as most intellectual property clauses are difficult to enforce. It has always amazed me how one of the most heavily negotiated terms (and one that results in significant blood pressure escalation) is so difficult to enforce and receives so little scrutiny in practice. Think about it: once consultants tender a deliverable and it is accepted by the client, the deliverable is completely out of the consultants' control. As they have most likely moved on to their next engagement, they have no ability to monitor whether their work product is properly utilized internally; if it is shared with third parties including competing consulting firms that are engaged elsewhere within the client organization; if their ideas, methodologies, or approaches are cut and pasted into other documents (without any ownership disclaimer) that are utilized by the client's staff or any third parties; and if their work product is reproduced, modified, or sold in a manner that would violate the terms of the license contained in the master services agreement. I am not suggesting that a client would intentionally take its consultant's work product and utilize it outside the boundary of the license it has been granted, but Fortune 500 client organizations are large, and e-mail and intranets help facilitate the wide dissemination of data without any guidelines as to future use. On that note, it is always amazing to me how copyright markings and restrictive legends regarding modification or reproduction seem to disappear from documents. This omission occurs within large Fortune 500 companies on a daily basis; think about the last time someone forwarded you a PowerPoint, logo, or other document that you utilized without even considering the origin and potential restrictions on use.

Despite these significant challenges in enforcement, most consulting firms will still propose a very restrictive intellectual property provision in which they retain ownership to all work products delivered under the engagement as seen here:

> **Client understands and agrees that all reports, analyses, and other material provided by consultant including ideas, know-how, concepts, approaches, techniques, methodologies, models, tools, software, documentation, diagrams, specifications, schematics, blueprints, expression of consultant's findings, analyses, conclusions, opinions, recommendations, designs, programs, enhancements, generic industry information, knowledge, and experience possessed by Consultant prior to, or acquired and developed by Consultant personnel (alone or jointly with the Client) in connection with the services, are solely for Client's information and use in connection with the engagement, will remain the property of Consultant, and may not be delivered to any third party without the prior written consent of Consultant, except as required by law. Subject to payment of any services fees required under this agreement, Consultant grants Client a nonexclusive license to use any of the foregoing for its internal business purposes. To the extent Client acquires any rights in the intellectual property, Client hereby assigns those rights to Consultant.**

This provision is pretty clear on its face: anything that the consultant delivers incidental to service delivery will remain the property of the consultant, and the client will be given a license to use the work product for its internal business purposes only and will not be able to share any work product with third parties without the prior written consent of the consultant. While this approach serves the consultant well, it may not be in the best interests of the client, as it is making a significant investment in the work product associated with a strategy, design, or implementation engagement for which it will only receive a limited use license in return, even for those items that are first produced during the course of the engagement.

What Protections Are Offered Under Copyright Law?

Before I discuss the approach that will be proposed by most Fortune 500 companies, or at least what they will accept as a part of the master agreement process, let's briefly discuss copyright law and its implications with regard to professional services deliverables. A *copyright* is a legal device that is defined as the exclusive right of the author or creator of a literary or artistic property such as a book, movie, or musical composition to print, copy, sell, license, distribute, transform to another medium, translate, record, perform, or otherwise use. Once a work is created, it automatically has federal copyright protection. A notice should be affixed to any such work, stating the word "copyright" or the "©" symbol along with the name of the creator of the work and the date of the copyright.

For copyright purposes, a work created by an employee within the scope of employment or a work created by a consultant under a written contract is deemed to be a "work for hire." Under federal copyright law, the owner of a work made for hire is considered the author of the work and thus owns the copyright. For example, if a client hires a consulting firm to create a strategic planning document, the client would own the copyright in the completed work to the extent that it contains content that is first produced during the engagement.

Given these basic rules, it would appear that the client should have ownership of all work product and deliverables created by its consultants and delivered during the engagement. The only rub is that the intellectual capital being developed by a management consulting firm under a strategy, design, or implementation engagement contains both new and preexisting work product that is typically commingled within the deliverables. That is why professional services firms strongly prefer to retain ownership of all work product (even that which is first produced), with the exception of any client information contained therein, and grant the client a perpetual and nonexclusive license to use the work product for its internal business purposes. The rationale being asserted by the management consulting firms is that the methods, tools, and thought leadership they bring to bear in every services engagement have been developed over time through their completion of similarly situated industry-specific client engagements, the ownership of which cannot be relinquished, as it benefits clients and yields a distinct competitive advantage in the market.

To find some middle ground on this issue, it has become somewhat of an industry standard to accept an intellectual property provision under which the client will own all work product "first produced" under the engagement, that the client will own its confidential information, that the consultant will own its preexisting work product, and that the client will be granted a nonexclusive license to use any preexisting work product embedded in any deliverables for its internal business purposes. To avoid ambiguity, it is also important to define what is meant by the terms *work product*, *preexisting work product*, and *internal business purposes* because they can be subject to multiple interpretations. A sample provision that captures this approach is shown here:

> **The intellectual property that each party or an applicable third party owns shall remain the property of that party. Unless agreed to otherwise in a statement of work, all work product of any type or kind whatsoever, whether tangible or intangible, which Consultant, invents, creates, composes, authors, discovers, or otherwise produces hereunder for Client shall be considered works made for hire to the fullest extent accorded the meaning of that term under the Copyright Laws of the United States and otherwise under any other applicable statutes, case law, common law, and/or common usage, and the entire right, title, and interest, whether in the nature of patent, trademark, copyright, trade secret, or any other form of intellectual property or other proprietary rights, in and to all such work product shall belong to Client.**

Notwithstanding the foregoing or anything to the contrary, Consultant shall retain all right, title, and interest to all of its preexisting material and, to the extent such material is incorporated in a Deliverable, Consultant grants Client a perpetual, royalty-free license to use and reproduce such material for its internal business purposes; further Client understands and agrees that all reports, analyses or other material provided by Consultant are solely for Client's information and use in connection with the assignment and may not be delivered to any third party without the prior written consent of Consultant, except (i) a third party who requires such disclosure in order to perform its services for Client's internal business purposes, provided such party has been informed of the confidential nature of the report or analysis and has agreed in writing to abide by the confidentiality restrictions herein; or (ii) as required by law. Consultant shall retain all rights to concepts, approaches, methodologies, models, tools, generic industry information, knowledge, and experience possessed by Consultant prior to, or acquired by it during, the performance under the Agreement.

While this approach seems to address the competing viewpoints in this area, it is still extremely difficult to put into operation and to enforce in practice. I assure you that a provision quite similar to what you just saw exists in the master services agreements that have been executed between the major consulting firms and their Fortune 500 clients. I can also assure you that deliverables are being developed under strategy, design, and implementation engagements that consist of content that was first produced under the engagement sitting right alongside the preexisting work product of the consultant. Most importantly, I can assure you that when deliverables are submitted to these clients, the text is all in the same color, and it is impossible to distinguish those components of the work product that have been first produced and are, therefore, owned by the client versus those for which they have been granted a license to use for internal business purposes. The bottom line for both clients and consultants is to agree upon an approach that reasonably protects intellectual property rights, that can reasonably be enforced, and that supports the development of quality and repeatable solutions that facilitate timely, quality, and cost-effective delivery.

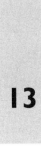

13

Pricing and Payment

In later chapters, we will spend a lot of time discussing the actual rates that the major strategy, design, and implementation providers are able to command across the consulting lifecycle and the competitor set against which any proposed rates will be benchmarked. We will also discuss the best way to effectively negotiate a rate structure with procurement that is commensurate with the nature of the services being provided and competitive with other vendors in the market. For now, I will address the price and payment terms contained within a typical master services agreement.

While you might think that pricing, rate structure, and payment terms would be fairly straightforward, a number of issues may arise during the term of the master agreement that extend well beyond negotiating a rate card that contains labor categories and corresponding rates. These issues include rate escalation clauses that will take effect on an annual or otherwise agreed-upon basis, invoice issue and payment due dates, prompt payment discounts, late payment interest charges, applicable taxes, form of payment, payment currency, staffing across geographic boundaries, staff promotions, and expenses. Each of these issues must be addressed when negotiating a master agreement. Failure to do so will result in significant ambiguity, which may result in potentially adverse financial consequences for both the consultant and the client. Let's discuss each of these areas in more detail.

Rate Escalation, Payment Frequency, Taxes, and Currency

Rate escalation clauses are always important when negotiating a master services agreement. Most Fortune 500 clients will typically request that the initially agreed upon rate structure remain valid for either a single- or multiyear period, after which time they will be subject to an escalation factor. Most master agreements have an initial period that ranges from one to three years followed by a number of one-year option periods that will automatically renew upon the anniversary date of the agreement. As master agreements with Fortune 500 entities have no minimum order requirement or volume commitment, they typically will continue in perpetuity unless either of the parties chooses to exercise its rights under the termination provisions of the agreement. A recent trend has been to extend the term of this initial period to three years in an effort to minimize any rate escalation until year four.

In terms of the escalation factor itself, it is typically expressed as either a flat percentage that will take effect annually on the contract execution anniversary date, or it will be tied to a macro-level or geographically specific cost of living index mutually agreed to by the parties. My target when negotiating with procurement organizations was to achieve a 5 percent to 8 percent annual escalation factor throughout the life of the agreement. Although it's not optimal, I would accept as low as 3 percent depending upon the strategic importance of the client, the anticipated transaction volume, and the structure, flexibility, and level of profitability built into the rate card.

The next issue to be addressed in this area is how often invoices will be issued, the level of detail provided, and the payment due dates. Invoice issuance will vary depending upon the services being delivered, but a general rule is that invoices will be issued on a monthly basis for time and materials work or in accordance with the milestone deliverable or progress payment plan agreed to by the parties for fixed price engagements. Payment terms will also vary ranging from due upon receipt to due within thirty days of receipt or invoice issuance. Many professional services firms will also offer an additional 1 percent to 2 percent discount for prompt payment via electronic fund transfer within ten days of receipt. Similarly, many master agreements will contain an interest penalty for payments that are not received in a timely manner.

Despite the inclusion of this provision, I cannot recall one instance in which I have pursued interest charges from any Fortune 500 company under a master agreement, even in those circumstances where they were quite delinquent from a payment perspective. In addition to the payment terms themselves, it is critical to agree upon the level of detail that will be required for an invoice to be deemed acceptable by the client.

In addition to the invoice itself, it is important to address any taxes that will be applicable to the services being delivered as well as the currency in which payment will be made. In terms of taxes, most consulting firms will provide a rate structure that is exclusive of any indirect taxes including sales, value-added, goods and services, or otherwise. To address this issue in a master agreement, language similar to the following should be included:

> **Professional services fees are exclusive of any VAT, GST, sales tax, or other applicable indirect taxes. If such taxes are applicable, they will be charged in addition to professional fees. In the event that consultant is not registered to collect such taxes, the client agrees to self-assess those taxes, to properly make the requisite payment to the appropriate taxing authority, and to provide the consultant with documentation evidencing such payment.**

Of significant importance is the issue of the currency in which payment will be made. This is particularly relevant when providing services under a global master agreement where services will be delivered across multiple regions and in which staff will be providing services outside of their respective home geography. To avoid any questions regarding the currency in which the invoice will be issued, the agreement should contain a provision which states that the consultant will invoice the client in local currency, which is defined as the currency customarily used by consultant for charges to its other customers in the territory in which the billed item is provided. One exception to this rule is with regard to staff crossing geographical boundaries for delivery. To avoid any currency fluctuation exposure as a result of staff incurring costs in local currency within the operating entity to which they report and being paid in the local currency of the geography in which the services were delivered, it is critical to include language in the agreement which states that the consultant's home location, not the location where services are being delivered, will determine the currency in which the client is billed for that particular resource.

Other Pricing and Payment Issues

Two other critical areas that must be addressed include staff promotions that occur during and expenses incurred during service delivery. Staff promotions that occur during delivery is an area that is typically overlooked when negotiating the terms and conditions of a master agreement. Absent any language to the contrary, the consultant will most likely invoice the client at the higher labor category rate once the promotion has taken effect. Depending upon the size and scope of the project and budget, and the number of consultants receiving promotions, the impact can be significant, and clients may consider this to be a tactic their consultants utilize to generate incremental revenue during the course of an engagement.

To mitigate any uncertainty in this area, the agreement should state that consultants receiving promotions will continue to be invoiced at their current rate either until the statement of work in which they are engaged is completed or until the end of the current month. Fortune 500 clients may also request detailed information for each labor category including education and experience requirements to mitigate any concerns regarding arbitrary promotions.

Travel and expenses have also become an area that receives a tremendous amount of scrutiny from Fortune 500 procurement organizations. Historically, travel and expenses were invoiced to Fortune 500 clients as a flat percentage of professional fees. The typical range was anywhere from 15 percent to 20 percent of total professional fees; under this approach, the consultant would simply include a line item on the invoice for this amount, and no supporting documentation was required for payment. The consultant could, therefore, travel and incur expenses in any manner and class they deemed appropriate and had no reporting obligation to the client. It was even possible to generate additional margin on expenses to the extent that actual costs incurred did not rise to the agreed-upon threshold. This trend changed quite drastically with the centralization of corporate procurement organizations. While expenses may still be invoiced as a percentage of professional fees in some master agreements, the relative range that is acceptable to many Fortune 500 clients has decreased significantly and is in the 10 percent to 12 percent range.

The more common approach has been to reimburse consultants for travel and related expenses at actual cost in a manner consistent with the *client's* travel policy and to require the submission of detailed supporting documentation with each invoice including receipts for any items costing in excess of anywhere from $25 to $75. Typically, these policies mandate the class of travel for which they will provide reimbursement as well as a list of preferred hotels where they maintain pre-negotiated rates for their staff and consultants. Don't think about having steak and lobster for dinner, as many Fortune 500 clients have also imposed daily per diem amounts for meals and incidental expenses that are geography-specific in nature. Clearly, the administrative costs associated with this approach are significant and do not always parallel the consultant's travel policy. As a result, many consulting firms have chosen to accept a lower fixed percentage and simply manage their expenses and travel style more prudently.

The only other issue that is typically addressed in the payment clause is the applicability of any volume discount. We will discuss volume discounts in more detail when we discuss rate card negotiations, but suffice it to say that most consulting firms will offer Fortune 500 companies a volume discount as a mechanism to entice them to increase their transaction volume under the master agreement. The volume discount is usually calculated based upon the total professional fees incurred on an annual basis, may run as high as 10 percent or greater depending upon actual volume, and is typically returned to the client in the form of an actual rebate check or as a credit against future services. While the credit against future services is much more advantageous to the consultant, handing a client a substantial rebate check goes a long way in creating client goodwill and setting a strong foundation for partnership.

Two other issues that most Fortune 500 clients like to address within the payment clause include a most favored customer provision as well as a term that relieves them of their right to pay for any services that are not invoiced within 90 days of delivery. I have always refused to agree to either of these provisions. While the 90-day provision is clear on its face, the most favored customer provision is not; in practice, it requires the consultant to notify the client if it is providing the same services to another client at a more favorable price. To the extent this is the case, the consultant agrees to immediately reduce its price to that level. My rationale on the 90-day rule is that if you deliver the service, then you are entitled to payment even if there is some issue with regard to issuing an invoice in a timely manner. While I understand the need for timely invoices and certainly strive to achieve this objective, the penalty for failing to invoice as a result of a clerical error should not be to completely relieve the client of its payment obligation.

With regard to the most favored customer provision, my position is that all professional services agreements and transactions are different in that they contain different levels of risk inherent in delivery, different delivery terms and conditions, different product and service offerings, and different delivery timelines. Given this variability combined with the fact that a large consulting firm can have hundreds if not thousands of active engagements ongoing at any time, signing up to this type of provision is neither administratively feasible nor advised. A sample payment clause that addresses many of these issues is as seen here:

Client shall pay the professional fees as specified in the applicable statement of work and this master agreement, subject to the Rate Schedule and Volume Discount Schedule attached to this agreement.

INVOICING: Within ten (10) days after the last day of each calendar month, Consultant shall submit an invoice to Client in accordance with the labor category rates and milestone deliverable schedule set forth in each statement of work. Client will pay all undisputed invoices within thirty (30) days after the invoice date. Client shall be entitled to an additional one percent (1 percent) discount if payment is received by Consultant within ten (10) days after the invoice date. Consultant may impose a late payment charge of 1 1/2 percent per month or, if less, the maximum rate allowed by law on all undisputed past due outstanding balances. Payments must be in the same currency specified on the invoice and are nonrefundable. Client shall be liable for and account for all charges and taxes (including any sales tax, use tax, value-added tax, or any equivalent local tax or government charge) Consultant becomes obligated to pay by virtue of this agreement, exclusive of taxes based on the net income of Consultant. Payment will be remitted to the address or the electronic transit routing indicated on the invoice.

INVOICE DETAILS: Consultant shall provide invoices with varying degrees of detail, as agreed upon by Client and Consultant. All invoices must conform to Client invoicing requirements, including those invoicing requirements set forth in the relevant statement of work. As a condition to Client's payment obligations hereunder, all Fees must be properly invoiced within ninety (90) days after the applicable Service is provided or charge is incurred, and Client shall not be obligated to pay any Fees that are not properly invoiced within such ninety (90) day time period.

REIMBURSABLE EXPENSES: Unless otherwise agreed in the applicable statement of work, Consultant's expenses shall not exceed 15 percent of the total professional fees for each statement of work. Consultant shall invoice Client for actual expenses incurred and will retain receipts for all expenses incurred greater than $75, which can be reviewed by Client to the extent any such expense amount is the subject of a good faith dispute. Consultant shall utilize Client's negotiated rates for air, rental car, and hotel accommodations wherever possible.

ADMINISTRATIVE EXPENSES: Except as expressly set forth in this Agreement, all costs and expenses relating to Consultant's performance of the Services, including but not limited to cell phone charges, copying, printing, faxing, personal digital assistant costs, and administrative and office support are included in the rate schedule attached to this agreement and shall not be charged to or reimbursed by Client.

> **PRICE GUARANTEE:** Consultant agrees that Client shall be treated as a most favored customer of Consultant, and to this end Consultant shall promptly provide to Client the Consultant's best pricing, service availability, service quality, and service responsiveness and new service offerings as they become available. Consultant guarantees that Client is receiving the Services and Deliverables hereunder at rates no higher than those charged by Consultant to its other Client's as of the Effective Date. If, at any time during the Term, Consultant charges any other Client for services or products similar to the Services and Deliverables at rates lower than those charged to Client hereunder, Consultant will immediately (a) notify Client and (b) reduce the rates charged under this Agreement to rates no higher than those charged to such other Client.

Pricing and payment terms are extremely critical components of any services agreement. As you can imagine, pricing receives an inordinate amount of scrutiny in the negotiation process. In the more than 100 master agreements I have negotiated with Fortune 500 companies, the time spent negotiating a rate structure outweighs the time spent negotiating legal and business terms and conditions by a margin of at least three to one. We will discuss pricing and procurement later in the book. With regard to payment terms, it is critical to realize that payment extends well beyond the dates invoices will be issued and paid. Failing to address substantive issues such as currency, taxes, travel and incidental expenses, staff promotions, and most favored customer status will result in ambiguity and uncertainty with regard to these issues and will ultimately have a detrimental financial impact upon both parties to the transaction.

14

Termination

As we discussed in previous chapters, many of the terms contained within a master services agreement with a Fortune 500 company are there simply to prepare for a worst-case scenario. Once the negotiation process is concluded and the agreement is executed, it is typically placed in a binder and not pulled out unless some delivery challenge or dispute arises. The only portions of the agreement that are really scrutinized during the period of performance are the payment provisions, rate cards, and travel and expense policies that are necessary for proposal submission and payment. To the extent that a worst-case scenario should arise, the termination provisions articulated in the master agreement take on a renewed level of importance and, therefore, must be carefully considered during the negotiation process.

Termination is not really good for either party unless it is an absolute necessity. It is not optimal for the client, as finding an alternate service provider will result in incremental cost and an extended delivery timeline. It is not optimal for the consultant, as it has to address staffing and other mobilization costs it may have undertaken to commence the delivery process. Nonetheless, the exercise of termination rights is not that uncommon and is a right that will be reserved by Fortune 500 clients and their preferred services providers.

Typical termination provisions will allow the parties to terminate for a material or repeated breach or default of the other party's duties or obligations under the agreement, to terminate for convenience, and to terminate in the event that either party becomes or is declared insolvent or bankrupt. A termination for breach or default could occur if one of the parties to the transaction materially or repeatedly defaults in performing its duties or obligations under the agreement and fails to cure the breach within the contractually stipulated cure period, which is typically set at 30 days.

Termination for Breach

Under a termination for breach, the nonbreaching party will notify the breaching party in writing by specifying the nature of the default. To the extent that the default is not substantially cured within 30 days after receiving the written termination notice, or if the breaching fails to provide a reasonable plan and completion date for curing such breach and fails to proceed with all due diligence to cure the breach in accordance with the plan, then the party not in default may terminate the agreement as of the date specified in the termination notice. Unlike termination for breach or default, termination for convenience is exactly how it sounds; it allows a party to the transaction to terminate the agreement or any statement of work issued thereunder with some notice period, typically 30 days, as specified in the agreement. Termination rights will also generally be available to either party in the transaction if the other party is liquidated, insolvent, or becomes bankrupt.

Termination for Cause or Convenience

Assuming there will be a termination for cause, convenience, or adverse business consequences like bankruptcy, the important issues to be addressed include the payment of any costs incurred by the consultant up to and including the date of termination as well as any demobilization costs, the development of an effective transition plan, the handling of any unaccepted deliverables or other work in progress, the return of any confidential information, and the maintenance and survival of any confidentiality provisions contained in the agreement. A sample termination provision for a master services agreement that would address most of these issues is seen in the following:

(A) Except as provided in Section (B), in the event of any material breach of this Agreement by a party, the nondefaulting party may terminate this Agreement with respect to that party, in whole or in part, by giving thirty (30) days prior written notice; provided, however, that this Agreement will not terminate at the end of the thirty (30) day notice period if the party in breach has cured the breach of which it has been notified prior to the expiration of the thirty (30) day period.

(B) In the event that Client fails to make payment of any undisputed, invoiced amounts due hereunder, and such failure continues for a period of thirty (30) days after Client's receipt of written notice thereof, Consultant will have the right to terminate the statement of work to which the payment default relates upon an additional sixty (60) days prior written notice unless the payment default has been cured before the end of such sixty (60) day period.

(C) Notwithstanding any provision of this Agreement to the contrary, Client may terminate this Agreement or any statement(s) of work upon ten (10) days prior written notice. Client agrees to pay Consultant for all Services performed up to the effective date of such termination at the agreed upon rates, provided that all such Services are in conformity with the specifications for such Services set out in the applicable statement of work. Notice of termination of any statement of work will not be considered notice of termination of this Agreement unless specifically stated in the notice.

(D) Either party may terminate Services in whole or in part immediately upon notice if the other party (i) is liquidated, dissolved, or adjudged to be in a state of bankruptcy or receivership, (ii) is insolvent, unable to pay its debts as they become due, or makes an assignment to or for the benefit of its creditors, or (iii) ceases to conduct business for any reason on an ongoing basis leaving no qualified successor to perform its obligations hereunder.

(E) In the event that Client terminates this Agreement in whole or in part pursuant to Section (A) or Section (D): (i) Client may, at its sole option (A) return any previously unaccepted Deliverables, in whole or in part, at Consultant's expense, and destroy all copies thereof, and Consultant will promptly refund any fees paid for such Deliverables, or (B) keep the Deliverables, in whole or in part, upon payment of the applicable portion of the fees incurred as of the date of such termination; and (ii) Consultant will promptly issue a refund of any prepaid fees unearned as of the date of such termination.

In this sample termination provision, the consultant may want to address a number of areas in the negotiation process. Specifically, while either party may terminate the agreement for breach, only the client can terminate the agreement for convenience. This is fairly typical, as I have yet to encounter a professional services firm that would terminate an agreement unless the client was not paying its invoice, met an unfortunate financial fate as articulated in Section D of this sample provision, or engaged in some other act that would result in their decision to terminate service delivery.

It is also important to note that under Section B of the agreement, the consultant may only terminate the particular statement of work for which it is not receiving undisputed payments in a timely manner, and not the entire master agreement. While this may be acceptable to the consultant, as there are likely multiple buyers with whom the consultant is engaged across the client buying community, it is sometimes difficult to treat each active statement of work in isolation. Finally, Section C only provides the consultant with ten days notice for a termination for convenience; given the potential size and scope of many engagements, this may not be a sufficient amount of time to disengage accordingly.

Like the payment term we previously discussed, the termination provisions of a master agreement must be carefully reviewed prior to contract execution. It is critical to consider the ramifications that may occur if a strategic engagement is terminated for cause, convenience, or adverse financial consequences. At a minimum, both parties to the transaction should make sure that the termination provisions are clear on their face, that they articulate which parties may terminate and under what consequences, that they address how work-in-process should be handled, and that they specify any ongoing obligations of the parties post-termination.

15

Warranty

Everyone understands the concept of a warranty. Let's assume you go to the local car dealer and purchase a new car. In exchange for your investment, you have an expectation that the car and all of its components will properly function for as long as you own the vehicle. In their attempt to satisfy part of your expectation, the manufacturer will offer a warranty which states that upon your accepting and taking delivery of the vehicle, they will, at no cost to you, correct and repair any defect, malfunction, or nonconformity that prevents the car from conforming and performing as warranted for some period or mileage threshold.

While this concept of warranty is pretty clear when purchasing a car or household appliance, it can be somewhat ambiguous when the commodity being purchased is a group of consultants delivering a strategy engagement or implementing a software product that is complex in scope, that contains hardware and software provided by third parties, and that involves staff from a number of disparate organizations and geographies. Under these circumstances, it can be quite difficult to identify the party who is responsible for the nonconformity and who should be responsible for satisfying the client's warranty claim. When negotiating a warranty provision, it is important to consider the length of the warranty period under which the consultant will correct, repair, and replace the nonconforming item at its expense and the standard of performance, or lack thereof, that will trigger a potential warranty claim.

When executing a master services agreement with a Fortune 500 company, the consultant will typically offer the client a number of warranties including that it is authorized to enter into the agreement; that its obligations under the agreement are not in conflict with its obligations under any other agreement; that its consultants have the requisite training and background to complete their tasks; that the services delivered will be performed in a professional manner in accordance with industry standards; that any deliverables being provided will not violate or infringe the patent, trademark, or copyright of any third party; and that at the time of acceptance and for some contractually defined period thereafter, any deliverables will conform to the specifications articulated in the applicable statement of work.

When I prepare to negotiate any warranty provision, I always temper my stance and approach based upon the output of the engagement. The first question to be asked is if any of the deliverables have moving parts and must function in some capacity to help power the client's business. It is important to distinguish this type of design or implementation engagement from one in which the deliverables are the time being expended by the consultants or any paper-based deliverables developed during service delivery. It is impossible to discuss warranty provisions without discussing acceptance criteria, as conformity with these criteria will drive the viability of any warranty claim. When it comes to acceptance criteria, you need to know only three words: *objective*, *measurable*, and *verifiable*. All acceptance criteria must meet this standard and be free from any ambiguity. As soon as the criteria become subjective, immeasurable, and unverifiable, both parties have different expectations with regard to delivery output, and I assure you that chaos will definitely ensue. So, if you learn nothing else from this book, the next time you are agreeing to acceptance criteria, please make sure they fit within these guidelines.

Tailoring the Warranty Based Upon the Engagement Output

So, under that mantra, let's first discuss the warranty typically being offered with regard to a services-only engagement where the output is paper-based deliverables, and there are no functioning items and no moving parts.

The problem with regard to the warranty clauses that are typical for these types of engagements is that they tend to be quite ambiguous and subjective in nature. Consider the options seen here:

All Services will be rendered by competent professionals who possess the skills outlined in the applicable statement of work, with the degree of skill and care that is required by current good and sound professional procedures and practices in accordance with highest professional and industry standards and will conform to Client's requirements hereunder.

Consultant warrants that it shall perform the Services and produce the Deliverables in all material respects in accordance with the applicable statement of work and the prevailing reasonable commercial standards applicable thereto.

All Services will be performed in a professional manner by qualified personnel, and are and at all times will be, with respect to quality, timeliness, and qualification of the Consultant performing the Services, comparable to or better than services offered by Consultant to any of its commercial customers who are similarly situated to Client with respect to types and volumes of services purchased.

Consultant agrees to undertake this assignment on a best efforts basis and that its findings and recommendations will reflect its best judgment based on the information available to it.

As you see, each of these provisions provides a standard of service that will serve as the hurdle for a successful warranty claim. In addition, the statement of work for an engagement of this type may specify some acceptance criteria with regard to the deliverable output to be provided to the client. While acceptance criteria are usually easily measured, delivery standards that are embodied in terms such as "current good and sound professional procedures, highest professional and industry standards, and prevailing reasonable commercial standards" are extremely ambiguous in nature, extremely subjective, and difficult to measure. The final option really provides no substantive warranty at all, as it simply states that the consultant will use its best efforts in delivery. Can you imagine attending a client meeting, telling them you gave it your best shot but failed, and requesting immediate payment?

Despite the ambiguity contained in these warranty provisions and their violation of my objective, measurable, and verifiable standard, the resolution of warranty claims in this area tends to be fairly straightforward. Consider an engagement in which the consultant will be developing a strategic plan surrounding its client's plans to launch a new product on a global basis, and the only deliverable is the strategic plan document itself. Once the contract is executed, the consultant fields a team and deploys them to a number of client offices to conduct local market competitive assessments and to interview key executives as to how the new product will complement the existing product suite. Assume that upon deployment, the client executive lead is unhappy with the performance of a member of the consulting team and feels he does not have the requisite level of experience for the work in which he is engaged, does not feel he is a good fit with the client's staff, and believes that he is not meeting the "highest professional and industry standards" performance standard contained in the warranty provision of the master agreement. Typically, they would raise this issue with the consultant's executive leadership for resolution; in effect, they have filed an informal warranty claim. In this case, it is not uncommon for the consultant to pull the implicated team member from the engagement and to deploy a replacement resource. Of course, there may be an issue around payment for the allegedly substandard hours provided by the consultant before he was removed from the engagement. This is not an uncommon occurrence and is typically dealt with in a fairly expeditious manner.

The bigger challenge would result if the team completed the engagement, provided the strategic plan, and the client was unhappy with the output and did not believe it met the ambiguous acceptance criteria identified in the statement of work. These types of warranty claims may be more difficult to address, as the consultant has already incurred significant cost over many months of effort and delivered the work product to the client for acceptance. The challenge when a client expresses concern over the quality of the final deliverable in an engagement of this type is that, like the ambiguous acceptance criteria, their concerns tend to be quite subjective in nature.

Most statements of work that are strategy focused do a great job of articulating the activities, data analysis, and reviews that the consultant will undertake with regard to articulating its solution, but do not contain a clear set of acceptance criteria that will serve as the benchmark for acceptance by the client. Failing to meet 100 percent of the client's expectations in this instance is not uncommon, and the consultant will typically, at its own expense, repair the document to bring it into conformity with the expectations of the client.

The bigger challenge is that most warranty provisions fail to address what will happen if the consultant repairs the deliverable, retenders it to the client, and the client still deems it unacceptable. Under these circumstances, it is always prudent to make sure that the warranty provision includes an escalation process that allows for a more objective review of the work product to determine if it meets whatever standard is articulated in the statement of work. Failure to provide such an escalation process can result in an endless cycle of tender, reject, repair, and retender for the consultant and client. A provision that would mitigate this occurrence might state that upon receipt of a deliverable, the client would have a contractually stipulated time window in which to review the deliverable and evaluate the services in question. If the client determines that the deliverable does not meet the relevant acceptance criteria, it will file its warranty claim in writing with specific documentation as to the deficiencies. Upon receipt of the warranty claim, the consultant will repair the deliverable at its own expense and resubmit it for acceptance to the client.

Once the deliverable is resubmitted, a fresh time window will commence. If the client is still unable to accept the deliverable even after the consultant's attempt to cure the deficiency, then the deliverable and acceptance criteria will be submitted to an independent internal review board for review. The board will consist of three nonproject members from each organization who will evaluate the deliverable in conjunction with the relevant acceptance criteria. If the board is unable to reach a majority opinion as to the validity of the warranty claim, the client may then pursue additional external remedies. Alternatively, the consultant and client could agree upon an independent third party review board to render a binding decision as to the conformity of the deliverable. It is therefore critical to articulate what will happen if a deliverable fails to meet the acceptance criteria, is repaired by the consultant, is retendered, and is still deemed to be nonconforming. Of course, the client could always seek other remedies in this instance, including termination for breach, but many warranty provisions seek to limit the remedies available for this type of warranty claim.

One of the other remedies that a Fortune 500 client may wish to embed within its warranty term is a provision that would allow for the cost of cover (explained shortly) if the consultant is unable to deliver its products or services in accordance with the acceptance criteria contained in the agreement. Even with the inclusion of an objective and independent escalation and review process, a stalemate scenario could arise as to whether the work product meets the acceptance criteria contained within the applicable statement of work. To mitigate the risk associated with this contingency, the client may seek to have the consultant compensate it for its *cost of cover*— the difference between what it was going to pay the consultant for the services and what it actually costs the client to obtain the services of another provider to complete the work product or services in a manner that conforms with the acceptance criteria contained in the contract.

I am not a proponent of cost of cover provisions, as I believe that objective, measurable, and verifiable acceptance criteria will substantially mitigate the need for this contingency and will drive the appropriate outcome to the extent that a dispute should arise. To the extent that the consultant would agree to this provision, its impact should be evaluated in light of the limitation on liability provisions contained within the master agreement.

Despite the ambiguity that typically surrounds pure strategy engagements where the output may be time and paper-based deliverables, I have only seen a few instances in which any nonconformities raised by the client were not successfully repaired by the consultant, retendered to the client, and accepted. Unfortunately, this is not always the case when the output of the engagement is a functioning object or system that has lots of moving parts.

What About Deliverables That Must Function?

As I mentioned previously, deliverables that must function, such as critical enterprise resource planning software or other information systems, create a whole new set of issues from a warranty perspective. Unlike their paper-based deliverable counterparts, they are complex in nature and not always easy to repair. In addition, there may be multiple deliverables specified in the statement of work that are all interconnected and part of a larger implementation timeline. For engagements of this type, the period in which the client must accept a tendered deliverable is critical; failure to do so may result in a completely derailed project plan and implementation timeline, and may also impact the ability of the consultant to recognize revenue in a timely manner.

These types of warranties are much clearer on their face and are similar to what a car buyer might receive from any of the major automobile manufacturers. For these types of deliverables, the key factors with regard to the viability of any warranty claim are going to be the conformity of the product or system with the acceptance criteria, the impact of any third-party hardware or software that is a part of the overall solution, and the term of the warranty being offered. A Fortune 500 client will most likely try and secure a warranty for a software product being developed and implemented by a consultant similar to what is seen here:

> **For a period of six (6) months following acceptance by Client (the "Warranty Period"), any software (and associated documentation) developed by Consultant for Client as part of the Deliverables will be free from significant programming errors and from defects in workmanship and materials, and will conform to the performance capabilities, characteristics, specifications, functions, and other descriptions and standards applicable thereto in all material respects. In the event of a breach of the foregoing warranty during the Warranty Period, Consultant will promptly remedy such breach at no additional expense to Client. Notwithstanding the foregoing, Consultant will have no obligation or liability to Client under this warranty to the extent that a defect results directly from (i) Client's use of such software in a manner inconsistent with the documentation; (ii) alterations or modifications made to such software by Client without the approval of Consultant; (iii) malfunctions of Client's computer hardware occurring through no fault of Consultant; or (iv) storage, operation, use, or**

maintenance of such software in a manner or in an environment inconsistent with the specifications and instructions of Consultant.

The parties understand that any work product delivered under this Agreement may specify that Client procure certain third-party hardware and/or software products. It is acknowledged by Client that Client shall be solely responsible for obtaining licenses to such third-party software, if such software is not already in Client's possession, including the right to incorporate such software into its systems. Consultant makes no warranties or representations hereunder, express or implied, as to the quality, capabilities, operations, performance, or suitability of any third-party hardware or software, and the quality, capabilities, operations, performance, and suitability of such third-party hardware or software lies solely with Client and the vendor or supplier of that hardware or software.

In addition to the general warranty provisions I have just articulated, there will always be a *warranty disclaimer*, which states that the consultant is not offering additional warranties other than those specified in the warranty provision of the agreement as seen here:

Unless otherwise expressly set forth herein, vendor hereby disclaims all other warranties, express or implied, including without limitation, the implied warranties of merchantability and fitness for a particular purpose.

The best guidance I can provide around warranty claims is to carefully focus upon the acceptance criteria that will trigger the warranty provisions. Acceptance criteria must be objective, measurable, and verifiable for all types of engagements, even those in which the output is time and paper-based deliverables. Carefully review the hurdle that must be crossed to trigger a warranty claim and the period under which the warranty will run. Also, make sure that the contract is clear as to what remedies the client can pursue in the event it finds a deliverable to be nonconforming as well as the escalation process for those deliverables that have been retendered and still are deemed to be unacceptable by the client. Finally, be cognizant of the nature of the services being provided and the amount of risk inherent in delivery. Temper your negotiating stance based upon the complexity of the solution being delivered, the number of moving parts involved, and your historical ability to deliver a similarly situated solution in a timely, quality, and cost-effective manner. Most important, warranty provisions can yield significant financial exposure for a consultant, so carefully think through the implications that warranty provisions can have in the delivery and acceptance process.

16

Confidential Information and Data Protection

During the course of a consulting engagement, significant amounts of confidential information are exchanged between both parties to the transaction. The nature of the information can be extremely sensitive depending upon the service offering and could have a significant detrimental impact upon the client in the case of unauthorized disclosure. Given the sensitivity of the information being exchanged, the potential inclusion of employee or customer personally identifiable information, and the risk associated with unauthorized disclosure, there has been a renewed focus upon confidential information and data protection rights when executing agreements with Fortune 500 companies. Much of this renewed focus has been the result of a number of highly publicized data loss incidents involving professional services firms.

When negotiating the manner in which confidential information will be exchanged between the parties, the first order of business is to identify what type of information will be deemed to be "confidential" under the terms of the agreement. Most agreements will stipulate that any information exchanged between the parties is marked "confidential," will be kept confidential by the receiving party, and will be utilized in an authorized manner that is typically defined as furthering the performance of services by the receiving party. Confidential information that is exchanged under a typical engagement may include:

- Lists of, or other information relating to and identified with customers, former or prospective customers or applicants

- Business volumes or usage

- Financial information

- Pricing information

- Information related to mergers or acquisitions

- Security procedures

- Information concerning business plans or business strategy

- Patent, copyright, trade secret, and other proprietary information

- Software and software documentation

- Data

- Inventions

- Know-how

- Processes

- Information related to the party's current, future, and proposed products and services

- The subject matter of the master agreement itself

On the other hand, there will be no restrictions placed upon information:

- That is in the public domain at the time of receipt or that came into the public domain through no fault of the receiving party

- That was in the receiving party's possession prior to its receipt by the disclosing party

- That was disclosed with the prior written approval of the disclosing party

- That was developed independently of any disclosures made under the agreement

- That was lawfully disclosed to the receiving party by a third party that was not subject to any restrictions on disclosure

- That is required to be disclosed by the receiving party by order of a court or administrative body of competent jurisdiction provided that the receiving party notifies the disclosing party and provides them with a reasonable opportunity to oppose any such order

What's the Proper Standard of Care?

Once the buckets of what is and what is not confidential information are identified, the next question to be addressed is the standard of care by which confidential information will be handled by the receiving party. Typically, the receiving party will be contractually bound to protect the disclosing party's confidential information with at least the same degree of care and confidentiality by which it protects its own confidential information that it does not want disclosed to the general public. In addition, the typical master agreement with a Fortune 500 company will state the information will only be provided to the consultant's employees solely as necessary (a need to know basis) to meet their obligations under the agreement. To the extent that any confidential information must be shared with any third party, the receiving party will require that third party to execute a nondisclosure agreement under which any confidential data will be protected and utilized in a manner similar to the conditions contained in the master agreement.

Despite the fact that significant amounts of sensitive information may be exchanged during the course of the engagement, the agreement will specify that the receiving party in no way obtains any right, title, or interest in the confidential information. To that end, the parties must agree on a policy by which any confidential information exchanged during the course of the agreement is either returned to the disclosing party or destroyed. This can be accomplished through the inclusion of a provision similar to the following language:

> **Within sixty (60) calendar days after termination of this Agreement, each party shall certify in writing to the other that all copies of Confidential Information in any form have been destroyed or returned to the disclosing party, unless explicitly permitted in writing otherwise by the disclosing party.**

In addition to the these standard provisions, many master agreements will also require the receiving party to maintain information security programs and administrative and physical safeguards intended to prevent the unauthorized disclosure, misuse, alteration, or destruction of confidential information, and require that any security breach or other incident involving possible unauthorized disclosure of or access to confidential information be immediately reported to the disclosing party. To ensure that these guidelines are adequately satisfied, it is not uncommon for Fortune 500 companies to include a provision in their standard master agreement under which they require their vendors to comply with their internal information security standards surrounding accessing, processing, and storing confidential information. Service providers will be required to meet these standards within a contractually stipulated period and are subject to physical inspection audits and reviews of system configurations. In addition, strict notification procedures will apply to the extent that there is any unauthorized access to any system or network utilized by the consultant to access, process, or store any confidential information of the client. A sample confidential information provision that addresses many of these issues is as seen here:

> **(A) Consultant and Client acknowledge that by reason of their relationship under this contract, they may have access to and acquire knowledge from, material, data, systems, and other information concerning the operation, business, projections, market goals, trade secrets, computer programs, software, documentation, formulas, data, inventions, techniques, marketing plans, strategies, forecasts, customer lists, employee information,**

financial information, work product, research, development, engineering, purchasing, manufacturing, accounting, marketing, selling, leasing, financial affairs, products, customers, and intellectual property rights of the other Party that may not be accessible or known to the general public ("Confidential Information"). The term "Confidential Information" shall mean: any and all information which is disclosed by one ("Disclosing Party") of the Parties to the other ("Receiving Party") verbally, electronically, visually, or in a written or other tangible form which is either identified as or should be reasonably understood to be confidential or proprietary.

(B) During the term of Consultant's relationship with Client, and indefinitely thereafter, Consultant will not, except as otherwise expressly directed in writing by Client, use, copy, disclose, or permit any unauthorized person access to any Confidential Information.

(C) Consultant may disclose Confidential Information or trade secrets to the extent that they are required to be disclosed pursuant to a requirement of a governmental agency or law, provided that: (i) Consultant has given Client prior written notice of such disclosure prior thereto and takes all available steps to maintain the confidentiality of the information disclosed; and (ii) Client has been afforded a reasonable opportunity to contest the necessity and scope of such disclosure.

(D) The Receiving Party further agrees to use the Confidential Information only for the purpose of performing this contract. In addition, the Receiving Party shall not reverse engineer, disassemble, or decompile any prototypes, software, or other tangible objects which embody Confidential Information and which are provided to the Receiving Party thereunder. Whenever requested by the Disclosing Party, the Receiving Party shall immediately return to the Disclosing Party all manifestations of the Confidential Information or, at the Disclosing Party's option, shall destroy all such Confidential Information as the Disclosing Party may designate.

(E) Consultant will, in advance, require each of its employees, permitted subcontractors, and their employees who are assigned to perform services or who are likely to be in a position to obtain any Client information or materials required by the terms of this Agreement to be kept confidential, to execute a confidentiality agreement. Consultant will provide Client with a true signed copy of each such confidentiality agreement upon request. Consultant further agrees to take any other steps reasonably required and/or appropriate to ensure compliance with the obligations set forth herein.

(F) Consultant acknowledges and agrees that, in the event of a breach or threatened breach of any of the foregoing provisions, Client will have no adequate remedy in damages and, accordingly, will be entitled to injunctive relief against such breach or threatened breach in addition to any other remedies available at law or in equity.

(G) The Receiving Party's obligations listed above shall not apply to Confidential Information which: (i) is or becomes a matter of public knowledge through no fault of or action by the Receiving Party; (ii) was rightfully in the Receiving Party's possession prior to disclosure by the Disclosing Party; (iii) subsequent to disclosure, is rightfully obtained by the Receiving Party from a third party who is lawfully in possession of such Confidential Information without restriction; (iv) is independently developed by the Receiving Party without resort to the Disclosing Party's Confidential Information; or (v) is required by law or judicial order, provided that prior written notice of such required disclosure is furnished to the Disclosing Party as soon as practicable, and prior to disclosure occurring, in order to afford the Disclosing Party an opportunity to seek a protective order or other legal remedy to prevent such disclosure, and that if such order or remedy cannot be obtained, disclosure may be made without liability.

Other Safeguarding Tactics

Two other tactics that have been utilized by Fortune 500 clients with regard to safeguarding their confidential information include background checks on any consultant staff that will be working under the engagement and strict covenant not to compete guidelines for staff that are deployed to provide services during the term of the master agreement and for some period thereafter. While background checks may have historically been reserved for executing master agreements with financial services entities, they have become much more prevalent across all major commercial industries.

The rationale behind the background checks is to maintain the reliability, safety, and integrity of the client's business and assets. A number of issues arise with regard to client-specific background checks including who will bear the cost and the level of potential intrusion to which the impacted consultant's staff may be subjected.

The importance of these two issues should not be underestimated. Given the potential scope of services to be delivered under a master agreement, the level of staff to be deployed can be significant, and the cost associated with completing a background check for each staff person can be substantial.

While this may be an issue for the negotiation process, most clients consider the background check to be a cost of doing business and will stand firm in their position that the cost associated with the background checks should be absorbed by the consultant. The requirements of background checks themselves are not cursory in nature and at a minimum will include verification of names, dates of birth, home addresses, criminal history, social security number, driver's license number, and any authorized work permits. In addition to the preceding, staff that will have access to any financial data or monetary assets will be subject to a credit check and review of court records for prior bankruptcy proceedings. Some organizations may require verification of professional certifications, physical examinations including drug testing, and other background investigations as necessary and appropriate given the nature of the work being completed and access to client facilities. These requirements are typically much greater than those conducted by most of the major consulting firms during the hiring process and may not be acceptable to each staff person who is scheduled for deployment to the client account team.

Another area that has received tremendous focus and that raises client blood pressure levels is the area of covenants not to compete. As we all know, competition among many Fortune 500 companies is quite fierce, and the unauthorized release of confidential data, particularly regarding strategic initiatives, to a key competitor could result in a significant competitive disadvantage in the market. This level of competitive intensity resonates throughout all hierarchical levels of these companies. You can imagine that companies in heated competition like Pepsi and Coca-Cola, and FedEx and UPS want to keep any information regarding their company and its strategy and operations out of the hands of their most fierce competitors, and they expect their consultants to adhere to a similar practice.

The challenge is that most of the large consulting firms have limited management and staff that have the requisite industry and functional expertise to deliver services to these clients. Given the fact that consulting staff typically serve multiple clients within their respective industry, Fortune 500 clients are concerned that their confidential information may be inadvertently shared across account teams. To address this dynamic, some consulting firms, depending upon the depth and breadth of their relationship, will make a business decision to serve a specific client and agree not to provide any services to a named competitor set. Other consulting firms will agree to implement an internal barrier between account teams to ensure that staff and project information are never commingled during the current periods of performance and for some contractually stipulated period into the future.

The key issues to be negotiated for these noncompete provisions include the staff that will be subject to any restriction (all staff deployed to the account or just individuals named as "key" personnel), the term of the restriction (anywhere from six months to multiple years), and the list of competitors to which the restriction applies. Each of these issues can significantly impact the viability of a consultant's practice in a particular industry, so it is critical to balance the restrictions of the covenant with current staff size and capabilities, the extent of the relationship and transaction volume with the client proposing the restriction, and the potential for lost opportunities with the named competitors subject to the restriction. A sample covenant noncompete provision is as seen here:

> **Unless specified in an applicable statement of work or as confirmed in writing by an authorized representative from Client, Consultant agrees that it will not assign any Consultant personnel performing services under the statement of work to perform the same or competitive services to other Consultant clients which are the direct competitors of Client as listed below for a period of twelve (12) months following the completion of such person's services under the applicable statement of work unless otherwise agreed to by Client and Consultant in such statement of work.**

During the course of a typical strategy, design, or implementation consulting engagement, it is not uncommon for highly sensitive and proprietary information to be exchanged between the parties. Given the highly proprietary nature of this information and the detrimental impact of unauthorized disclosure, this area has received a tremendous level of scrutiny in recent years. Technology advances are also responsible for this renewed focus, as jump-drive and other portable storage devices have complicated the exchange and identification process and facilitated the risk of unauthorized disclosure. Given the highly competitive landscape within the commercial markets, a limited number of quality service providers, and a number of highly publicized data loss incidents, Fortune 500 companies are requiring their vendors to take extreme measures with regard to protecting their proprietary information. As we have discussed, these measures may vary from the benign identification of the standard of care by which such information should be handled to the more aggressive requirements to implement information security programs and physical safeguards, to require extensive background checks for personnel, and to adhere to rigorous covenants not to compete. Given the level of sensitivity in this area, it is critical that both parties to the transaction clearly understand the protective measures in place and adhere to them accordingly.

17

Other Key Contract Issues

In addition to the most heavily negotiated provisions listed throughout Part 3, a few other key contractual provisions tend to receive a significant amount of scrutiny and to elevate the blood pressure levels of management consultants as well as Fortune 500 procurement and legal staff. Those provisions include the areas of acceptance, payment, liquidated damages, client obligations, engagement governance, change orders, order of precedence, nonsolicitation clauses, audit rights, third-party beneficiaries, business continuity and disaster recovery, the utilization of subcontractors in the delivery of services, publicity, and dispute resolution.

We discussed acceptance in our review of warranty claims, as the two issues are intertwined. Agreeing to a narrowly tailored statement of work with objective, measurable, and verifiable acceptance criteria is an absolute necessity, as those criteria will serve as the baseline against which the viability of a warranty claim will be measured. The best counsel I can provide in this area is to carefully review the statement of work and acceptance criteria and to make sure that they are free from ambiguity. I am a big fan of the *four corners rule*, which simply states that a document should be interpreted based upon what is contained within its four corners and not based upon any extrinsic factors such as any of the circumstances surrounding its writing or any prior dealings of the parties to the transaction.

To interpret a contract in this manner, it is critical that the document stand on its own. Over the years, I have been handed countless statements of work to review prior to client submission. In the majority of instances, the recurring comment I make is that the statement of work is not narrowly tailored, and the criteria that will measure success are ambiguous. In response to that comment, I am frequently told that the statement of work has been reviewed with the client with whom we have worked for years and that everyone has clear expectations as to the deliverables and corresponding acceptance criteria that will govern the engagement. While this may be the case, the bottom line is that staff turnover is a common occurrence within both Fortune 500 companies and management consulting firms, and conversations during meetings and prior dealings are simply not sufficient when executing agreements for the delivery of services that may span multiple years. Don't get me wrong; I do believe that some flexibility is necessary to successfully put into operation the terms and conditions contained within the contract. But it is important to carefully manage where that flexibility lies; as we discussed previously, the most common reason projects fail is scope creep. Scope creep results when statements of work are not narrowly tailored, and the measuring stick used to ensure success, the acceptance criteria, are vague and ambiguous. So when you think the statement of work and acceptance criteria are clearly defined, take one more look from the perspective of an objective third party who is not familiar with the scope of services being rendered, but nonetheless who might be asked to render a decision to adjudicate a dispute between the parties sometime in the future.

When I conduct this review, I ask myself one question: could my mom review this document and tell me exactly what is being delivered and how success will be measured between the parties? If my answer to this question is yes, then I feel confident that the statement of work can stand on its own and easily facilitate any dispute resolution. I know I seem to be dwelling on this point, but I cannot stress how important it is to properly define how success will be measured for any consulting engagement. Spending an extra hour reviewing the statement of work will save time and money and preserve references and relationships downstream.

We discussed payment terms in detail during our discussion of price. The only issue I would reiterate is the fact that payment is much more than agreeing upon the dates in which invoices will be issued and the payment due date. A number of other issues including prompt payment discounts, interest charges for late payments, payment currency, payment method, taxes, invoice requirements, and travel and expense policies must be carefully considered during the negotiation process. Failure to do so can have a significant detrimental impact upon the client's budget and the consultant's financial performance on the engagement.

A Fortune 500 company may seek to introduce a liquidated damages provision within a particular statement of work executed under a master services agreement. Under a liquidated damages provision, the parties agree to the payment of a fixed amount as satisfaction for a breach by the other party. This type of provision is typically utilized in contracts where the damages that would result from a breach are uncertain and unable to be reasonably estimated by the parties. The inclusion of such a provision within a services agreement of this type will depend upon the nature and scope of the engagement as well as the ability of the parties to ascertain the damages that would result upon a breach of the agreement.

For a liquidated damages provision to be legally binding, the consequences of the breach and the resulting injury must be difficult to quantify, the amount must be reasonable and proportionate to the potential harm caused by the breach, and the damages must not be meant to function as a penalty. Unlike liquidated damages, a *penalty* is a sum that is not proportionate to the actual harm that may be caused as a result of the breach and is used as a deterrent against the occurrence of a breach.

While a liquidated damages provision is not applicable to all engagements, it is not uncommon to see the inclusion of such a provision when the services being contemplated include the implementation of a software product in accordance with a contractually stipulated go-live date. A liquidated damages provision in this context might state that if the consultant fails to implement the system on or within a specified number of days of the go-live date articulated in the statement of work, liquidated damages will be assessed on a monthly basis until such time as the system is accepted and in production. Under this scenario, the potential liability of the consultant could be unlimited if the liquidated damages provision was listed as a carve-out to the limitation on liability term contained in the master agreement.

A more likely scenario might be a one-time fixed payment that would be assessed upon the consultant for failing to meet the go-live date. Under this approach, the parties are effectively agreeing to an acceptable settlement related to a potential breach versus having to pursue what would definitely be a much more costly and lengthy litigation or arbitration process. While neither scenario is optimal for the consultant, this fixed liquidated damages payment provides the consultant with the ability to better gauge the amount of risk inherent in delivery and to more accurately determine the potential cost of nonperformance. A sample liquidated damages provision is seen here:

> **Consultant agrees that in addition to all other remedies available to the Client, the Client may collect Liquidated Damages in the amounts specified under the following circumstances:**
>
> **If the Consultant fails to implement the system on or within twenty (20) calendar days of the production installation date, liquidated damages in the amount of $300,000 per month may be assessed from the production implementation date. The production installation date will be the date articulated in the statement of work and milestone delivery schedule contained therein.**
>
> **To the extent that the Client exercises its right under this provision, it may deduct any amount owed for the liquidated damages from invoices as necessary to offset the full amount owed.**

Clearly articulating the level of cooperation and obligations of the client is a critical part of any engagement. Any professional services engagement, irrespective of where it falls within the consulting lifecycle, requires that the client provide qualified and capable resources that are relieved from their day-to-day obligations where appropriate and dedicated to working with the consultant to achieve timely, quality, and cost-effective delivery. Almost all professional services firms take the position that they have been engaged to *assist* and *partner* with the client to solve some business problem. Successful engagements do not occur with the consultant working in isolation. While the consultant's team may be experts in a designated functional area and have extensive industry and technical knowledge, they do not have an equivalent level of client institutional knowledge.

Therefore, in any engagement, the consultant's level of success will be very tightly aligned with the quality, capability, and dedication of the client resources with which it is engaged. In addition to the size and capabilities of the resources that the client will make available during the course of the engagement, it is critical to clearly articulate any other client obligations that impact successful delivery. A sample listing of client obligations might typically include the language seen here:

During the course of service delivery, the Client shall be responsible for:

1. **Designating a single point of contact for each statement of work to whom all Client communications may be directed and who has the authority to act on all aspects of the services. The primary contact will be identified in each statement of work and will be available during normal business hours.**

2. **Designating a back-up contact when the primary contact is not available.**

3. **Participating in regularly scheduled meetings with the consultant to discuss delivery status, and to address and resolve any problem issues as well as any other duties and tasks set forth on the applicable statement of work.**

4. **Providing adequate access to the Client's premises and equipment reasonably required for performance of the services.**

5. **Assigning specific managerial, technical, and user personnel as reasonably requested by consultant to participate in essential project activities including preparation and review of specifications, testing, migration activities, data conversion, training, operations, and project administration. The Client shall ensure that all such staff have reasonably adequate skills and experience for their respective functions and will comply with the reasonable directions and requests of the consultant with regard to service delivery.**

6. Supplying any and all required information, data, and documentation required for consultant to successfully perform the services under the agreement.

7. With respect to any software, documentation, information, interfaces, data, or specifications supplied by the Client, providing a warranty to the consultant that it has the right to use and to disclose to the consultant all such information and that the information will be complete, accurate, and prompt.

8. Inspecting and reviewing all reports prepared by the consultant within a reasonable (as stipulated in the contract) time after receipt. Failure to reject any such report on a timely basis shall constitute acceptance.

While these obligations may seem quite reasonable, they are not always quickly agreed upon in practice. I have been a party to a few transactions in which the Fortune 500 client with whom I was negotiating was unwilling to agree to a provision which stated that any information they provided to the consultant during the course of delivery would be complete, accurate, and prompt. While this refusal may not be the industry norm, it is critical that both the consultant and client clearly articulate the delivery obligations of both parties before service delivery commences.

Closely related to the area of articulating client obligations is the area of governance. Given the size, scope, cost, and complexity of most engagements, project timelines are tight, and scheduling delays are not easily absorbed. To that end, it is critical that the agreement provide for a strong governance process by which deliverables are reviewed and approved, project-level decisions are made, and problems and issues that arise between the parties are escalated for resolution. As we have previously discussed, the review and approval process for milestone deliverables will typically be stipulated in the acceptance provisions of the agreement.

With regard to project-level decisions, it is advised to include a framework within the master agreement that specifies the prioritization of issues based upon their level of importance and time sensitivity and the timeline under which the client must respond to the consultant with an answer. In addition, a dispute resolution process should be included within the agreement that identifies the escalation process to be followed by the parties prior to initiating any formal arbitration or adjudication process. I find the inclusion of this type of governance process can be extremely helpful, as it escalates problem issues to the appropriate hierarchical level before they spiral out of control and detrimentally impact delivery. A sample issue resolution clause is as seen here:

Prior to the filing of any claim with respect to a dispute, the aggrieved party ("Invoking Party") will call for progressive business management involvement in the dispute resolution process by providing written notice to the other party. Such a notice will be without prejudice to the Invoking Party's right to any other remedy permitted by the Agreement.

The parties will arrange personal meetings and/or telephone conferences as needed, at mutually convenient times and places, between the parties at the following successive management levels with the associated allotted times:

MANAGEMENT LEVEL	CONSULTANT	CLIENT	ALLOTTED BUSINESS DAYS
Level 1	Delivery VP	Program Executive Sponsor	Five
Level 2	Portfolio or Industry VP	Steering Committee Lead	Seven
Level 3	Executive/Regional VP	CIO or CFO	Fifteen

The allotted time for the first-level discussion will begin five (5) business days after the other party receives the Invoking Party's written notice. If the dispute is not resolved by negotiators at any given management level at the end of their allotted time, then the allotted time for the negotiators at the next management level will begin on the next business day. Each party agrees to negotiate the claims in good faith. Pending final resolution of any dispute, the parties agree to proceed with performance of the Agreement.

In addition to client obligations and decision-making and issue resolution governance, it is critical that any agreement for the delivery of think, build, or run services contain a well-defined change-order process. As discussed earlier, the primary reason projects fail is scope creep, and scope creep typically occurs when both consultants and clients deviate from the statement of work and fail to execute a change order.

Many clients see a negative connotation to the change order process, as they feel consultants use this tactic to significantly increase the initially agreed upon cost associated with delivery. There is certainly plenty of historical evidence to support this assertion. That fear is best embodied in a photo that hung in the office of one of my former staff members; it depicted a small and rather modest boat that was named *Prime Contract* and a large and lavish 100-foot-plus yacht named *Change Order*. While this may represent an extreme example of a change order process gone wrong, the bottom line is that the change order process, when utilized in accordance with a narrowly tailored statement of work, will facilitate changes in scope and ultimately support timely, quality, and cost-effective delivery.

When executing a master agreement, it is important to clearly articulate the timeline and mechanics around the change order administration process. Given the complexity of many engagements and the number of concurrent activities in the project plan, it is critical that any change order requests be dealt with in an expeditious manner so they do not have a detrimental impact on the project timeline. Let's first define a change order. A *change order* is a document executed by both parties to the agreement that changes the method, manner, performance, specifications, or terms and conditions of the statement of work initially agreed upon by the parties.

An efficient change order process is one under which both parties to the transaction are clear that there will be no deviations in scope unless a written change order has been executed between the parties. No exceptions to this rule are allowed, irrespective of the exigency of the circumstances. I assure you that if you allow for exceptions, you are walking a tightrope over the Grand Canyon with no net. An efficient change order process is also one that places time constraints around the request, proposal submission, review, negotiation, and acceptance process. A sample process might state that any changes in project scope should be requested by the client in a timely manner and submitted in writing to the consultant for review. Within 15 days of receipt of the request, the consultant will provide the client with an updated cost proposal and revised project plan, and the client will have an additional 15 days to review the proposal, negotiate any issues related to the price and project plan, and execute the change order. This process could result in a 30-day window under which a change order could be executed. It may be prudent to allow for a fast-track process for mission-critical change orders, as a 30-day window will not always be feasible, especially for complex implementation engagements under which deviations to the schedule can impact project success.

The other issue to be addressed around the master services agreement change order process is the order of precedence or conflicts provision that will typically be contained within the master agreement. This provision simply states which terms, those contained in the master agreement itself or those contained in a statement of work or change order executed thereunder, will take precedence in the event of a conflict. It is important to be cognizant of this provision when executing a change for a particular statement of work that may conflict with the terms and conditions agreed upon in the master agreement. A sample order of precedence provision is seen here:

> **In the event of a conflict between or among the provisions of this Agreement and specific provisions set forth in a statement of work, the provisions of such statement of work will take precedence over this Agreement if such provisions specifically reference the provisions of this Agreement that are inconsistent therewith. In all other cases, the terms of this Agreement will prevail.**

The bottom line on change orders is that they are a necessity for success. Make sure the process is formal, is understood clearly by both parties, allows for a fast-track process where appropriate, and is followed in all instances. A sample change order process that captures most of these areas is as seen here:

> **If Client shall, at any time during the Term of Agreement, require any additions to or changes in the scope of the Services articulated in the statement of work, then it shall request the same in accordance with the provisions below.**

(a) Client may request modifications to any statement of work agreement by submitting a change request order to Consultant. Consultant, at its sole discretion, may elect to implement and perform such modifications or reject the request.

(b) Consultant shall have a period of fifteen (15) days within which to respond to Client requests for the provision of the modified services. Consultant shall provide an estimate of the date by which Consultant will be able to implement such request and a quotation for the price to be paid by Client and terms in respect thereof. Client shall, within fifteen (15) days of receipt of such estimate and quotation, notify Consultant in writing whether or not Client accepts the same.

(c) Both Consultant and Client agree to undertake all reasonable efforts to expedite the review and approval of any scope changes that will detrimentally impact the project schedule as mutually agreed by the parties.

(d) Consultant and Client shall negotiate in good faith in an attempt to agree on any changes in terms of price and scope as are reasonably necessary for Consultant to provide the modified services.

(e) Each Change Request Order, which is duly authorized in writing by both Consultant and the Client, shall constitute a formal modification to and shall become a part of the applicable statement of work. In no event shall the statement of work or any other obligations of Consultant be deemed amended except through a Change Request Order approved by Consultant and the Client in accordance with the provisions of this Section.

Another area that typically receives some scrutiny in the negotiation process is the nonsolicitation clause. With regard to these clauses, it is important to make sure that you can actually monitor and enforce the provisions contained in the master agreement. Given the decentralization of the hiring process within most companies and the size of their staff, it is important to be able to draw some reasonable boundaries around the policy and to communicate it to all impacted parties. My counsel would be to limit any such nonsolicitation clauses to the key personnel from both the client and the consultant who are leading the delivery process. In addition, try to avoid any blanket no-hire clauses, and focus on those which exclude hiring activities that result from advertising, job postings, unsolicited résumés, or other generic methods that are targeted to the general public. A sample nonsolicitation provision is seen here:

> **During the term hereof and for a period of one (1) year thereafter, each party shall not, without the prior consent of the other party, intentionally solicit for employment any personnel of the other party who have been directly involved in the provision and/or receipt of services under this Agreement. "Intentionally Solicit" shall not include consideration of responses to advertising or job postings directed at the general public or of unsolicited résumés. The parties agree to inform their personnel of the terms of this section.**

Other Key Contractual Provisions

A few other key areas that tend to receive some focus during the master agreement negotiation process include audit rights, third-party beneficiaries, business continuity and disaster recovery, the utilization of subcontractors, publicity clauses, and dispute resolution. When it comes to audit rights, Fortune 500 companies want to retain the ability to audit the consultant's financial records, facilities, information systems, and business process to the extent that these items impact the consultant's ability to perform and comply with the terms and conditions of the agreement. Such provisions have become quite common and are generally acceptable as long as they contain some reasonable-notice provisions and limitations on the scope and frequency of any such audit.

The applicability of any third-party beneficiaries is also an important issue that must be addressed when contracting for services. As it is not uncommon for the work product of consultants to be shared with third-party consultants or others, it is important to clearly articulate in the master agreement that the work product being produced under the agreement is intended to be solely for the benefit of the buyer and that no third parties can rely on any work product or obtain any benefits, make any claims, or be entitled to any remedy under the agreement. This provision is most critical for the consultant, as it wishes to limit the scope of its liability to the client with whom it is engaged and not to any third parties that may have relied upon the findings in their work product for some other purpose. A sample clause that would achieve this objective is seen here:

> **Consultant and Client mutually agree that this Agreement, or any statement of work, is intended by them to be solely for the benefit of Client and Consultant and that no other entities may rely on any reports, analyses, or other material provided by Consultant or shall obtain any direct or indirect benefits from the Agreement, have any claim, or be entitled to any remedy under this Agreement or otherwise in any way be regarded as third-party beneficiaries under this Agreement.**

Another important area of scrutiny is in the area of business continuity and disaster recovery. Given the critical nature of services being provided to Fortune 500 companies, it is a mandatory requirement that the consultant be able to continue to perform its obligations under the contract in the event of a disaster with minimal disruptions or delay. The requirements and specificity of any business continuity provision will vary depending upon the nature of the services being provided and their level of criticality to the ongoing business operations of the client. Two other areas we should briefly discuss include the utilization of subcontractors and publicity. Most Fortune 500 companies will require the consultant to obtain written consent before utilizing the services of any third-party subcontractor or using their name, logo, or trademarks or in any way publicizing any information related to the nature of services being provided under the agreement.

Dispute Resolution

Finally, let's discuss dispute resolution. Many agreements with Fortune 500 companies will simply specify the governing law and jurisdictional venue for any disputes that may arise during the course of the agreement. To the extent that the parties cannot resolve their dispute, they can immediately pursue their remedies accordingly. In an effort to mitigate dispute resolution through a formal legal process, many agreements will require that the parties pursue mandatory binding arbitration or follow an internal governance process to address any disputes that arise under the agreement. Under such a provision, the parties may agree to appoint a designated individual who will be responsible for negotiating a resolution for the dispute with their counterpart. If both designates, after negotiating in good faith, agree that an amicable resolution of the matter will not result through continued negotiation, then the issue can either be escalated to the next level of management as outlined in the governance process, or either party may demand immediate arbitration in accordance with the rules of the American Arbitration Association.

Conversely, the agreement may specify that the parties will bypass any governance process and submit all disputes, with the exception of any carve-outs, directly to binding arbitration for resolution. Consultants will typically prefer that an all-encompassing arbitration provision apply to services delivery versus more formal resolution through the judicial system. As we all know, pursuing a dispute through the judicial system can be quite costly. Arbitration can definitely be less costly and more expeditious than litigation, but it does not always produce a legally correct result. To gauge their desire to agree to a binding arbitration provision, both parties should consider their answers to the following questions:

- Do we want to get the dispute resolved in an efficient manner, or are we more concerned with obtaining the right legal result?

- Are the underlying issues that may be in dispute over the course of the contract of significant importance to our business?

- Will we need confidential information from the opposing party to resolve the dispute?

- How important is it for the dispute to be confidential?

If the parties seek efficiency, the underlying issues of dispute are not material, confidential information from both parties is not anticipated to be required to resolve the dispute, and the dispute should be kept confidential, then arbitration would be an appropriate solution. However, if the parties are more focused on achieving the proper "legal result," the issues are of significant importance to both parties and may have a material financial impact, extensive information will be required to resolve the dispute through the discovery process, and allowing the dispute to be litigated in open court is an acceptable option, then the judicial system may be a more appropriate alternative.

Depending upon the nature of the services, and the issues raised by the preceding questions, the parties should effectively negotiate the method by which disputes shall be resolved. It should be noted that if the parties agree to binding arbitration, they must be willing to accept the decision of the arbitrator as final. Once the arbitration process is complete, neither party will be able to pursue the matter through the judicial process. It is therefore critical to consider the terms of the arbitration and any potential areas identified as carve-outs that will not be subject to the binding arbitration process. A final alternative might be the inclusion of a nonbinding arbitration process under which the parties submit the claim to arbitration, the result of which will be nonbinding.

To the extent that the aggrieved party is not satisfied with the result, it could still pursue the resolution of its claim through a more formal judicial process. While it may seem as if this would always be the likely course of action for the aggrieved party to follow, this is not necessarily the case. While certainly not a guarantee, the arbitration process may yield a result similar to a court of law on the substantive issues. Given the cost associated with pursuing the claim through judicial means, the aggrieved party would carefully evaluate its likelihood of success prior to commencing any formal legal action.

So we have discussed the most heavily negotiated terms and conditions as well as a number of other issues that you will absolutely have to address during the master agreement negotiation process with a Fortune 500 company. While I have provided some sample terms and counsel regarding industry best practices, we have also addressed the notion that no two professional services agreements are the same. Given the nature and complexity of the services being provided, the delivery capabilities of the consultant, the motivations of the parties, and the respective negotiating leverage and alternatives of each party, each master agreement negotiation process will be different. To that end, every time you take a seat at the negotiation table, you will have to adapt your approach accordingly. Following my approach will serve you well in this regard:

- Temper your approach based upon the amount of risk inherent in delivery.

- Temper your approach based upon the geographic region in which you are engaged.

- Temper your approach based upon the individual who is sitting across from you at the negotiation table.

In the spirit of George Mitchell, remember that "conflicts are created, conducted, and sustained by human beings and can be resolved by human beings."

Part

4

Procurement and Pricing

18

Paying Homage to Corporate Procurement

If you ask any business development or delivery executive at any of the brand-name consultancies the one entity they don't want to encounter when selling and delivering within their respective Fortune 500 account base, their answer will most likely be procurement. Over the past few years, there has been a fundamental change in the way Fortune 500 companies procure consulting services. The net effect of the change is that Fortune 500 clients, irrespective of industry and geography, have become much more sophisticated buyers of corporate strategy, design, and implementation services. The major components of the change include the streamlining of the vendor base; the identification, through a competitive request for proposal process, of a set of preferred vendors across a variety of service lines; the comprehensive use of master services agreements; the implementation of a vendor performance management system; and the implementation of a more rigorous and disciplined buying process with aggressive negotiating tactics in the areas of pricing and terms and conditions. The entity at the intersection of each of these focus areas is corporate procurement. Many of those same business development or delivery executives will tell you that successfully selling management consulting services is based upon developing and cultivating relationships within their respective client base.

Even though this assertion is correct, the needle has moved significantly in the past few years toward the best value end of the continuum. While relationships still play a significant factor in selling corporate strategy services to C-suite executives, the farther you move to the right in the consulting lifecycle, the more influence corporate procurement organizations will exert in the buying process. Even the major strategy providers have taken steps to expand their service offerings and delivery footprint, so an encounter with procurement may be inevitable. The bottom line is that the relative influence and power of corporate procurement organizations have grown significantly in recent years, and they have been empowered, through chief procurement officers reporting directly to the CFO or CEO, to aggressively pursue their agenda.

Given this dynamic, it is no longer a viable solution to rely completely upon client relationships or prior performance for success. The only exception to this rule might be some of the brand-name corporate strategy providers, as I am aware of a number of instances in which they have chosen to opt-out of a procurement-driven request for proposal process for all management consulting services, but were not detrimentally impacted for so doing. However, the long arm of procurement has finally reached their door, and they are all reevaluating their strategy and approach in this area. Given this dynamic, prudence requires developing a strategy through which corporate procurement organizations can be effectively leveraged to facilitate the business development and footprint expansion process. A few years ago, I met with a senior procurement representative at a leading oil and gas company that spends well over $100 million per year on corporate strategy and information technology services. My primary objective in that discussion was to focus on footprint expansion beyond the strategy domain and to leverage procurement to assist me in facilitating that objective.

During the discussion, I was shocked to learn that 65 percent of the buying community that sought out the counsel and guidance of her team were new buyers and had no preconceived notions as to the vendor best suited to deliver the services articulated in their statements of work. This metric made it clear to me just how important it would be to make sure that she understood the nature of the services my firm sought to provide, our value proposition, our global delivery capabilities, and our ability to deliver strategy, design, and implementation services in a timely and quality manner that was commensurate with the nature of the services being provided and priced competitively with their other preferred vendors. It was my absolute intention to utilize the services of that procurement organization to assist with my business development and footprint expansion efforts.

This new buyer dynamic is not unique to the oil and gas industry. Many sales executives fail to realize that within many Fortune 500 companies, new buyers comprise anywhere from 35 percent to 60 percent of the overall buying community. It is not uncommon for these new buyers to develop a statement of work and to seek out the guidance and counsel of their procurement leadership as to which vendors would be best suited to deliver the services contemplated in their statement of work and should be included in the request for proposal process. Not being included in the request for proposal pipeline can be disastrous from a footprint expansion perspective, particularly for a consultancy wishing to cross over the strategy, design, and implementation domains, as full insight into the pipeline of current and future opportunities is critical for success. It is therefore essential that procurement organizations understand your service offerings, delivery capabilities, and value proposition, and hopefully reach a determination that your firm can deliver in a timely, quality, and cost-effective manner. Given the level of influence they wield, my approach has always been to make every attempt to build strong relationships with corporate procurement organizations and to let them serve as an extension of your business development capabilities in properly educating their buying community as to your delivery capabilities.

Frankly, I struggle to understand why all vendors would not pursue a similar strategy. I can assure you from personal experience that if procurement does not reach these conclusions with regard to your firm and its service offerings, and particularly if they believe you are not cost-competitive, business development and footprint expansion will absolutely be a steep, ugly, uphill battle. To assist in effectively working with Fortune 500 corporate procurement organizations, I have focused my efforts on understanding what they want, what motivates them, and what they are trying to achieve. In my experience, the agenda of the typical Fortune 500 procurement organization is not that much of a mystery; specifically, they want:

- To optimize their global consulting spend and share best practices across their organization

- Fewer and more strategic preferred vendors with broad delivery capabilities

- Vendors with "skin in the game"

- Aggressive pricing (OK, as cheap as they can get) with volume and other discounts in exchange for the "preferred" vendor label

- A pricing structure that is commensurate with the nature of services being provided and competitive with the other preferred vendors—separate rate schedules for strategy and IT engagements

- Vendors that deliver best value—timely, quality, and cost-effective delivery

- Competition among vendors for commodity-like services

- An increase in compliance and reduction in maverick spending

- Efficiency gains (reduced cycle time), cost savings, and control over the buying process through the implementation of an e-procurement solution

- A performance management system under which vendors are evaluated across quality, time, and cost parameters and stripped of the "preferred" label if they fail to meet performance standards

- Business and legal terms and conditions that yield an acceptable level of risk and reward

Working Effectively with Procurement

Now that we have a better understanding of the agenda that is actively being pursued by Fortune 500 procurement organizations, a viable go-to-market strategy and approach can be crafted that will facilitate working in partnership with procurement for the mutual gain of both parties to the transaction.

Before I discuss what I believe to be an effective strategy with regard to each of these agenda items, let's briefly review the procedural process you are likely to encounter when negotiating terms and conditions and rates for a master services agreement. The process is typically commenced with the issuance of a formal request for proposal (not for a specific opportunity but for the sole purpose of identifying preferred vendors across the various service lines for which services will be procured) that is distributed to potential vendors or by invitation or mutual agreement through the natural evolution of delivering recurring services to the company. Many Fortune 500 procurement organizations have licensed web-based e-procurement applications to facilitate the sourcing event surrounding the release of the RFP. These applications allow for a consistent communication mechanism and procurement process for all potential vendors that are responding to the solicitation. The request for proposal will require that any potential vendors provide qualification data—financial data, delivery capabilities and methodologies, and references—that will be utilized in any down-select process. Once the initial down-select process has occurred, many procurement organizations are utilizing these same applications to conduct an auction process through which the vendor selection process is finalized and delivery rates are established.

Fortune 500 companies have embraced only recently the auction process for determining which vendors will receive "preferred" vendor status for the delivery of management consulting services. Once procurement has completed its initial screening and evaluation of potential vendors, a select group will be invited to participate in the ensuing auction process. During the auction process, which typically lasts for an hour, each vendor will be given the opportunity to provide additional discounts to the rates that were initially submitted in their proposal response. During the auction process, each vendor will be able to see their respective rank in relation to the other vendors participating in the auction. The ranking will be provided on both a country and service line basis. At the end of the auction period, the top five vendors (or whatever number is specified in the auction rules) with the lowest total evaluated price for the categories and volume estimates utilized in the auction will be given "preferred" vendor status.

Fortune 500 procurement organizations strictly adhere to the results of the auction process; only those vendors that fall within the specified range will be given preferred status. The assumption being made by procurement is that all of the vendors that advance to the auction process meet the requisite qualification standards across the service lines and geographies in which they seek to sell and deliver services; they simply use the auction process as the final price shootout to determine the winners. Irrespective of the final rankings, preferred status is contingent upon successfully negotiating delivery terms and conditions.

In almost every instance in which I have negotiated a master services agreement, the company with which I was affiliated had been previously engaged with the client, so they had a good understanding of our delivery capabilities and some recent intelligence regarding our pricing structure and the terms and conditions under which we were willing to contract. Despite this prior history, the process for executing a master agreement, irrespective of whether it was by invitation or via request for proposal, always seemed like starting from scratch. Previously agreed-to terms and conditions and rates were almost always set aside as the master agreement process commenced. I attribute this dynamic to the fact that procurement centralization is a recent trend, and procurement leadership is looking to set aside the decentralized ways of the past in favor of a more structured and disciplined process over which they exert significant control.

The master services agreement process with any Fortune 500 company, irrespective of industry, typically starts with an introductory meeting with procurement representatives. In my meetings, I always kick things off with a brief PowerPoint presentation, a required component of any client meeting if you work for any of the big consulting firms, which provides a macro-level update regarding firm financial or organizational issues, recent awards received, global delivery capabilities, firm mission and high-level strategy, active and prior engagements that have been successfully completed for the client, competitive differentiators, client satisfaction ratings, service offerings, the specific delivery points (strategy, design, and implementation) at which the firm was currently engaged across the consulting lifecycle and aspirations regarding footprint expansion, and references that would speak to delivery capabilities and domain and industry expertise.

My preference is to conduct these introductory meetings on my own because bringing along a delivery partner would almost always result in three things: (1) they would spend too much time talking about their relationships within the client and their delivery acumen; (2) they would offer discounts and give things away before the negotiation process even commenced; and (3) they would bring a lengthy PowerPoint presentation that would tend to derail the conversation and not allow for sufficient time to gain an understanding of procurement's agenda and any burning platform issues upon which they were focused. Frankly, procurement never seems to care about the delivery partner's relationships and delivery acumen, at least not at this point in the process; is not really interested in reviewing a lengthy

PowerPoint presentation; and offering any discounts or other concessions is simply premature at this point in the process. There have been many instances when I tried to nudge my delivery colleagues under the table (as they wanted to play Santa Claus well before Christmas was even visible on the calendar), but they were simply too far out of reach. So I perfected the art of quickly changing the topic and deferring any such conversation to a more appropriate time in the negotiation process. I also use this introductory meeting to begin building what I hope will grow into a trusted advisor relationship with the client's procurement leadership that can be leveraged as appropriate during the business development and delivery lifecycles.

This introductory meeting embodies the overarching strategy that I pursued with procurement organizations across the Fortune 500 client base. The crux of the strategy is simple and straightforward: build a relationship with procurement that would parallel that of the delivery leadership. They could remain focused on delivery, on up-selling new opportunities, and on cultivating the client relationship. They could focus their discussions regarding their reference base, delivery acumen, and results to their respective client. They could set expectations regarding delivery, but would steer clear of procurement and comply with the terms and conditions and rate structure contained in the master agreement. This parallel relationship track worked well, especially when it came to taking a firm position during the negotiation process or playing the "bad cop" role regarding the enforcement of terms and conditions or adjudicating a dispute. With this approach, I could fulfill that role without jeopardizing the overarching delivery relationship with the client that had been established over time and was critical to preserve.

By adhering to this strategy, the master agreement negotiation process became much more objective in nature; as I did not have a lengthy delivery history with the client, I was able to approach the process in a dispassionate and unemotional manner and focus solely upon negotiating an agreement that was acceptable to both parties. Building this relationship with procurement worked extremely well. Not only did the relationship help downstream to the extent that any challenges or problems materialized during the course of delivery, but it also helped tremendously in the business development and footprint expansion process. Do you remember the new buyers I mentioned earlier? Building strong relationships with procurement and educating them as to your delivery capabilities will result in your firm being included on the list of potential vendors that might be able to fulfill the requirements specified in their statement of work.

For any firm that is trying to cross over a major delivery divide—from strategy into design and implementation or vice versa—I assure you that it will be extremely difficult if you fail to build a strong relationship with and educate procurement as to your value proposition and delivery capabilities. Despite what you might think, this is most difficult when trying to move farther downstream in the consulting lifecycle. As we previously discussed, the strategy wallet is relatively small, and the engagements are usually under the purview of senior-level executives within the C-suite. For these opportunities, procurement is typically not heavily engaged, as there tends to be parity among the rate structures of the major providers, and the selection process will almost always be relationship driven. The strategy providers are quite comfortable with that dynamic. However, in recent years, they have decided they want a piece of the bigger wallet—the implementation of the programs and initiatives they identified during their strategy engagement. But unfortunately, they have typically received quite a surprise once they traverse that line of demarcation. Crossing over into the world of design and implementation engagements can be extremely challenging. Procurement is heavily involved and influential in the buying process, relationships are not all-telling, rates are heavily scrutinized, brand awareness and a strong reference base are most critical, the services tend to be more commodity based, and competition for opportunities is fierce. Under these circumstances, a strong relationship with procurement is a necessity. Without it, there is a substantial likelihood that you may not even be included in the request for proposal process.

The Impact of Procurement's Agenda on the Negotiation Process

So, we have been invited into the master agreement process or made the down-select through a more formal request for proposal and have conducted an introductory meeting. We left the delivery executives and any lengthy PowerPoint presentations at home and have begun to build a relationship with procurement executives. Now the real fun begins, as we are about to embark on what can be a very difficult, frustrating, and lengthy journey to negotiate a rate card and delivery terms and conditions. Over the next few chapters, we will discuss each of the main agenda items of a typical Fortune 500 procurement organization so we are prepared for how they may impact the negotiation process.

Let's start with the optimization of global consulting spend and the sharing of best practices. Even as recently as just a few years ago, many procurement organizations within Fortune 500 companies were very decentralized from an organizational structure perspective and had little influence and control over the procurement of management consulting services. They were much more focused upon the procurement of commodities including desktop and laptop computers, paper, coffee, and other similar items. When it came to the procurement of professional services, a budget was typically established at a global level that was disseminated out to regional or functional leadership to utilize as they deemed appropriate.

Under this model, the role of procurement was very much administrative in nature; they would assist with the execution of purchase orders and the like, but would not become engaged with regard to the vendors being utilized and the rates, terms, and conditions that would govern delivery. Given the size of the third-party consulting budget for both strategy and IT services within many of these entities (in many cases more than $100 million a year), it was not too long before finance and procurement organizations recognized the potential cost savings that could be realized by centralizing the procurement process, streamlining the vendor base, and leveraging their global consulting spend when negotiating terms and conditions and rate structures. In addition, the centralization of this process would facilitate the sharing of best practices among what were previously disparate operating units in terms of the sharing of intellectual capital and knowledge received from their professional services vendors.

When it comes to optimizing their global consulting spend with a particular vendor, most procurement organizations will expect to receive an additional discount based upon historical transaction volumes they incurred with the vendor with which they are negotiating. Under the old decentralized model, professional services firms were able to price their services under discrete engagements, and the rate structure under which they were operating on the other side of the world was pretty much irrelevant, as the engagements were negotiated and managed in isolation. Under the centralized model, procurement will expect something, typically in the form of an additional discount, in exchange for contracting volume they incur with your organization. They will never commit to any guaranteed volume, but will spend lots of time talking about their pipeline of opportunities and how you can be well positioned to capture a piece of that pie in exchange for an additional concession. As we walk through their agenda, you will quickly see that expecting additional discounts and concessions is a recurring theme that weaves its way through each of their agenda items.

While procurement wants to achieve each of the agenda items I just articulated, they are motivated by and recognized and rewarded for obtaining cost reductions from their vendor community—hard stop. Think about it; who doesn't want to go back to their boss, most likely the CFO, and wave a flag that says they were able to negotiate an additional 5 percent discount from one of their largest preferred vendors. While 5 percent may seem nominal in nature, the savings can become significant given the size and scope of many engagements and the annual transaction volume with their larger vendors.

Procurement executives always like to talk about how much they have spent with your firm in prior years, and how much they intend to spend, not necessarily with you, in the coming year. They will talk about all of the large and strategic projects they have coming up in the pipeline and how well suited and positioned your organization may be to capture a portion of the revenue associated with those opportunities. I usually simply listen carefully to the potential opportunities and then let them continue on about how such large contracting volume should get them something in return. Then I tell them that I stand ready, willing, and able to provide additional discounts if they could guarantee me a piece of the aforementioned work or some other volume commitment over the course of the year. As I know they are unwilling to offer any sort of guarantee, we then usually discuss the idea of a volume discount that would be contingent upon meeting some predefined materiality thresholds—usually maxing out at an additional 5 percent discount once annual volume had exceeded some mutually agreed upon threshold—and then moving to the next item on their agenda.

The next item, fewer and more strategic preferred vendors with broad delivery capabilities, is another carrot that is dangled by procurement to entice master services agreement vendors to offer a greater discount in exchange for the hunting license they have been granted. Under the decentralized model, regional and functional leadership had complete autonomy with regard to the vendors they would utilize for the delivery of business unit strategy and self-contained design and implementation engagements. Under that construct, the quality, timeliness, and cost-effectiveness of delivery for similarly situated services were inconsistent across the vendor base. This spotty delivery certainly had a detrimental impact on the return on investment and client satisfaction realized in the postdelivery environment.

With centralization came the desire to streamline the vendor base, to identify a set of preferred vendors that would provide their services through global master services agreements, and to carefully monitor performance across quality, time, and cost parameters. Having fewer vendors ultimately gave Fortune 500 companies better quality control, more attractive pricing, and the ability to develop trusted advisor relationships with their vendors. To the extent that the preferred vendors have broad delivery capabilities and can cross over the strategy and IT divide, any knowledge loss that is typically realized during that handoff is eliminated. Let's be clear; while procurement may ask for a lot in return, receiving the "preferred" label is a valuable asset for the vendor as well. While it does not guarantee any specific transaction volume, it does provide a hunting license and an expedited sales cycle through the master services agreement. The best part of the "preferred" label is that it is limited; many Fortune 500 companies have a small number of preferred vendors, and entry is by invitation only. It also carries a lot of weight and credibility within the buying community, as centralization has brought much more rigor, structure, and discipline, and buyers are prohibited from and potentially even penalized for utilizing nonpreferred vendors. While there may be exceptions to the rule, receiving and maintaining the "preferred" vendor label will give you a captive audience when it comes to marketing and selling your service offerings to new prospects. So the "preferred" label can be a valuable asset and should be treated accordingly. Based upon my experience, it is the key to selling (with the only exception being corporate strategy services being delivered to the C-suite) within the Fortune 500 client community and may be worth some additional consideration in the pricing and negotiation process.

The next agenda item that procurement wants to prosecute is not just having a limited set of preferred vendors, but having a group of vendors that will share risk and reward and have a vested interest, some skin in the game, with regard to the successful completion of the programs in which they are engaged, and be accountable for realizing the projected value proposition and return on investment associated with the engagement. I have always been a proponent of incentive-based contracting, but it should be used only in those instances where it is commensurate with the nature of the services being provided and carefully contemplated by both parties. The feedback I have received from a number of procurement executives is that there should actually be some delivery risk associated with the fees in question; it seems that many firms like to propose the concept of incentive-based contracting, but restrict its usage to those instances in which the level of risk to which they will be subject is minimal.

So if you want to have skin in the game, then utilize this approach when you will truly be sharing risk and reward with the client. Clients are typically willing to offer significant reward to a vendor that is willing to absorb an enhanced level of delivery risk. For any incentive-based agreement to be successful, the appropriate structure must be in place to measure the pay for performance criteria as well as the timing and measurement methodology. For a performance-based agreement to be successful, the vendor must be in a position where the depth and breadth of the engagement are such that the vendor can influence the results it requires for success. As you can imagine, the ability to influence results flows back to the requirement that the statement of work be narrowly tailored and that roles and responsibilities and acceptance and decision-making criteria are clearly defined because they will impact the ability of the vendor to meet and exceed its performance benchmarks.

For any performance-based engagement, the parties must also agree upon how the at-risk fees will be addressed in the event of termination or a dispute regarding success. Unfortunately, there have been many instances in which the incentive contract has been misused to the detriment of both parties to the transaction. Most of the major professional services firms will agree to an incentive-based contracting scheme—and many even prefer to tie their pay to performance—under which all or a portion of their fees are at risk and subject to the results (both the upside and downside) and return on investment achieved through delivery.

For an incentive- or performance-based agreement to be successful, it is critical that the parties be able to agree upon a set of objective, measurable, and verifiable performance criteria, benchmarks, or targets that can be measured within a specified timeframe and that will be used to define the success of the engagement and ultimately determine how much of the at-risk fees, and any premiums or penalties applied thereto, the vendor will receive. The possibilities for structuring a performance-based agreement are endless; there could be a single performance indicator such as achieving a targeted savings percentage over some period for a particular expense item, or multiple performance indicators such as sales, margin, or customer satisfaction that will be measured to determine the return on investment realized from the implementation of the initiative. I was always willing to agree to the concept of incentive- or performance-based contracting to the extent that it was appropriate given the nature of the services being provided and based upon objective, measurable, and verifiable performance criteria.

As we have discussed previously, most business development or delivery executives at any of the brand-name consulting firms want to avoid procurement during the sales and delivery process. While this might have been a viable approach five years ago, this is clearly no longer the case given the influence procurement wields in the preferred vendor selection and overall buying process. Given this dynamic, it is much more prudent to craft and pursue a sales and delivery strategy that aligns with procurement's strategic agenda and is focused on attaining preferred vendor status, being accountable for delivering on your value proposition, and partnering with procurement for success.

19

Price Negotiations

Now we get to the most important procurement agenda item and the one to which all roads lead—the rate structure under which services will be delivered. So what exactly does procurement want when it comes to price? The answer is fairly straightforward: they want cheap prices with aggressive discounts in exchange for the "preferred" vendor label and a pricing structure that is commensurate with the nature of the services being provided and that is competitive with their other preferred vendors. Alternatively, you may simply be providing a price for a stand-alone engagement that is not tied to a master agreement. This is a critical distinction, as the mechanics and implications of each are quite different.

With a stand-alone procurement, your pricing scheme may be based upon a number of factors including:

- The competitive nature of the opportunity and its strategic importance to your firm

- Your competitive positioning relative to any other potential vendors in the market

- The operating tenure and strength of your relationships within the client

- Your staff size, composition, geography, and availability

- The ability to utilize preexisting intellectual capital during the course of delivery

- The size of the client's budget

- The client's level of price sensitivity

- The current and anticipated transaction volume with this client

- The client's expectations with regard to your pricing structure that have been developed through prior dealings

- The size and duration of the engagement

- The leverage model (ratio of senior-level to junior-level staff which may be in the 6–10 to 1 ratio for strategy engagements and as high as 35–50 to 1 for design and implementation engagements)

- The potential for follow-on engagements

- Your relative level of experience in delivering similarly situated services

- The contract type

- The terms and conditions that will govern delivery

- Any financial incentives or discounts you may wish to offer to improve your probability to win, expand your market share, geographic presence, or delivery footprint

The key differentiator is that the procurement is stand-alone in nature and will not obligate your organization for any downstream opportunities. While you might be setting some precedent with regard to your pricing scheme, labor categories, and leverage model, the rate structure proposed will be solely limited to this particular engagement. It is important to compare and contrast the single-procurement environment with that of a multi-year master services agreement. While many of these same considerations will be applicable when negotiating a master agreement, it is important to be cognizant of the fact that the master agreement rate card will be the standard against which all engagements will be delivered globally—typically a one- to three-year base period with a number of one-year option periods thereafter. Any rate increases will be limited to the escalation clause contained in the agreement, typically 5 to 8 percent at best, and will not be open to additional negotiation despite market conditions.

Given these considerations, I urge you to think very carefully of the long-term pricing ramifications associated with a multiyear master services agreement. Despite all of the blood pressure elevation, focus, and energy expended on contractual terms and conditions, the rate card is the area where you will spend the majority of time when negotiating a master services agreement. The objective is to propose a pricing scheme that is commensurate with the nature of the services being provided, competitive with other preferred vendors, and that falls within a range that is acceptable to procurement. At the same time, the rate schedule proposed must meet any economic guidelines or financial targets established by your organization and remain viable for the term of the agreement.

The standard pricing structure for most of the major professional services firms, for strategy, design, and implementation engagements, tends to be fairly straightforward. It typically consists of a set of labor categories, which may include a description of the types or activities in which that individual may be engaged, as well as any educational or experience requirements and the associated standard or rack rate for each category that is expressed on an hourly, daily, or weekly basis. In addition, the rate structure will typically vary depending upon the country or region in which the consultants reside and the location of service delivery. In its simplest form, the negotiation of rates (or a corresponding fixed price) for either a stand-alone or master agreement is simply determining how much discount, if any, will be offered from those standard rates during the period of performance. As I like to say, it is that simple and that complex. The complexity comes in the form of the multiple factors that must be considered when making that determination. You can ask executives at most of the brand-name management consulting firms if price is a determining factor in the award of consulting engagements, and you will most likely hear "no" at least half of the time. In my opinion, the answer to that question will vary depending upon the nature of the services being provided. As we have discussed, I believe the general rule to be that the farther you move to the right in the consulting lifecycle, the more commodity-like the service and the more that price will be a deciding factor in the award process.

Ultimately, I believe the selection process is a combination of a number of factors including functional and industry expertise, the technical approach to deliver the services, the quality of the team that will be deployed for delivery, the consultant's expertise in delivering similarly situated solutions within the client's industry, the level of executive involvement in the proposed solution, the level of relationships and trust between the parties, any client perceptions regarding the capabilities of the consultant, any prior delivery history, and of course, price. Most of those executives I mentioned believe that their relationships are ironclad and will be the driving force when decision-making time rolls around. While I believe relationships are extremely important, they must be augmented with a strong track record of delivering sustainable results. Although I do believe that a trusted advisor relationship with a client will give you a seat at the table, a first look at new opportunities, and insight into the client's agenda and priorities, it is by no means a guarantee of success. This position was confirmed for me recently at a sales conference when a senior executive at one of the largest suppliers of building materials was asked what factors most influenced his leadership team when evaluating consulting, technology, and outsourcing providers for mission-critical programs within his organization. His answer was simply: "Trust matters, but it is the deal that counts."

Price Discounts

When it comes to price negotiation, I am not a fan of what I like to call "sport-discounting." If you are going to provide a current or prospective client a discount, make sure you are doing it for some legitimate business reason—to enter a new account or market, to capture a must-win or strategic opportunity, to compensate for a lack of functional or industry expertise, or to achieve some viable future return on that investment. It takes zero negotiation skill to provide a current or prospective client with what you believe to be a competitive price for your services if you only intend to discount those rates by 30 percent two weeks later in the negotiation process. In my opinion, this serves no purpose other than completely undermining the integrity of your rate schedule and implying that your rates were overly inflated in the initial submission. Frankly, that does not go a long way in establishing trust with procurement or with the client. When it comes to discounting, I usually follow a few simple rules. They are as follows:

- A nominal discount (10 percent or less) can be used effectively to close a deal and generate goodwill with a client. A volume discount (based upon contractually stipulated volume thresholds that are measured on an annual basis) can also be used as an effective tool at the negotiation table.

- Offering a mid-size discount (10 percent to 30 percent) is not an effective negotiating strategy. Not only does it erode margin, but it also causes clients to question the integrity of the original bid. In my experience, it does not result in a greater win rate than the nominal discount referenced earlier.

- Extreme discounts (>30 percent) should be offered only in extreme circumstances. When I say "extreme," I mean only in very unique circumstances to achieve some strategic advantage—to establish a reference and build expertise in a specific industry or functional area, where the opportunity is simply a "must-win" and discounting at this level is required for award, where there is a significant follow-on opportunity under which the discount will be recovered, or where there is some other viable payback alternative.

With that being said, let's shift our focus to negotiating a rate card for a master services agreement, an area where I guarantee you will be heavily pressured to offer significant discounts to your proposed rate structure. The first thing you have to assume is that the company with which you are negotiating already has a number of preferred vendors that are delivering services in conjunction with a global rate card in a timely, quality, and cost-effective manner. Those vendors may be large brand-name consultancies or smaller niche providers. In either case, the client already has an expectation as to the market rates for similarly situated services and will utilize their existing rate cards as the benchmark by which the rates you propose will be evaluated. Given the current economic climate, they will most likely expect a rate structure that is more favorable than that of their preferred vendor base.

The Dual Rate Card Structure and Resource Commingling

While there may still be instances where a client requests one composite rate for all services across the consulting lifecycle, most Fortune 500 procurement organizations are cognizant of the different engagement parameters—the ultimate client and engagement type, the team size and project duration, and the staff type and capabilities—between a strategy and design and implementation engagement, and, therefore, they are strong proponents of a dual rate card structure. It is a certainty that no client wants to pay premium pricing for commodity-type services. Under this dual rate card structure, it is extremely important to set the client's expectation as to the applicability of the various rate cards. Of critical importance: once the dual rate card structure is established, you never, and I mean never, under any circumstances commingle the resources that will be delivering services under each rate card. Keep the strategy staff separate from the design and implementation staff and vice versa, at all costs. If you commingle staff (allowing premium-priced staff to deliver commodity-like services and vice versa), you will completely undermine the integrity of the dual rate card structure, and you will find yourself in a very deep hole with no way out. From a procedural perspective, I would usually suggest including a footnote which states that the consultant and client will mutually agree upon the rate card to be utilized based upon the nature of services provided as articulated in the applicable statement of work.

You might ask why the commingling issue is so critical. The answer is the major fundamental difference between strategy and design and implementation engagements and the rates under which they are delivered in the market. Strategy rates are market driven and may vary anywhere from $250 to $300 per hour for a recent MBA graduate to anywhere from $900 to $1100 for a senior partner or director. Design and implementation rates tend to be more cost driven (based upon an individual's cost rate (salary/ 2080 hours) plus a multiplier for any indirect costs (fringe, overhead, and general and administrative) plus any fee or profit, and may range anywhere from $75 to $100 per hour for a low-level specialist or analyst to $350 to $500 per hour for an experienced architect, subject matter expert, or project manager. So it is clear why having the strategy consultant deliver nonstrategy services would be a cause for serious concern by the client. If you were to consolidate all of the engagements being provided across the entire vendor community, I would estimate that the average rate range for strategy (think), IT (build), and systems integration (run) services would be approximately $300 to $350, $150 to $200, and $100 to $150 per hour respectively.

So we know we will have two rate cards contained within the master agreement, and we will provide the client with a qualitative description of the engagement parameters that go along with each rate card and a representative listing of sample engagements that can be shared within the client buying community. We will stress repeatedly that there will be no commingling of resources across the two domains. If your only takeaway from this book is that you will never commingle strategy and IT staff, I will consider it a huge success, as this simple principle is the reason so many firms are unable to create differentiated pricing, move up- or downstream within the consulting lifecycle, and expand their delivery footprint. We also know that whatever rates we provide will be benchmarked against the prevailing rate cards of the client's existing strategy and design and implementation providers.

When it comes to strategy rates, there tends to be parity among the major providers in the marketplace, which are McKinsey & Company, Bain & Company, The Boston Consulting Group, and Booz & Company. Procurement will still expect discounts from any standard rate structure, but there is a little more reasonableness when it comes to negotiating a strategy rate card. As we have discussed, the level of negotiation and involvement of procurement when negotiating a strategy rate card will vary depending upon the ultimate client for which the work will be delivered. To the extent that the services are being conducted for the CEO, procurement will have little involvement, most likely serving in an administrative role, and the rates will be given very little scrutiny. Just think about my former colleague, who was a director at one of the major strategy firms, who told his client that the cost for the job was $1 million, which was his cost, and that his team was free. Given this dynamic, it is not uncommon for some of the major strategy providers, especially where they are well entrenched within the C-suite, to simply refuse to participate in any of the procurement-sponsored master services agreement activities. Although this has been the historical approach taken by some of the large strategy providers, they are currently rethinking this strategy as procurement's reach is beginning to break the barrier into their domain.

Where the real challenge lies is within the benchmarking of design and implementation rates. Benchmarking can be a dangerous game because this is where procurement organizations tend to lump services together and treat the entire IT lifecycle as one big commodity. When a procurement representative is buying a commodity, he will set the barrier for entry at a rate no higher than what he is currently paying for what he perceives to be the same service. Clearly, treating all IT services as a single commodity is not a reasonable proposition, as the IT lifecycle is vast, and services and market rates will vary fairly dramatically from the assessment, analysis, design, and development phases on the left to the ultimate implementation of a solution and the ongoing maintenance, operations, and support on the right. It is therefore extremely critical to articulate to procurement where your service offerings reside in the IT lifecycle and to make sure they are benchmarking your rates against what are truly similarly situated providers.

If your services tend to be farther to the left in the IT lifecycle (more strategy-like in nature) and your rates are being benchmarked against the implementation rates of an Accenture, IBM, or Deloitte, the variance might be too significant to overcome. I can't stress this point enough: do whatever it takes to distinguish your service offerings and to avoid the commodity label because once you become a commodity, it is likely that there will always be a lower-cost provider. So, make every attempt to level the playing field; by doing so, you will hopefully put yourself within the relative range of the other preferred vendors. If, after going through the negotiation process, you are still higher priced in relation to their existing vendors, you may still have a fighting chance by relying on your brand awareness, the quality of your products, and the strength of your reference base for delivering similarly situated services.

20

Negotiating an Additional Discount

At this point in the master agreement process, we have effectively communicated our value proposition to procurement, and they have a clear understanding of the services we provide across the consulting life-cycle. With this understanding, they will hopefully be able to properly benchmark the competitiveness of our rate structure against that of their other preferred vendors. To kick off the negotiation process, the vendor will typically provide an initial submission of its rate card proposal in accordance with any structural requirements mandated by procurement.

Those structural requirements may include:

- The countries, geographic regions, and service lines for which rates should be submitted

- The designated labor categories and descriptions including any corresponding educational, experience, or certification requirements

- The manner in which the rates should be expressed—hourly, daily, weekly, or team-based

- Any limitations on the number of hours that can be billed each week

- The time period—one year or multiple years—for which rates should be submitted

Labor Category Descriptions and Upward Slotting Mobility

One of the key departure points from a structural perspective is the labor categories that will be contained within the rate card. Some procurement organizations will mandate the labor categories and corresponding descriptions and requirements that must be utilized in the rate card submission, while others will accept the standard labor categories and descriptions utilized by the consultant. This is a critical distinction, as spoon-fed and procurement-mandated labor categories will require the consultant to map its standard labor categories to those mandated by the client. If all else were equal, the mapping exercise itself would not be a big deal, but the client may also mandate specific labor category requirements from an experience, education, or certification perspective that are greater than those utilized by the consultant as a matter of standard practice. Such narrowly tailored labor category descriptions restrict the mapping flexibility afforded to the consultant and mitigate its ability to utilize upward slotting mobility to its advantage. *Upward slotting mobility* simply gives the consultant the ability to map and invoice a particular staff person based upon her ability to perform a function as articulated in the labor category description, not based upon her years of experience or the number and type of degrees or certifications that she holds. Effectively utilizing upward slotting mobility to your advantage can have a significant impact on the financial viability of the rate card.

Let's look at an example. Assume that the consultant has five labor categories and associated standard rates within its organization. The consultant also follows an up-or-out performance management model that is skill- and experience-based as seen in Figure 20.1 on page 191.

As a part of the master agreement process, let's assume procurement mandates that all prospective bidders must map their standard labor categories in accordance with the following labor category breakdown:

LABOR CATEGORIES	CAPABILITIES
Partner/director	Responsible for the overall client relationship at the executive level. Partners/directors will work closely with the client and provide overall project and engagement leadership. Partner/directors are accountable

LABOR CATEGORIES	CAPABILITIES
	for successful delivery and value generation for the client. These resources typically have deep strategic knowledge of the client's industry and are able to support strategic client initiatives.
Principal consultant	Responsible for developing strategic opportunities to enhance client revenues, expand services, reduce costs, and manage risk. Principal consultants will lead and assist project teams with planning and estimating projects and will bring advanced problem-solving skills to bear during delivery. These resources may lead multiple project teams and will typically be responsible for timely, quality, and cost-effective delivery.
Project manager	Responsible for leading project teams to meet project deliverable requirements. Project managers will provide analytical, business, and management expertise to their team and will utilize independent judgment to make decisions where no clear precedent exists. Project managers will demonstrate in-depth industry or functional expertise and typically have broad business and management experience. They can utilize complex delivery methodologies and innovative approaches across a diverse range of projects.
Senior consultant	Responsible for taking a senior-level role on a project team and bringing the requisite experience to bear and for making complex decisions to deliver solutions for the client. Senior consultants must be able to develop relationships with and work effectively with client project teams to deliver results. Senior

consultants will have limited project management capability, but can effectively manage a group of junior consultants to deliver in accordance with the project plan.

Junior consultant   Responsible for completing project assignments and providing technical and analytical support. Junior consultants will gather information within the client organization, perform data analysis, develop results, and communicate with the client as directed. Junior consultants typically have limited industry and functional expertise.

Under this construct, the labor categories provided are purely skills-based and do not specify any experience, education, or certification requirements. Given a labor category breakdown of this type, the consultant could be extremely aggressive in its labor category mapping and utilize upward slotting mobility to its advantage. By adhering to this approach, the consultant would be able to maximize the financial viability of the rate card

Labor Categories	Hourly Rate	Years of Experience
Vice president	$800	10+
Director		7+
Level 4	$650	
Level 3	$600	
Level 2	$550	
Level 1	$500	
Senior manager		5–7
Level 3	$450	
Level 2	$400	
Level 1	$375	
Associate		3–5
Level 3	$350	
Level 2	$325	
Level 1	$300	
Analyst		0–3
Level 2	$200	
Level 1	$165	

Figure 20.1   Sample consultant rate card

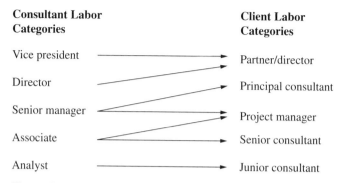

Figure 20.2   Aggressive labor category mapping

during the course of the agreement. Of course, the utilization of the upward slotting mobility technique is predicated on the fact that the lower-level staff person in your hierarchy is capable of meeting the requirements articulated in the category to which he will be mapped. An aggressive mapping might look like Figure 20.2.

Most of the major management consulting firms have different cohort levels within each major hierarchical category. For example, there may be four different levels of director or three different levels of senior manager through which an individual must progress before she can advance to the next level. This type of cohort structure definitely supports an aggressive upward slotting mobility strategy as seen in Figure 20.3.

Given this hierarchical structure, utilizing an upward slotting mobility strategy will provide the consultant with the ability to aggressively map its level-4 director, level-3 senior manager, and level-3 associate to a more senior category under the client's mandated labor category structure. As you can imagine, this will definitely impact the financial viability and attractiveness of the rate card for the consultant.

In an effort to mitigate the consultant's ability to utilize upward slotting mobility to its advantage, procurement organizations will provide very prescriptive labor categories for both strategy and design and implementation staff. In the preceding example, they would include degree requirements, years of experience, and even certification requirements for each level. Under this construct, it is likely that the consultant would be limited to a much more traditional, and not as financially lucrative, mapping as seen in Figure 20.4.

Limiting the flexibility of the consultant provides procurement with the ability to effectively benchmark rates for similarly situated resources across

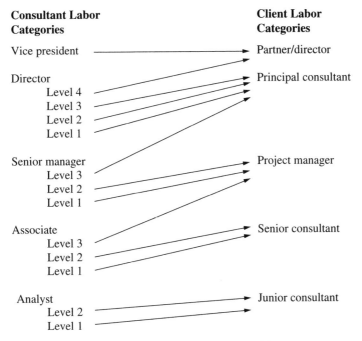

Figure 20.3   The cohort structure and aggressive labor category mapping

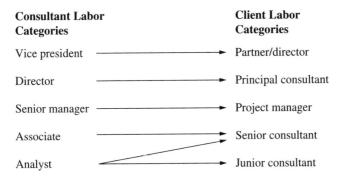

Figure 20.4   Prescriptive labor category mapping

its vendor base. In these instances, the best alternative for the consultant is to map its resources in as aggressive a manner as possible under the constraints articulated in the labor category descriptions, or to request some modification to the labor category requirements such that years of experience can serve as the equivalent for specific degrees or certifications.

While the consultant may be somewhat limited based upon restrictive labor category requirements, it will typically have flexibility in a number of other areas including the format by which its rates are expressed—hourly, daily, weekly, or team-based—the thresholds at which any volume discounts may be offered, annual escalation factors, how promotions will be handled, the currency in which the rates are expressed, and the geographic applicability (country or region) of the rate card. Although hourly rates are most common, daily or weekly rates are also a viable option, as they avoid conflict with any foreign labor laws and eliminate the need to limit the number of billable hours in the workweek. A team-based billing structure is also a workable option and will provide a number of options given the level and number of resources required. In an effort to make their rates look more competitive, some firms will take their weekly rates and dilute them by 60 or 65 hours, what they claim to be their average workweek, to achieve what appears to be a much more competitive rate when evaluated on an hourly basis. Irrespective of the method, procurement is savvy enough to do some simple math and will conduct an apples-to-apples comparison.

The Counteroffer

Once the initial rate card structure has been submitted by the consultant, procurement will typically review the proposed rate structure, conduct its benchmarking analysis, and respond back to the consultant with its feedback on the rates and what amounts to a counteroffer for each of the categories and rates contained in the initial submission. I can assure you there is always a counteroffer. I have negotiated many master agreements across all industries and have never received feedback from procurement that the rates were acceptable and that we could move forward with contract execution. You can be assured that procurement will identify a gap between the price points submitted by the consultant and the target rates they are trying to achieve.

Many procurement organizations utilize a stoplight approach under which they identify three relative ranges—red, yellow, or green—for each service line being proposed and plot the consultant rate submission accordingly. A "green" rating means that the rate structure fits within the acceptable range, that procurement will endorse and support the consultant's rate structure within the buying community, and that the consultant should be able to effectively compete with the other preferred vendors. A "yellow" rating means that the proposed rates fall outside the acceptable range, that procurement may be neutral or negative in its support of the consultant's rate structure within the buying community, and that the ability of the consultant to effectively compete with other vendors may be detrimentally impacted. A "red" rating means that the proposed rates fall significantly outside the acceptable range, that procurement will not support, through actively discouraging buyers from contracting with the consultant, the rate structure, and that the rate structure will detrimentally impact the business development efforts of the consultant.

Once the counteroffer has been received from procurement, the consultant will have to evaluate the rate structure, analyze the financial and economic implications of the counteroffer, and respond accordingly. All of the issues I addressed in this chapter, including the following, must be considered before rendering a decision on the viability of the counteroffer:

- The competitive nature of the opportunity and its strategic importance to your firm

- Your competitive positioning relative to any other potential vendors in the market

- The operating tenure and strength of your relationships within the client

- Your staff size, composition, geography, and availability

- The ability to utilize preexisting intellectual capital during the course of delivery

- The size of the client's budget

- The client's level of price sensitivity

- The current and anticipated transaction volume with this client

- The client's expectations with regard to your pricing structure that have been developed through prior dealings

- The size and duration of the engagement

- The anticipated leverage model (ratio of senior to junior staff) that will be utilized in delivery

- The potential for follow-on engagements

- Your relative level of experience in delivering similarly situated services

- The terms and conditions that will govern delivery

- The nature of the services being provided

- Any financial incentives, discounts, or other concessions you may offer to improve your probability to win or expand your market share, geographic presence, or delivery footprint

Most importantly, be cognizant of the fact that this is just round one of the pricing negotiations.

The first step when evaluating the counteroffer is to identify the variance between the initial submission and the rates proposed by procurement. I suggest conducting this analysis on a category-by-category basis. As we previously discussed, strategy rates tend to be market driven, and the variance analysis against list price or standard rates is fairly straightforward. Based upon the labor category structure we identified earlier, that analysis might look like what is seen in Figure 20.5.

Based upon this analysis, the counteroffer proposed by the client results in an attractive strategy rate card for the consultant. While every category is not profitable, the key is to model the proposed rate structure against the typical team that the consultant would field for potential opportunities under the master agreement and to determine the profitability of future engagements. By evaluating team size, duration, and the amount of senior-level time, the consultant can carefully model the viability and sustainability of the rate card during the course of the master agreement.

As we also discussed, design and implementation rates tend to be cost based, and a similar rate analysis can be conducted. Unlike the strategy rate evaluation in which a variance against list price is determined, the design and implementation analysis will be focused upon analyzing the cost

Client Labor Category	Consultant Labor Category	Standard Rate	Counteroffer	Premium/ Discount
Partner/Director	Vice President	$800	$750	−6%
Partner/Director	Director 4	$650	$750	15%
Principal consultant	Director 3	$600	$580	−3%
Principal consultant	Director 2	$550	$580	5%
Principal consultant	Director 1	$500	$580	16%
Principal consultant	Senior manager 3	$450	$580	29%
Project manager	Senior manager 2	$400	$380	−5%
Project manager	Senior manager 1	$375	$380	1%
Project manager	Associate 3	$350	$380	9%
Senior consultant	Associate 2	$325	$315	−3%
Senior consultant	Associate 1	$300	$315	5%
Junior consultant	Analyst 2	$200	$185	−8%
Junior consultant	Analyst 1	$165	$185	12%

Figure 20.5 Strategy rate structure variance analysis

associated with the specific individuals contained within the labor pool from which you will be drawing resources. Let's assume that I have proposed one design and implementation labor category to the client called Subject Matter Expert, and the labor pool from which I will be drawing the staff is as seen in Figure 20.6.

When considering offering an additional discount to a client, or evaluating the financial viability of its counteroffer for any design and

Name	Salary	Cost Rate	Fully Loaded Hourly Rate	
Jones	$325,000	$156.25	$625	
Smith	$300,000	$144.23	$577	
Jackson	$265,000	$127.40	$510	75% = $502
James	$250,000	$120.19	$481	
Davis	$250,000	$120.19	$481	50% = $466
Stevens	$235,000	$112.98	$452	
Wilson	$225,000	$108.17	$433	25% = $425
Canton	$220,000	$105.77	$423	
Green	$210,000	$100.96	$404	
Williams	$195,000	$93.75	$375	

Figure 20.6 Design and implementation rate analysis

implementation staff, it is important to determine at what percentile you can draw a line within the labor pool and still deliver a mix of resources in a profitable manner during the course of service delivery under the terms of the master agreement. In this case, I have calculated a fully loaded cost rate using a 4.0 cost multiple, which includes any fringe, overhead, general and administrative costs, and profit associated with deploying that staff person to the client. Let's assume that I proposed a rate of $580 for the Subject Matter Expert labor category. Based upon the labor pool identified above, this cost would cover all of the staff within the pool with the exception of Jones, whose fully loaded rate is $625. Let's also assume that the client has counteroffered with a rate of $485 for this category. When evaluating the client's counteroffer, it is important to consider the viability of that rate given the fully loaded costs of the individuals from which you can draw during the course of delivery. At a rate of $485, I would be at slightly less than the 70th percentile for this category and unable to provide my most senior level staff in a profitable manner. While I don't need to be at the 90th percentile, it would be prudent to try and negotiate a rate for this category in the $525 range; achieving that objective would allow me to staff some 80 percent of the labor pool during the course of delivery. Of course, the analysis here would also be based upon some assumptions regarding resource availability and the team size that would be deployed during the course of delivery. A similar analysis would be conducted for each design and implementation labor category, and a determination would be made as to the viability of the counteroffer.

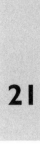

21

How to Handle Price Resistance

In my experience, there will be multiple iterations of the rate card, the contractual document that articulates the labor categories and corresponding rates under which you will deliver services across the consulting life-cycle, before you reach an agreement on the rate structure. As we have discussed, procurement organizations within Fortune 500 companies can be relentless when it comes to seeking additional price concessions from their consultants. It is one of their primary motivators and one of the key measures utilized internally to gauge their effectiveness. They usually bring plenty of evidence to the table to support their position; I have had procurement representatives provide me with the actual rate cards for their preferred vendors across the strategy and design and implementation domains, and tell me that I had to either meet those rates or be within the relative range—a 5 percent to 10 percent variance at most—to move forward with the master agreement and have their support.

In addition, it is not uncommon for procurement to provide market-based salary and other data, including publicly available pricing information from the General Services Administration Advantage website, to support the rate structure contained within their counterproposal. This is where the "commodity" label really comes into play. The more procurement believes the services being contemplated are commodity-like, the more difficult it will be to justify any price premium. That is the sole reason why it is important to pick your delivery sweet-spots, articulate your value proposition, and make every attempt to avoid being viewed as a commodity. This approach is not always easy to follow, as some services are truly commodity-like in nature, and multiple service providers are available in the market.

You might be a great negotiator and have great client relationships, but it will be extremely difficult to convince a procurement representative or your client that you command a 20 percent price premium over the competition for an IT architect, or any other labor category for that matter, that has the same qualifications in terms of years of experience and certifications. It is a losing proposition. The key to success is to rely upon the notion that the whole delivery package your firm brings to bear is greater than the sum of the parts, and that the other factors, including your value proposition, relationships, brand awareness, reference base you reputation for delivering similarly situated services in a timely and quality manner, will more than justify any price premium, even for those services that might seem to be more commodity based. Let's be clear; some services are commodities and will have to be priced accordingly. The key is to make sure that the client is paying premium prices for premium services and that the prices they are paying for commodity services are competitive, that they are adjusted with some price premium given the "other" factors articulated earlier, and that they are financially viable and fit within your economic model.

What if You Reach an Impasse?

That being said, you may reach a point in the negotiation process where you may have to tell procurement that enough is enough and that your rates are firm. I have served as the lead negotiator on a number of master agreements where an impasse was reached, and my firm made a conscious decision to move forward with a rate structure that contained specific labor categories and even complete service lines that were deemed to be very "red" by procurement, or even quite yellow with some near-red tendencies. Of course, procurement strongly advised against this approach in every instance and reiterated what it would mean in terms of its support with new buyers, the potential detrimental impact it might have across the buying community, and on any business development and footprint expansion capabilities. It is in these instances that you must make a decision as to the relative weight of the yellow or red rating versus your brand awareness, reference base, relationships, and history of delivering in a timely, quality, and cost-effective manner. Just like in any game of poker, you have to know when to draw a line in the sand and "call" your opponent. Unfortunately, I can't provide any surefire method as to how to effectively deal with procurement when it comes to negotiating rate cards under a master agreement, but some general rules you should adhere to are as follows:

1. Insist upon multiple rate cards—at a minimum one for strategy and one for IT-related services. There can be no exceptions to this rule.

2. Clearly articulate the different engagement parameters and the ultimate client (C-suite or otherwise), engagement type, team size and project duration, staff type and capabilities, and service line—strategy, human resources, IT, finance, and so on, associated with each rate card, and agree to mutually work with the client to identify the appropriate rate card that is applicable to each new opportunity.

3. *Never* under any circumstance commingle resources from one rate card to the other. If you commingle resources, you will completely undermine the integrity of the pricing structure, and that is a problem from which you will be unable to recover.

4. To the extent that procurement is benchmarking your rates, make sure you are being evaluated against similarly situated vendors delivering similarly situated services. Work diligently with procurement on this issue.

5. Be clear regarding the firmness of the rates contained in the master agreement. Many procurement organizations encourage their buyers to consider the rate card to be merely a departure point for additional price concessions. This will clearly impact the negotiation process.

6. Carefully review client mandated labor category descriptions, seek relief where appropriate, and map your internal labor categories as aggressively as possible.

7. Where labor category descriptions are purely qualitative in nature, utilize upward slotting mobility where appropriate.

8. Where labor categories are not client-mandated, keep the structure simple and straightforward. Fewer categories allows for much greater flexibility in the delivery process. In addition, provide labor category descriptions that are skills-based and that are not tied to years of experience, degrees, or certifications.

9. Think carefully about the composition of the typical team you will deploy during the period of performance, and structure any specific labor category discounts accordingly.

10. Express rates in a daily, weekly, or team-based structure—shift the emphasis from the hourly rate to doing whatever it takes to deliver results.

11. Offer volume discounts where appropriate based upon a set of predefined contracting volume materiality thresholds, based upon the duration of the engagement, or based upon the size of the team (more staff deployed for a longer term will most likely result in a greater discount). Offer the discount as a credit against future work (rather than as a cash rebate) to ensure a long-term pipeline with the client. But in any event, keep the discounting scheme as simple as possible.

12. Make sure to include an annual rate escalation factor, as it will serve as the only price increase you will receive during the course of the agreement.

13. Provide a rate card structure that serves all contemplated delivery geographies, and provide rates in local currency that are commensurate with your cost profile in that country or region.

14. Agree upon the prevailing rate card (home location versus location where services are being delivered) for resources that will be crossing geographic boundaries for service delivery.

15. Agree upon a policy for the timing of rate increases and labor category re-slotting resulting from staff promotions during the course of the engagement.

16. When considering the rate structure for a long-term master agreement, think carefully about the types of opportunities in which you will be engaged, the team size and leverage model that will be required for delivery, and the other preferred vendors that you will be competing with for opportunities.

17. When evaluating strategy rates, calculate the variance to standard across each labor category, and determine the viability of the potential rate card given the opportunities and leverage model against which you intend to deploy during the term of the master agreement.

18. When evaluating design and implementation rates, carefully review the resources, and their fully loaded cost rates, contained in the labor pool from which you will draw resources during the course of delivery. Carefully determine at what percentile you can draw a line and still deliver in a profitable manner during the term of the agreement.

19. Clearly stipulate that the rates do not include travel and related expenses and that they will be invoiced separately as specified in the contract.

20. Know when to hold the line, say "no," and tell procurement that your rates are firm. This rule is becoming increasingly difficult given the current economic climate in which it is not uncommon for Fortune 500 clients to come back to every master agreement holder and request an additional across the board discount to all rates contained within the master agreement. If you are faced with this issue, I would suggest going back to the top of this list and pursuing any strategies that might result in a cost reduction to the client that do not have a corresponding detrimental impact on the financial viability of the rate card. Or, if you decide to offer an additional discount, make sure that you are getting something in return.

How the Master Agreement Process Complements Procurement's Strategic Agenda

Through the master agreement process, procurement organizations hope to make progress in achieving three items on their agenda:

- Identifying a preferred vendor community that delivers in a timely, quality, and cost-effective manner

- Developing competition among vendors for similar services

- Securing business terms and conditions that yield an acceptable and predictable level of risk and reward for their organization

Ultimately, the use of master services and frame agreements has become the cornerstone of the sourcing strategy being implemented across all industries within the Fortune 500 client community. Given this dynamic, it is critical to hold master services agreements with all strategic clients, to build relationships with procurement executives that may influence the buying process, and to deliver in a manner that will result in the preservation of the "preferred" vendor label.

22

How to Reduce Maverick Spending and Implement e-Procurement

The other major items contained on the typical agenda of a Fortune 500 procurement organization include compliance, efficiency gains, cost savings, e-procurement, and performance management. When it comes to compliance and control, Fortune 500 procurement organizations have implemented fairly stringent policies with regard to engaging third-party consultants. A policy similar to the following is not uncommon:

> Our procurement department has heightened its focus on the management of its outside consultant spend and on ensuring strict compliance with internal policy in the process of engaging consultants. We have made several important process changes to our policy for engaging consultants, and you are strongly encouraged to review and fully understand how we will engage consulting firms for future services. The process changes will also help provide consistency with respect to invoice payment and tracking during the term of the engagement. Key elements of the revised policy are:

- All consulting engagements must be approved by the chief executive officer, executive leadership team member, or regional managing director prior to the commencement of work.

- A minimum of three bids must be obtained for all consulting services.

- An approved contract and statement of work is required for all consulting engagements and must be fully executed prior to the commencement of work.

- The consulting engagement process will be overseen by the procurement department.

- Any consulting engagement of $500,000 or greater must be reviewed and approved by the procurement department and the global consulting oversight board.

- Any material changes to existing engagements that include scope expansion or cost increases in excess of 10 percent or $50,000 require an amendment to the contract and approval by the procurement department.

- To ensure that payments to your firm are made on a timely basis, please confirm with your project sponsor that all required paperwork has been completed and approvals obtained prior to the commencement of work.

As you can see, this policy puts the procurement organization right in the middle of the contracting process for third-party consultants. In addition to being applicable to all new opportunities, the reach of the policy includes any material changes made to existing engagements. This policy is distributed not only internally within the client buying community, but also to the vendor base as well. The purpose of that broad distribution is encapsulated in the last bullet point, which speaks to vendor payments. It is clearly putting all third-party consultants on notice that they will not be paid if this process is not followed by their project sponsor. Some procurement organizations have even instituted penalties that are charged directly to the offending business unit for failing to adhere to the policy.

Implementing e-Procurement and Compliance

When it comes to efficiency gains, cost savings, and control over the buying process, procurement organizations have aggressively pursued the implementation of e-procurement solutions. E-procurement has revolutionized the method and cycle time by which goods and services are procured and received. Not only does it simplify the procurement process, but it also dramatically reduces cycle time. Even though complex consulting services might not be ordered solely in conjunction with the review of an online catalog, a robust e-procurement system will significantly reduce the cycle time associated with identifying a need and having consultants on the ground delivering services. Ultimately, an e-procurement solution will enable a distributed but controlled purchasing environment. It automates the process from requisition to payment by streamlining operations, shortening cycle time, and reducing costs. The process is seen in Figure 22.1.

As you can see, an e-procurement solution will streamline the procurement process, generate better management reporting and intelligence, optimize spend, and empower the client buying community. It will yield an increase in process efficiency by reducing the administrative cost, in the form of error rates and processing time, for each transaction shifted from paper to the electronic channel. It will yield an increase in contract compliance

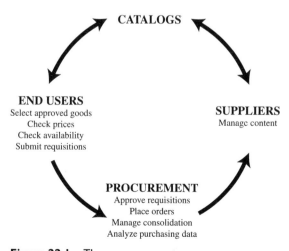

Figure 22.1   The e-procurement process

through the increased use of preferred suppliers and a reduction in off-contract spending, processing errors, and the ultimate costs for purchased goods and services. It will also yield an increase in purchasing power leverage by capturing the consolidated details of actual spend with each supplier that can be utilized in the negotiation process, as well as actual spend in each product and service category that can be used to determine where additional preferred vendors may be needed.

The reason Fortune 500 procurement organizations are so concerned with compliance is that a significant portion of the projected return on investment associated with an e-procurement system consists of the volume discount pricing and favorable terms and conditions they hope to secure by executing master agreements with their preferred vendor community. A lack of compliance within the buying community will result in a loss of that portion of the projected return on investment and a much longer than expected payback period. It is therefore critical that procurement motivate the buying community to embrace the e-procurement system and to engage only preferred vendors for the delivery of consulting services. While procurement can certainly promulgate a strict control policy regarding the utilization of preferred vendors, it is critical that they obtain internal buy-in, as the cost of noncompliance is significant. The compliance multiplier effect, as articulated in Table 22.1, reflects the bottom-line impact of noncompliance.

Given the extensive cost associated with noncompliance, procurement organizations will educate their internal buying and preferred vendor communities as to the appropriate process that should be followed before the

**Table 22.1   The Compliance Multiplier Effect
($ to the Bottom Line for Each $10 Million of Spending)**

	% COMPLIANCE WITH NEW CONTRACT TERMS AND CONDITIONS				
COST SAVINGS	25%	50%	75%	85%	95%
5%	$125,000	$250,000	$375,000	$425,000	$475,000
10%	$250,000	$500,000	$750,000	$850,000	$950,000
15%	$375,000	$750,000	$1,125,000	$1,275,000	$1,425,000
20%	$500,000	$1,000,000	$1,500,000	$1,700,000	$1,900,000
25%	$625,000	$1,250,000	$1,875,000	$2,125,000	$2,375,000
30%	$750,000	$1,500,000	$2,250,000	$2,550,000	$2,850,000

delivery of services commences. It is clear that an e-procurement solution is a key tenet of the typical Fortune 500 procurement agenda. It enhances the value of the preferred vendor label, as it strongly discourages and may even penalize members of the buying community from utilizing the services of nonpreferred vendors. Ultimately, every dollar that is kept out of the hands of a nonpreferred vendor is another that can be captured by a member of the preferred vendor community. So I suggest you strictly comply with the processes and procedures being promulgated by procurement in this area.

e-Procurement and Cost Savings

The reason Fortune 500 procurement organizations are so focused on implementing an e-procurement solution is that the savings are significant. Companies that adopt e-procurement solutions report efficiency gains of 50 percent with regard to the time spent sourcing goods and services. As we have discussed, the full value of the savings and cost reductions will not be realized without compliance from the internal buying community and external vendor base. In a 2003 study, the Aberdeen Group found that companies that had adopted e-procurement solutions could save an additional 7 percent if suppliers would comply with existing contracts. Other studies report that 20 percent to 30 percent of unrealized savings are due to noncompliance by suppliers and employees continuing to order from nonpreferred vendors. It is this type of data that has resulted in procurement being so highly motivated to streamline their vendor base; to identify, cultivate, and measure the performance of a set of preferred vendors; to execute master services agreements; and to achieve compliance from its internal buying community as well as its external vendor base. Through aggressively pursuing this agenda, procurement organizations within Fortune 500 companies hope to achieve the following:

- Strong compliance for both direct and indirect spend, which allows for the recapture of unrealized savings from the implementation of the e-sourcing solution

- A streamlined and structured process by which risk is proactively managed in existing and prospective sourcing agreements

- Detailed and accurate reporting regarding current sourcing spend and proactive statistics on systems and controls compliance

- Reduced financial, technical, legal, and delivery risk

- An empowered client buying community

- Clear and unambiguous policies, procedures, and risk guidelines by which third-party goods and services are procured based upon the size, scope, and complexity of the transaction

- Objective, measurable, and verifiable criteria by which third-party vendor performance is gauged across time, quality, and cost parameters

Given the level of motivation by which procurement is pursuing its agenda, the internal recognition and performance incentives they may realize through achieving cost savings, and the level of empowerment they have been given through the reporting hierarchy, executing master services agreements and building enduring relationships with procurement organizations is becoming a required rite of passage if you want to successfully sell services within the Fortune 500 community. The only real exception to this rule that I have encountered is if you are selling only high-level corporate strategy services directly to the C-suite and have no aspirations to expand beyond that delivery footprint. But even that strategy can yield some less than desirable results. As we have discussed previously, the high-level corporate strategy providers rely upon their C-suite relationships to secure new business opportunities. Some of them simply refuse to participate in the master agreement process, and by doing so, they completely circumvent procurement. While they may still be able to secure sole-source high-level strategy work with this approach, I am unclear as to what can possibly be gained by ignoring and creating a potential adversary in Fortune 500 procurement organizations. Such actions may serve no purpose other than to compel them to undertake efforts to mitigate your respective share of future consulting spend. If you follow this approach, don't even think of expanding your delivery footprint to any downstream opportunities.

For the rest of the professional services vendor community, I encourage you to embrace the master services agreement and preferred vendor process and to build upon existing relationships and to cultivate new ones with the procurement organizations within the Fortune 500 client community. Having been at the intersection of this strategy, I can assure you that it will yield a significant return on investment in the form of new client business development, existing client footprint expansion, and an enhanced reference base.

Part 5

The Competitive Landscape

23

Who Is the Competition?

The competitive landscape for both strategy and design and implementation consulting services is extremely well populated. Irrespective of where your service offerings reside across the consulting lifecycle and the industry in which you are engaged, fierce competition from both a technical and price perspective will be prevalent. This highly charged and competitive environment exists for all service providers, including those that have strong brand awareness; a history for delivering in a timely, quality, and cost-effective manner; and a strong industry-specific reference base. Whenever you are competing for a new opportunity, trying to expand your delivery footprint, responding to a master services agreement request for proposal, maintaining your position as a firmly entrenched provider, or negotiating a rate structure with a Fortune 500 procurement organization, it is critical to clearly understand the alternatives that the client can pursue if you fail to successfully negotiate an agreement.

If you have ever read any books published by the Harvard Program on Negotiation, you likely have encountered the acronym BATNA (best alternative to a negotiated agreement). In negotiation theory, BATNA is the course of action or alternative that will be pursued by a party if the current negotiations fail and an agreement cannot be reached. Properly evaluating your BATNA and that of the opposing party is the key to being a successful negotiator, as it will, if carefully estimated, clearly identify where the leverage points lie in the negotiation process. It is my intent not to discuss negotiation theory but to reinforce the fact that when you are negotiating with Fortune 500 procurement organizations, it is critical to understand their BATNA if you fail to reach an agreement.

Given the quite populated competitive landscape that I mentioned earlier, their BATNA will typically be to seek an alternative vendor that can deliver similarly situated services. To successfully evaluate the viability of the client's BATNA as well as your competitive positioning, it is critical to have a clear understanding of your competitors in the marketplace. To that end, this section of the book will provide a brief competitive snapshot of the major strategy, IT services, and outsourcing service providers across a number of parameters including to whom they sell, how they sell, their service offerings and delivery footprint, the markets and industries they serve, their pricing and contracting strategy, and the strengths, weaknesses, opportunities, and threats I perceive they will face given the current economic climate and the global consulting and IT services markets in 2010 and beyond.

I will start with the major corporate strategy firms including McKinsey & Company, Bain & Company, The Boston Consulting Group, and Booz & Company, and conclude with a review of Accenture, IBM, Deloitte, and HP, a good cross-section of the largest IT and outsourcing service providers. While there are certainly many more strategy, operations management, human resources, business advisory, multiservice, IT services, and pure play outsourcing firms that I could mention, a snapshot of these firms should provide some insight into the current pricing, delivery, and market conditions across the global consulting market. Having worked for a few of these firms, I can tell you that while their size, scale, prestige, and respective delivery sweet-spots may vary, they are all heavily focused on enhancing their brand awareness and reference base, building trusted advisor relationships with their clients, and delivering their respective solution in a timely, quality, and cost-effective manner that achieves the value proposition articulated in their proposal. Just to recap, the competitive profiles are based upon my experience in competing with these firms in the market as well as upon publicly available materials, which may include SEC filings, GSA Federal Supply Schedules, and industry publications.

24

McKinsey & Co.

McKinsey & Co. is the gold standard when it comes to providing corporate and IT strategy and operations management services to the Fortune 500 client community. They have extremely strong brand awareness, ironclad and trusted advisor relationships with C-suite executives, and are recognized as global thought leaders in the areas of strategy and operations management across all commercial industries and within the public sector.

While I use the term "ironclad," the strength of their relationships within the C-suite simply cannot be overstated. They are trusted advisors to CEOs, command premium pricing for their corporate strategy services, most of which are awarded on a sole-source basis, and even procurement defends their turf within the C-suite. Within some companies, it is not uncommon to have a McKinsey line item in the annual budget. Their primary competitors within the market, Bain & Company, Booz & Company, and The Boston Consulting Group, are focused upon trying to compete with and unseat them from this market-leading and heavily entrenched position. When I think of the position that McKinsey commands within the corporate strategy market, I think of sports dynasties that include the Boston Celtics of the 1960s, the UCLA Bruins of the late 1960s and early 1970s, and the Michael Jordan-led Chicago Bulls of the 1990s. But when it comes to the Fortune 500 strategy providers, everybody wants to be like McKinsey.

McKinsey was founded in 1926 by James O. McKinsey, who had an established practice that was focused on budgeting and finance. In the past seventy-five years, the firm has grown tremendously, and its current foot-print crosses over all geographies, industry boundaries, and the public and private sector domain. McKinsey does not disclose its client list, but does state that it provides services to more than 70 percent of the Fortune 1000 and three of the world's largest companies. As of April 2008, *Forbes* maga-zine reported that the five largest companies in the world, based upon sales volume, include Wal-Mart, ExxonMobil, Royal Dutch Shell, BP, and Chevron. The rankings are not relevant but embody the types of blue-chip and brand-name industry-leading companies that McKinsey helps to artic-ulate a strategy that will allow them to achieve their mission, vision, and growth aspirations.

McKinsey is a privately held company and is not subject to SEC filing requirements, but McKinsey employs a workforce consisting of more than 8,400 billable consultants (as reported in September 2009 by *Consulting Magazine*) generating in excess of $5.0 billion ($5.33 billion as estimated by *Forbes Magazine* in its November 2008 listing of America's largest private companies) in annual revenue. McKinsey has a very strong alumni network across the Fortune 500 client community and utilizes those relationships to their fullest extent, as many current clients are former McKinsey consult-ants. McKinsey is truly global in reach with over ninety-four offices spread across fifty-two countries.

Like many of its competitors, McKinsey's global footprint has expanded significantly in the past few years to the extent that McKinsey generates a sub-stantial portion of its revenue from clients outside the United States. In addi-tion, it has made significant inroads within a number of emerging markets including India and Japan and maintains a very strong presence in China. Evidence of its commitment to this region was clearly communicated to the market in 2004 when McKinsey established the Asia House, a program with offices in Frankfurt and Paris which serve as the gateway between McKinsey clients in Europe that wish to expand into the Asia Pacific market.

McKinsey's Strengths

From a delivery perspective, McKinsey has broad management consulting capabilities in the areas of corporate finance; corporate strategy; talent, organization, and human resources management; marketing, brand, and sales strategy; and operations management. Through its business technology office, McKinsey seeks to fuse its strategy expertise and capabilities with technology consulting in the areas of outsourcing and IT architecture, cost, governance, organization, and infrastructure. Although McKinsey is building a strong technology consulting practice, its sweet-spot still remains to the left of the line of demarcation between the strategy and design and implementation domains within the consulting lifecycle.

The bottom line is that McKinsey develops strategy—organization strategy, IT strategy, financial strategy, and marketing and brand strategy—and the programs and initiatives that will be required by the client to achieve their business objectives or growth aspirations within each of the functional disciplines just identified. To the extent the strategy requires implementing technology to achieve those objectives, it is a foregone conclusion that the client will seek out one of the major implementation providers to bring those programs and initiatives to fruition. Based upon its actions, McKinsey is fine with that approach, as it appears to have no interest in delivering services at that end of the consulting lifecycle. As I have previously mentioned, McKinsey has tremendous brand awareness in the market as the preeminent provider of corporate strategy services to the Fortune 500 client community. In addition, McKinsey is considered to be a key thought leader on issues that impact both public and private sector clients. It has established the *McKinsey Quarterly*, a newsletter that offers new ways of thinking about management in the public, private, and non-profit sectors, as well as the McKinsey Global Institute, which focuses on critical economic issues facing businesses and governments, through which it disseminates its research and viewpoints.

McKinsey in Government

One area where McKinsey has attempted to expand the depth and breadth of its delivery footprint is providing services to the U.S. federal government. It is these efforts that will provide us with some insight into McKinsey's rate structure. In terms of expanding its delivery footprint within the federal government market, McKinsey has entered into some strategic subcontractor relationships with some of the larger government contractors around the DC beltway, participated in activities that will advance its thought leadership agenda, leveraged its alumni and relationships, expanded its physical presence within the DC region, and entered into negotiations for and executed a contract under the General Services Administration MOBIS (Mission Oriented Business Integrated Services) contract, which is a vehicle through which contractors provide management and strategy consulting services to the major cabinet agencies.

As you may be aware, the General Services Administration, through its Federal Supply Schedules Program, establishes long-term contracts through which all of the executive agencies within the federal government may efficiently order goods and services directly from GSA Schedule Contractors at most-favored customer pricing under an expedited procurement cycle. While GSA Schedule pricing does not exactly mimic commercial pricing terms, it is a very good gauge of a company's commercial pricing practices. Within its GSA Schedule (#GS-10F-0118S) that was executed on January 27, 2006, and runs for a five-year period, McKinsey offers its services under different team constructs that are priced on a weekly basis. The contract states that McKinsey "works to help clients achieve substantial, lasting improvements in their performance. To do so, we establish working relationships with senior leaders, explore their aspirations and challenges, and jointly define engagements that have the potential for lasting impact. McKinsey Washington will provide expert consulting services to customers on issues such as strategy, organization, operations, and business technology." The team structure and pricing (effective May 2008) contained in the contract is articulated in Table 24.1.

Table 24.1   McKinsey GSA Rate Structure

TEAM TYPE	BRIEF TEAM DESCRIPTION	GSA WEEKLY PRICE
Team A	1 engagement manager, 1 associate, and engagement director support	$75,585.45
Team B	1 engagement manager, 2 associates, and engagement director support	$93,288.00
Team C	1 engagement manager, 3 associates, and engagement director support	$116,374.75
Team E	1 associate and engagement director support	$31,195.51

As we discussed previously, it is not uncommon to see management consulting firms express their labor category rates on an hourly, daily, weekly, or team basis, or some combination thereof. In an effort to allow a comparison between the McKinsey team rate structure and those of their corporate strategy counterparts, I will attempt to reverse engineer their weekly team rate structure to an hourly basis for each of the labor categories identified. I will assume that McKinsey invoices its clients for no more than 40 hours per week per individual, irrespective of the actual number of hours worked. With that being said, if you review the team compositions articulated in Table 24.1, the only difference between Team Types A and B and Team Types B and C is the addition of an associate-level staff person to the staffing model. If we look at the average price difference between these two teams, $(($93,288 - $75,585.45) + ($116,374.75 - $93,288) \div 2)$, the result is $20,395, which is assumed to be the cost of a full-time associate. Dividing that weekly rate by 40 hours yields an hourly associate billing rate of $510 per hour.

There also appears to be an alternative and more junior associate cohort rate; the fee variance between Team A and Team B is $17,702.55, which would equate to an hourly rate of $443 per hour and would represent the alternate associate rate. If we take the average cost of a full-time associate ($20,395) and subtract it from the total weekly rate for Team E ($31,196), we are left with the cost ($10,801) associated with the support provided by the engagement director. The schedule states that engagement directors and senior leaders allocate their time to between two and three engagements at any one time. Let's assume that the engagement directors and senior leaders spend 90 percent of the 40-hour week in a billable capacity and are focused on three engagements; this would equate to 36 hours, or 12 hours per engagement, for the week. If we take the $10,801 remaining cost in Team E and divide it by 12, we end up with an hourly rate of $900 for an engagement director or senior leader. Finally, once we have calculated the rate for the associate, engagement director, and senior leader, we can assume that the remaining cost for Team A ($75,585) - $10,801 (engagement director) - $10,801 (senior leader) - $20,395 (associate), or $33,588, is the cost associated with the fully dedicated engagement manager. Dividing this cost by 40 hours yields an hourly rate of $840 per hour. Based upon this analysis, the team composition and associated labor rates for each of the teams would be as seen in Table 24.2.

Table 24.2 McKinsey Team Structure Rate Buildup

STAFF LEVEL	WEEKLY HOURS	HOURLY RATE	FEE TOTAL
Team A Rate Buildup			
Associate	40	$510	$20,400
Engagement manager	40	$840	$33,600
Engagement director	12	$900	$10,800
Senior leader	12	$900	$10,800
Total Fees Team A			**$75,600**
Team B Rate Buildup			
Associate 1	40	$510	$20,400
Engagement manager	40	$840	$33,600
Engagement director	12	$900	$10,800
Senior leader	12	$900	$10,800
Associate 2	40	$443	$17,720
Total Fees Team B			**$93,320**
Team C Rate Buildup			
Associate 1	40	$510	$20,400
Engagement manager	40	$840	$33,600
Engagement director	12	$900	$10,800
Senior leader	12	$900	$10,800
Associate 2	40	$510	$20,400
Associate 3	40	$510	$20,400
Total Fees Team C			**$116,400**
Team E Rate Buildup			
Associate	40	$510	$20,400
Engagement director	12	$840	$10,800
Total Fees Team E			**$31,200**

As you can see, my hourly rate calculations reconcile with the weekly team rates contained in the McKinsey GSA Schedule. Whether my assumptions are correct is not that critical; I simply wanted to provide you with a ballpark estimate of the hourly rates being charged for strategy consulting services. Keep in mind that the rates being provided to the federal government are typically discounted rates, so adding a premium of anywhere from

5 percent to 10 percent or more (depending upon the labor category) would be appropriate to convert these to standard rates for a commercial client. We will compare these rates against the hourly rates contained in the GSA Schedules of Booz & Company and The Boston Consulting Group to assess the accuracy of my math and to gauge their validity.

Now that we have some indication of McKinsey's market position and their rate structure, let's discuss the strengths and potential weaknesses of their market position given the current economic climate and delivery landscape. Let's be clear about one thing: McKinsey has no risk of losing its status as the leader and preeminent provider of corporate strategy and operations management services in the global marketplace. Their ability to attract talent combined with their extremely strong brand awareness and trusted advisor relationships within the upper echelon of the Fortune 500 client community is extremely strong, and unseating them is not likely without a change in C-suite leadership. I have sat through many internal strategy meetings plotting their demise—or at a minimum how to capture some of their market share—and the results have been marginal at best. As I mentioned previously, procurement organizations within many Fortune 500 clients carefully protect the corporate strategy turf that is dominated by McKinsey and serve as an additional barrier to entry. In addition to their extremely strong C-suite relationships, McKinsey relies very heavily upon their alumni, many of whom serve in C-suite roles across the Fortune 500 and stand ready to procure services from their former employer. In addition to its corporate strategy and operations management delivery acumen, McKinsey has extensive IT strategy capabilities, which it delivers through its business technology office.

With that being said, I also believe that McKinsey faces some challenges given the current economy and delivery landscape. First and foremost, McKinsey is a corporate strategy and operations management firm and does not offer any downstream design and implementation capability. This limited footprint may impact their growth opportunities, as Fortune 500 clients seek out full lifecycle providers like Accenture or IBM that not only can develop the strategy but that also have skin in the game and the delivery capability to implement the programs, initiatives, and technology identified during the strategy phase of the engagement. Having a full lifecycle provider achieves a number of objectives: it provides the client with the ability to hold one party accountable throughout the engagement lifecycle; it allows the client to negotiate a rate structure that is commensurate with the nature of the services being provided; and it mitigates the knowledge gap that typically materializes during the transition and handoff from strategy to implementation provider.

Another challenge for McKinsey is that they provide services at premium prices; I am not questioning the value of their service offerings or the return on investment their clients will ultimately realize, but the current economic climate may severely impact the size of the corporate strategy wallet and the premium rate structure it embodies. The size of the Fortune 500 strategy wallet is also a limitation for a firm like McKinsey. Ultimately, the number of clients that have the resources to invest in a premium service provider like McKinsey is limited, and the level of competitive intensity within each of the major commercial industries is growing exponentially. At some point, a corporate strategy provider will be unable to deliver similar services to companies that are heated competitors with each other in the marketplace and will have to place its bets accordingly. While Chinese-like walls and other barriers can be implemented to insulate delivery teams and safeguard confidential information, it is simply a fact that companies such as Coke and Pepsi and UPS and FedEx don't want their strategy providers to be playing for the opposing team.

Ultimately, McKinsey is the dominant leader within the corporate strategy market, and as with the celebrated Celtics, Bruins, and Bulls teams mentioned earlier, their competitors are simply fighting for second place. McKinsey continues to receive high accolades in industry publications such as *Consulting Magazine*—where it ranked second in the "Best Firms to Work For" survey—and is recognized as the world's leading management consulting firm across the Fortune 500 buying community. While the wave of the future may be for Fortune 500 clients to seek out full lifecycle providers, I would view such a dynamic as a great opportunity for a firm like McKinsey.

The key differentiator for McKinsey is its unmatched brand awareness, trusted advisor relationships, and outstanding corporate strategy and operations management delivery capability; however, it lacks the downstream implementation capability that clients desire so they can hold their strategy providers accountable for results. Conversely, most of the full lifecycle firms have exceptional functional expertise and the capability to implement the programs identified during the strategy phase in a timely, quality, and cost-effective manner; however, they lack the upstream delivery capabilities and relationships that a firm like McKinsey brings to bear in the corporate strategy world. It is this dynamic that has most likely resulted in the bifurcated delivery landscape that we see today: Strategy firms develop strategy and implementation firms implement solutions. If you remember, words very similar to these embodied the launch of the one-firm evolution at Booz Allen Hamilton back in 2005. While Booz Allen Hamilton was ultimately unsuccessful in its efforts, McKinsey may want to revisit this strategy by entering into a robust alliance or partnership with one of the major implementation firms. In my opinion, such a strategy, if executed properly, would yield a market force that would be unstoppable.

25

Bain & Company

Bain & Company, like McKinsey, is also one of the preeminent providers of corporate strategy and operations management services across the Fortune 500 client community. Bain has long-term trusted advisor relationships with C-suite executives and has established extremely strong brand awareness in the market as a firm that shares risk and reward with and delivers results for its clients. Like McKinsey, it is heavily focused on providing strategy and operations management consulting services across all industries, but has significant depth and breadth within the financial services and consumer and media markets, as well as extensive cross-industry service offerings in the areas of private equity, mergers and acquisitions, valuation, due diligence, and advisory services.

While Bain (founded in 1973) may not have the history of McKinsey, it has established itself in the market as a firm that is objective, innovative, unbiased, and unyielding in its efforts to deliver results for its clients. Despite its global presence, it has been able to maintain a strong corporate culture that serves as a common foundation across its employee base. For those of you keeping score, Bain was recently awarded the top spot in *Consulting Magazine's* annual "Best Firms to Work For" survey; this is quite familiar territory, as it has held that position for seven consecutive years. Given this reign, I think it is safe to say that Bain has become the gold standard for where to work within the professional services industry. This survey has grown tremendously over the past few years, and the 2009 results reflected feedback submitted by some 10,000 random consultants across 236 firms. Bain finished first in the areas of career development and work/life balance, and second in the areas of leadership and compensation and benefits.

The strength of the Bain culture and its heavy focus on values, diversity, and the Bain family is definitely a contributing factor to its dominance in what is a very important survey across the professional services industry, especially given the data collection methodology. In a 2008 interview with *Consulting Magazine*, Bain & Company Worldwide Managing Director Steve Ellis addressed the critical importance of maintaining such a positive culture across the firm. He stated that "Results serve as the core of our culture. We are passionate about what we do, enjoy our work, laugh a lot, and celebrate success when we achieve it. And we have a culture of successful teaming and collaboration, both with the client and internally. We put the team first at the client level, within our local offices, and as we operate seamlessly across our 39 offices around the world." When he was recently interviewed after receiving top honors in 2009, Ellis stated "We're a global team that lives by this principle of a 'Bainie' never lets another 'Bainie' fail. This is true across geographies, cultures, languages, and over time and through generations."

For me, this strong culture and deeply rooted passion is reminiscent of my early years at PeopleSoft in the late 1990s. The PeopleSoft culture was a part of our fabric; irrespective of the size of the company, we had a common mission and vision and were a part of a team. To this day, I still wear my PeopleSoft team jersey, adorned with my employee number, #3021, with great pride. The culture was not something that was mandated by leadership—it ran through our veins and allowed us to achieve incredible growth over a short period. We very much followed a work hard/play hard mentality, and a similar construct seems to be flourishing at Bain. As you can tell, a lot of that PeopleSoft culture and pride is still inside me, even though it has been seven years since my departure from the company. To the extent that Bain has cultivated a similar dynamic across its employee base, it will provide a distinct competitive advantage in the market.

As I mentioned previously, Bain's brand awareness is very strong across the Fortune 500 buying community. Ask anyone within the corporate strategy buying community about Bain, and they will very quickly spout off the Bain tagline that "We put our money where our mouth is." This notion of placing fees at risk and sharing risk and reward with the client is another competitive differentiator for the firm. While contingency and value-based pricing is not out of the question for the other corporate strategy providers, Bain prides itself on aligning its fee structure with the success and return realized by its clients and on its ability to deliver on its value proposition, and this results-oriented approach is a key tenet of the Bain culture. According to Ellis, over one-third of Bain's global revenue is derived from client engagements where Bain places its fees at risk and aligns its financial incentives with those of the client; such an approach definitely fosters a sense of ownership and account-ability within all hierarchical levels across its project teams. It is therefore highly unlikely that a buyer can make the claim that Bain does not have skin in the game and is unwilling to put its money where its mouth is—there is that tagline again. Given the current economic climate, utilizing value-based pricing to its fullest extent and clearly aligning its fees with client return on investment and success should yield a distinct competitive advantage for Bain.

With regard to its overall delivery footprint, Bain is significantly smaller than McKinsey with some 3,500 billable consultants, (as reported in September 2009 by *Consulting Magazine*) and total annual revenues, as esti-mated by *Forbes Magazine* in its November 2008 report on America's largest private companies, in the $1.64 billion range. Bain has a smaller global presence than McKinsey, with some 40 offices spread across 27 countries with a North American- and Western European-focused slant from a delivery perspective. Despite this focus, Bain has, like all of the major consultancies, expanded its operations into emerging markets including Brazil, Russia, India, and China (BRIC) and has organized its operations across three regions including the Americas, Europe and the Middle East, and Asia Pacific. Like its corporate strategy brethren, Bain has a broad alumni network (in excess of 8,000) that is strategically placed across all industries and academia, which it utilizes to its advantage to promulgate its thought leadership agenda and to facilitate new opportunity capture. Like McKinsey, BCG, and Booz, Bain must continue to make investments in building out its IT consulting and strategy practice to augment its corporate strategy and operations management capa-bilities; ultimately, its inability to scale this component of its delivery portfo-lio may create a competitive challenge, as clients are seeking out management consulting firms that have the capability to bridge the gap between strategy and IT and to cross over a broader spectrum of the consulting lifecycle.

What Makes Bain Unique

Bain is unique among its competitor set in three major areas. The first is that Bain does not have a public sector business and appears to have no intention of growing its footprint or expanding its delivery capabilities within that market. To that end, Bain has no General Services Administration Federal Supply Schedule in place that would provide greater insight into its pricing structure and has no measurable footprint within the U.S. state and local or federal government marketplace. Based upon my interactions negotiating strategy rates with Fortune 500 procurement executives and speaking with consumers across the corporate strategy buying community, Bain's rate structure is on par with its primary competitor set; however, Bain seems much more willing to utilize value-based pricing to articulate its value proposition with existing and prospective clients, something that is paid a lot of lip service to, but not necessarily acted upon by its competitors.

Although Bain does not have a measurable footprint within the public sector market, it does provide pro bono strategy consulting services to a number of nonprofit organizations and maintains a strong partnership with The Bridgespan Group, a nonprofit organization that it founded in 2000, whose mission is to provide strategy and management consulting, executive search, and business advisory services to nonprofit and philanthropic organizations. Although the organizations are separate entities, Bain provides thought leadership, intellectual capital, and resources to help Bridgespan achieve its mission and vision.

Another major distinction between Bain and its primary competitors is its dominance in the area of private equity consulting. Bain has strong ancestral ties in this area as Bain Capital, one of the largest private equity firms in the world, which was founded in 1984 by a group of Bain & Company partners. Bain Capital has in excess of $60 billion in assets under management and has invested in many brand-name companies across all commercial industries. Although Bain Capital is an independent company, it clearly served as the catalyst for the creation of Bain's Private Equity Practice, which has a dominant presence in Europe and North America. Even though the private equity flow has narrowed over the past year, Bain has been able to realize significant growth given its private equity, mergers and acquisitions, due diligence, valuation, and management advisory capabilities. This has been especially true in a number of emerging markets where private equity funds are still flowing, including China and India. Its ability to deliver these types of services in a timely, quality, and cost-effective manner has given Bain immediate access to clients across a number of industries and geographies and has certainly helped expand the depth and breadth of their C-suite liaisons. This capability will continue to serve them quite well given market consolidation across all industries and a strengthening economy.

The third key differentiator is the composition of its client base; while Bain certainly serves a number of Fortune 500 brand-name clients, it derives a significant portion of its revenue from small- and medium-sized businesses. Bain, while smaller than McKinsey, has trusted advisor relationships, strong brand awareness and corporate culture, and takes a no-nonsense approach to aligning its financial incentives with those of its clients to deliver measurable results. In addition, Bain is very heavily focused upon maximizing client satisfaction, achieving extraordinary results, coaching, developing and training its staff, simplifying the organization to drive operational efficiencies, and capturing and disseminating best practices and driving consistency on a global basis. The bottom line is that Bain is an extremely strong competitor and brings a powerful arsenal to bear when competing for new opportunities.

Bain's Competitive Positioning

Bain & Company brings quality products, brand awareness, and a strong reference base to the table when competing for and delivering corporate strategy and operations management consulting services. Combine that with their extremely strong culture, and you have a force to be reckoned with. However, like McKinsey, Bain may face some challenges given current market conditions and the future delivery landscape. As I mentioned, Bain generates a significant portion of its revenue from small- and medium-sized businesses that may be struggling given the current economic climate. To the extent those clients must engage in broad-based cost reduction efforts to weather the storm, Bain's share of the strategy wallet may be impacted accordingly. In addition, Bain's client base and delivery model is focused very much on North America and Western Europe in scope; clearly, both regions are experiencing tremendous economic turmoil across all industries, with the potential exception of the public sector in which Bain has no measurable presence. Bain has expanded into the emerging markets including India and China but has trailed its primary competitors in doing so; ultimately, their delay may impact their ability to meet their growth aspirations from a market share perspective.

Finally, and possibly most importantly, Bain must continue to expand its IT consulting capabilities that have been the focus of many of their competitors including McKinsey and Booz & Company. Current buying trends clearly indicate that all clients, Fortune 500 or otherwise, are seeking out management consulting firms that can deliver services across the entire consulting lifecycle, or at a minimum, those that can bring delivery capabilities to bear that extend beyond the strategy realm into its intersection with technology. Although Bain has expanded its IT consulting capabilities in recent years, it must continue to heavily invest in this area to maintain pace and compete effectively with its primary competitor set. With full service providers like Accenture and IBM looking to expand upstream to capture a piece of the strategy wallet and bring their full lifecycle solution to bear, Bain's ability to achieve its growth aspirations could be at risk. As with McKinsey, it may be prudent for Bain to develop a strategic alliance with one of the large downstream implementation providers that have strong IT consulting capabilities; such a combination would yield a much more complete go-to-market strategy that would meet the demand of the buying community and minimize any extreme volatility in their portfolio.

26

The Boston Consulting Group

Like McKinsey and Bain, The Boston Consulting Group (BCG) provides strategy and operations management consulting services to a global client base that includes the Fortune 500, mid-sized companies, nonprofit organizations, and government entities across a variety of industries including automotive, financial services, technology and communications, healthcare, and consumer and media. Like both McKinsey and Bain, BCG has longstanding and trusted advisor relationships with its clients, and it is from those "clients for life" that the firm generates a substantial portion of its revenue.

BCG is privately held and was founded in 1963 by Bruce D. Henderson as the management and consulting division of the Boston Safe Deposit and Trust Company. With some 4,500 billable consultants worldwide (as reported in September 2009 by *Consulting Magazine*) and revenue in the $2.3 billion range (as estimated by *Forbes Magazine* in its November 2008 listing of America's largest private companies), BCG has strong brand awareness, maintains a position as a well recognized and highly respected thought leader, and has a reputation for delivering innovative and unconventional solutions to its clients. BCG also has a broad network of alumni with which it is in frequent contact. Like its competitors, BCG relies upon its alumni to facilitate the capture of new opportunities as either direct consumers of or as advocates within their respective organizations.

Like Bain, BCG also has a well-known tagline. If you ask around the corporate strategy buying community, it will not take long for someone to shout

out that BCG is "The Partner of Choice to Transform Business and Society."
Like Bain, BCG has performed remarkably well in *Consulting Magazine's*
"Best Firms to Work For" survey. They have done so well that they have
never dropped out of the Top 5 listing since the inception of the survey in
2001, held a firm grasp on the number two position in both 2007 and 2008,
and ranked third in the 2009 survey. In addition, BCG was just named third
on the list in *Fortune Magazine's* 2009 "100 Best Companies to Work For."
BCG is known for its strong culture, commitment to growing and mentor-
ing its staff through a number of programs including a significant investment in training, and for providing exceptional pay and benefits to its
employees. BCG is particularly committed to the career progression of its
staff, and that position was certainly reflected in a recent interview that Hans-
Paul Buerkner, BCG's CEO, conducted with *Consulting Magazine*. In that
interview, when asked about career development, Buerkner commented:

> That is one of the most important reasons why someone joins a
> consulting firm. So a lot of emphasis is placed on helping people
> learn, helping people develop their skill sets, developing their
> leadership capabilities. If you want to become a great leader in
> business, it's not sufficient to be a great intellect, you also need to
> have the capability to deal with people, lead them, mobilize them,
> motivate them, and I think that has become a real focus for us
> over the last several years.

Global Teamwork and Innovation

Another area where BCG has made great strides is in the area of bringing
its global capabilities to bear to deliver innovative solutions for its clients.
BCG respondents provided very positive feedback when asked about the
team-oriented culture of their firm. Buerkner went on to comment that
"The teaming aspect has been emphasized very strongly at BCG. So, teaming is key, not just on the local level but across offices, across practice areas,
and across different countries." Achieving this level of global teamwork is
critical in any consulting firm that is structured in a partner-led and team-
based environment. As we all know, this structure can definitely foster a

very partner-centric, P&L focused, and myopic view of the world. Ultimately, BCG's ability to break down any internal barriers and to team effectively across industry and geographic boundaries will yield a distinct
competitive advantage in the market in the areas of new opportunity
capture, delivery excellence, and client and staff retention.

BCG considers itself to be one of the founders and global leaders in the
field of strategy consulting, and unlike some of its competitors, still generates an overwhelming portion of its revenue from delivering strategic planning, organizational strategy, IT strategy, financial strategy, and marketing
and brand strategy. BCG has also built a robust IT practice that comple-
ments BCG's strategy, organization, and operations capabilities. Through
its IT practice, BCG is able to provide services in the areas of IT strategy,
transformation, sourcing, organization, and performance. BCG's commitment to bridging the gap between strategy and technology and implementation was clearly evident when it established a wholly owned subsidiary
called Platinion, an IT consulting firm headquartered in Germany that is
focused on developing and implementing the IT solutions that are identified during the strategy phase of an engagement. Although still relatively
small from a staffing perspective, Platinion provides its services across the
entire IT lifecycle and has a strong reference base within the energy and
utilities, telecommunications, banking, and insurance sectors. This ability
to augment its historical delivery sweet-spots and to deliver services at the
intersection of strategy and technology is another distinct competitive
advantage that BCG brings to bear in the marketplace and is a message that
is very well received within the global buying community.

To that end, BCG has established a broad global footprint with over
66 offices in 38 countries. While BCG has an established footprint in North
America, it has a very strong presence across Europe and the Asia Pacific
region. That EMEA (Europe, Middle East, and Africa) and APAC (Asia and
Pacific) focus was always quite evident to me when negotiating North
American strategy rates with procurement, as BCG was rarely the benchmark that was utilized to gauge price validity. To that end, BCG has focused
its business development and expansion efforts globally and has been able
to realize significant success and to substantially grow its revenue base by
penetrating the markets in Russia, Thailand, Australia, Korea, China, Japan,
Ukraine, Dubai, and Abu Dhabi.

BCG's brand awareness is enhanced by its ability to think outside the box and provide innovative solutions that are tailored to its client base. Some individuals across the corporate strategy buying community have the perception that the major providers have a tendency to recycle intellectual capital and to use generally accepted best practices for similarly situated clients within the same industry. That is clearly neither the case nor the market perception with BCG, as they tend to be much more creative in their problem-solving approach and strive to establish new "best practices" for their clients. When I think of BCG, I tend to think about the GM commercials that tout the fact that "this is not your father's Chevrolet." You should definitely not expect the status quo when contracting with BCG for the delivery of strategy services.

This unique approach is clearly embodied in its Strategy Institute, through which BCG takes a forward-looking view across a ten-year time horizon to identify the forces that will shape business strategy and competitive advantage in the future. By collaborating with a broad community of contributors across the business, academic, and scientific communities, BCG is able to collect wide-ranging insights into the nature of strategy and to apply those principles and findings across its client base. While other consultancies may engage in similar pursuits, BCG has taken a much more formalized approach to unlocking how strategy has and will evolve and how its clients can successfully compete in the global economy. Through its collaboration efforts with the Strategy Institute, BCG is able to bring innovative and forward-thinking solutions to its clients.

BCG Pricing Methodology

From a pricing perspective, BCG has a reputation for maintaining somewhat of a disparate pricing methodology depending upon the client and opportunity for which it is competing. They are known to discount heavily if necessary to capture new or strategic opportunities or to prohibit a competitor from penetrating an existing client. In terms of obtaining some insight into their rate structure, we can review their prior (they no longer have a GSA Schedule in place) GSA MOBIS schedule, which contained rates that were prevailing in the 2005 timeframe. Within that schedule, #GS-10F-0475N, BCG describes its primary service offering as "custom work for the senior leaders of an organization on their most important strategic, organizational, and operational challenges." The schedule contains a fairly comprehensive listing of those service areas where BCG can bring its experience to bear to assist public sector policymakers in achieving their respective mission and includes strategy and innovation, operational effectiveness, strategic management of human capital, change management, and IT navigation and e-government.

BCG's GSA Schedule consisted of seven distinct labor categories, three of which contained multiple cohort levels, with hourly rates ranging from $54.86 for an entry-level case team support specialist to $802.99 for a vice president. It is also important to note that the rates were based upon a 44-hour workweek for vice presidents and a 52-hour workweek for all other labor categories. As we discussed previously, many of the strategy consulting firms will dilute the rates (from a standard 40-hour week) contained in their rate schedule to more adequately reflect the actual number of hours worked on a weekly basis and to make the rates appear to be more cost competitive to the naked eye. While the GSA may not be too concerned with this issue, most Fortune 500 procurement organizations will conduct their benchmarking analysis based upon a 40-hour week and will use those rates as the basis for comparison and rate negotiation purposes. With that being said, the BCG GSA rate schedule can be seen in Table 26.1.

Each of the BCG labor categories contains a detailed labor category description that provides the minimum thresholds required, from both an education and experience perspective, for each labor category. A sample description for the manager category is as follows:

Manager: BCG managers are proven professionals with four to seven years of experience at the firm. They have established track records as both outstanding consultants (for two to three years at BCG) and successful project leaders (for one and a half to three years). They gradually take on larger project management responsibilities, eventually directing a number of client engagements. Over time, they also help link BCG's work on client projects to its broader business and strategic vision. They typically have deep expertise in one or more practice areas. They coordinate the work and output of multiple project teams and work directly with senior client executives. BCG managers ensure that our work consistently reflects the goals and agendas of our clients.

The GSA does not mandate a specific format for its GSA schedule holders; given that dynamic, it can be difficult to compare and contrast

Table 26.1   The BCG GSA Rate Schedule

Labor Category	GSA Schedule Rate*	Normalized for a 40-Hour Week	
Case team support specialist	$54.86	$71.32	
Research support specialist	$145.64	$189.33	
Associate I (0–12 months in role)	$147.63	$191.92	
Associate II (13–24 months in role)	$183.54	$238.60	
Consultant I (0–12 months in role)	$269.33	$350.13	
Consultant II (13–24 months in role)	$324.19	$421.45	→ McKinsey GSA associate rate: $443–$510
Project leader I (0–12 months in role)	$378.05	$491.47	
Project leader II (13–24 months in role)	$432.92	$562.80	
Manager I (0–12 months in role)	$486.78	$632.81	
Manager II (13–24 months in role)	$540.65	$702.85	→ McKinsey GSA engagement manager rate: $840
Manager III (25–36 months in role)	$595.51	$774.16	
Manager IV (37–48 months in role)	$650.37	$845.48	McKinsey GSA director rate:
Vice president	$802.99	$883.29	→ $900

*Based upon forty-four hours per week for vice presidents and fifty-two hours for all other labor categories

service offerings, labor categories, and their corresponding rate structures for different vendors. However, the GSA does require that all vendors establish commerciality—that they have sold similarly situated services to clients at similar prices—for the items that will be offered under the schedule. Given that commerciality requirement, GSA Schedules are a very good indicator, although they tend to be slightly discounted, of the standard rate structure being offered to Fortune 500 clients within the commercial markets. As you can see, a comparison between the BCG and McKinsey schedules reveals a fairly consistent rate structure between the two companies for similarly situated staff. Based upon the commerciality requirement and my experience in negotiating strategy rates, that level of consistency extends across all industries within the commercial markets.

Let's get back to BCG and their position and brand awareness in the marketplace. From a competitive perspective, the biggest challenge that BCG faces is the fact that they, like Bain, are a distant second to McKinsey when it comes to the pursuit and delivery of corporate strategy and operations management engagements. It is pretty much that simple and that complex. BCG has very strong brand awareness, long-term and trusted advisor relationships with C-suite executives within its client base, a strong corporate culture, an excellent reputation for delivering in a timely and quality manner, a strong and influential alumni base, deep industry knowledge, a competitive pricing structure, and a broad reference base across all of the industries it serves. So from my seat, the key is to figure out the secret sauce that will allow them to compete more effectively with and take market share from McKinsey. As we have previously discussed, that is not an easy undertaking—especially in an economy where high-priced strategy services may be viewed as an unnecessary luxury within the corporate buying community. Combine that with the global war for talent, limited IT capabilities in relation to some of its competitors, and full lifecycle firms with strong value propositions like Accenture and IBM looking to expand upstream, and you have a tall order to fill.

From a market penetration perspective, BCG has a strong presence in the Middle East, Eastern Europe, and Russia, all of which are experiencing strong growth in areas that definitely complement BCG's delivery sweetspots. To the extent that BCG can continue its penetration in emerging markets, continue to expand its IT capability, and close some of the gap with McKinsey, they should be able to deliver upon their value proposition and achieve their growth aspirations.

27

Booz & Company

While a distant fourth to McKinsey, BCG, and Bain from a revenue perspective, Booz & Company provides corporate, supply chain, IT, and sourcing strategy, and operations management consulting services to Fortune 500 companies across all geographies and commercial industries. The name Booz & Company is a recent addition to the corporate strategy provider landscape, as it was not launched until July 2008, when Booz Allen Hamilton formally separated its U.S. government and global commercial consulting businesses and sold a majority interest in its U.S. government consulting business to The Carlyle Group for $2.54 billion, resulting in a significant financial windfall for Booz Allen's roughly 300 partners worldwide. The years leading up to the formal separation reflected some rather contradictory and erratic behavior that fluctuated from a formal launch of the firm's "one firm" evolution in late 2005, a global initiative under which Booz Allen Hamilton completely redesigned and migrated its organizational structure and delivery model to a full consulting lifecycle approach that would span commercial and government domains as well as the rarely crossed strategy and design and implementation chasm, to a decision less than two years later that the businesses were quite different, placed constraints upon each other, and could not coexist under the same roof.

Having been at Booz Allen Hamilton during the two years following the "one-firm" launch, I could not disagree more with this conclusion and question what, if any, competitive advantage was achieved through the separation. As we have discussed, many Fortune 500 clients are looking for a one-stop shop, a full consulting lifecycle and global firm that can work with its leadership to develop its strategy and then undertake the programs and initiatives identified during the strategy phase to successfully transform the client to a desired future state. The ability to deliver services commensurate with (client and engagement type, staff type and capabilities, team size and project duration, and leverage model) the nature of the services being provided and priced competitively with other vendors offering similarly situated solutions is a key tenet of this approach. Booz Allen Hamilton was in a unique position to deliver upon this fully integrated value proposition, as it had the trusted advisor relationships; brand awareness; reference base; reputation for delivering in a timely, quality, and cost-effective manner; organizational structure; quality and repeatable solutions and best practices within the public and private sector; and global delivery capability to transform business and operations strategy into action.

This "one-firm" message was very well received by finance and procurement executives across the Fortune 500 buying community who want to get beyond the notion that strategy firms only deliver strategy, that technology firms only develop conceptual designs, and that implementation firms only implement solutions. It was also refreshing to the client buying community, as it provided them with the ability to leverage the full delivery capabilities and sweet-spots of its trusted advisors, to minimize delivery risk, to hold its vendors more accountable, to take advantage of the natural synergies that develop during the design and implementation of strategic initiatives, and to mitigate the knowledge loss that typically occurs during the handoffs between disparate strategy, design, and implementation providers. Based upon my experience articulating the "one-firm" value proposition, Booz Allen Hamilton was able to successfully capitalize upon the "one-firm" era by expanding its delivery footprint across the strategy, design, and implementation lines of demarcation within existing clients, generating net new tactical revenue, taking market share from entrenched competitors, establishing new client relationships, and capturing new opportunities across all industries within the commercial markets. These achievements were clearly evident in Booz Allen Hamilton's consolidated financial results, as their 2007 annual report reflected sales growth of some 24 percent ($3.3 billion in fiscal year 2005 to $4.1 billion in fiscal year 2007) during the "one-firm" era. Add to this a September 2008 article in *Consulting Magazine* in which Booz & Company's Managing Director of North America stated that its commercial business has realized a compounded annual growth rate of at least 17 percent a year for the last three years, and the results speak for themselves.

Despite this apparent success and most likely heavily motivated by the significant financial incentive realized through the Carlyle investment, Booz Allen Hamilton's partnership voted in favor of the separation. As a result, Booz & Company was formally launched in July 2008 and is now operating as a stand-alone entity. The financial incentive theory was clearly reinforced in an April 30, 2009, memorandum opinion written by Chancellor Chandler in the Delaware Chancery Court regarding Civil Actions No. 3878-CC and 3934CC. The case involved a claim made by two former partners that Booz Allen Hamilton's board of directors breached their fiduciary duty of loyalty, that Booz Allen Hamilton breached its implied covenant of good faith and fair dealing in connection with a retirement contract that was entered into between the company and the plaintiffs, and that Booz Allen Hamilton and its board was unjustly enriched as a result of its actions relating to this matter. While the facts of the case are not that important and the claims were ultimately dismissed, the memorandum revealed some interesting statistics regarding the valuation of a share of Booz Allen Hamilton stock both prior to and subsequent to the transaction with The Carlyle Group. In the opinion, Chancellor Chandler states that the Carlyle transaction generated a transaction price of more than $700 per share to Booz Allen Hamilton's stockholders, reflecting a minimum $537.54 premium over its pre-transaction book value of $162.36 per share. When you consider that the plaintiffs in this case owned a combined 104,000 shares of Booz Allen Hamilton stock and that the named directors as a group owned in excess of 300,000, it becomes quite clear how this premium could have served as a significant incentive to consummate the Carlyle transaction, irrespective of any benefits that had been achieved from and the viability of the one-firm strategy.

With some 3,300 billable consultants (as reported in September 2009 by *Consulting Magazine*) in 57 offices around the world and revenues in excess of $1 billion ($1.10 billion as estimated by *Forbes Magazine* in its November 2008 listing of America's largest private companies), Booz & Company provides corporate and IT strategy and operations management consulting services to nonprofit organizations, non-U.S. government entities, and Fortune 500 companies across the automotive, consumer and media, financial services, energy and utilities, and technology and communications industries. Although Booz & Company is relatively new to the mix, it has a deeply rooted history with Booz Allen Hamilton, which was founded in 1914 by Edwin Booz who, along with partners James Allen and Carl Hamilton, helped create the management consulting profession as we know it today. Prior to the formal separation, the consolidated Booz Allen Hamilton generated approximately $4.1 billion in total sales through an employee base of some 19,000 staff deployed across some 100 offices worldwide. While the two companies were still consolidated, they received plenty of accolades including a recurring spot in *Fortune Magazine's* "100 Best Companies to Work For" and *Working Mother Magazine's* "100 Best Companies for Working Mothers."

Booz Allen Hamilton GSA Pricing

From a pricing perspective, Booz Allen Hamilton holds a GSA MOBIS Schedule, GS-23F-9755H, that contains four strategy labor categories that are based upon a 40-hour week and priced on an hourly basis. While Booz & Company may no longer sell its strategy services through this GSA MOBIS schedule, it does provide some insight into its prevailing rate structure prior to its formal separation from Booz Allen Hamilton. The Booz Allen Hamilton GSA Schedule contains a 3.8 percent annual escalation for its strategy rates and provides unique labor category descriptions that cross over six parameters including thought, leadership, analysis, value, education, and experience. A sample labor category description is as follows:

EXECUTIVE/STRATEGY OFFICER

Thought: Works directly with senior level clients to set the project strategic agenda

Leadership: Drives the project team toward desired outcomes to achieve results for clients

Analysis: Ensures project objectives are delivered in the context of industry best practices

Value: Develops new knowledge and capabilities derived from a broad range of cross industry/functional experiences within commercial clients

Education: MBA or other graduate degrees. Some hold Ph.D. qualifications in economics, finance, organizational development, or other business-related specialties

Experience: Generally over 12 years of significant experience in multiple domains across a broad range of clients; Held consulting or leadership positions in major private or public organizations in areas such as Business Strategy, Manufacturing and Supply Chain Strategy, IT Architecture Strategy, Platform Strategy, Go-to-Market Effectiveness, Global Sourcing Strategy, and Innovation Strategy

The strategy labor categories and corresponding rates are as shown in Figure 27.1.

A comparison of the McKinsey, BCG, and Booz Allen Hamilton GSA MOBIS rate structures clearly reveals a significant level of pricing consistency for strategy services that will be provided to the U.S. government. Even though the BCG rates are dated, the McKinsey rates were reverse engineered from their team-based pricing structure, and Booz & Company may no longer be selling its services through the Booz Allen Hamilton MOBIS schedule, the variance is quite nominal. Although the GSA rates were discounted from standard or list price, they do provide a good indicator as to the relative range of the hourly rates being charged by these vendors when selling strategy and operations management services to Fortune 500 clients.

Booz & Company Delivery Footprint and Competitive Positioning

Although Booz Allen Hamilton and Booz & Company are privately held partnerships, the consolidated entity has historically published an annual

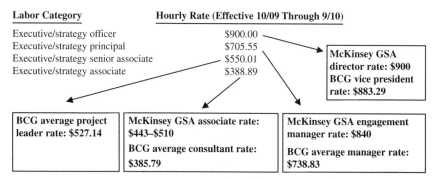

Figure 27.1   Booz Allen Hamilton GSA MOBIS strategy rates

report that identifies the primary service offerings that the firm delivers across the public and private sector. Those service offerings include strategy and leadership, corporate finance and business analysis, mergers and restructuring, organization and change, product and service innovation, marketing and sales, information technology, systems engineering and integration, operations and logistics, and public sector mission effectiveness. In addition to its core service offerings, the annual report spotlights many of the non-U.S. government and commercial client accounts for which Booz Allen Hamilton provided services during the reporting period. Those accounts include leading companies across all commercial industries as well as governments throughout Western Europe, the Middle East, and the Asia Pacific region.

The depth and breadth of its client relationships clearly provides Booz & Company with a strong reference base that it will heavily rely upon as it seeks to expand its global delivery footprint. It also has strong brand awareness (as a result of its more than ninety-year affiliation with Booz Allen Hamilton) and a reputation for delivering its services in a timely, quality, and cost-effective manner. Although it is relatively early in its tenure, Booz & Company was ranked number five in 2008 and number fifteen in 2009 in the "Best Firm to Work For" survey conducted by *Consulting Magazine*. Like the rest of their strategy brethren, they, too, have a strong alumni network that is strategically placed in senior-level positions across the public and private sector domains.

But despite this deeply rooted history, Booz & Company faces a number of significant challenges in the marketplace. By formally separating from Booz Allen Hamilton, Booz & Company's ability to position itself as a full lifecycle provider was severely detrimentally impacted. While the two firms will certainly collaborate with regard to new opportunities, the value of the "one-firm" value proposition has been diminished. The "one-firm" message resonated very strongly across the Fortune 500 procurement and buying communities and resulted in the generation of net new revenue for the firm. Without the ability to bring the downstream design and implementation capabilities of Booz Allen Hamilton to bear, Booz & Company has in effect taken the position that it will compete directly with McKinsey, Bain, and BCG for its share of the strategy consulting wallet. With BCG and Bain a distant second to McKinsey, that leaves Booz & Company with a tenuous market position. While Booz & Company has made great strides by expanding its delivery footprint into the Middle East, South America, and Asia Pacific regions, it lacks the scale of its strategy counterparts and many of the full lifecycle providers including Accenture and IBM. Clearly, Booz & Company is in its infancy stages as a stand-alone entity; time will be the ultimate judge as to whether severing the cord with the Booz Allen Hamilton mother-ship was prudent.

28

Accenture

Accenture is one of the leading management consulting, technology, and outsourcing services providers in the professional services industry. Accenture first arrived on the competitive landscape in 2001, but its roots can be traced back many years to Andersen Consulting and Arthur Andersen. Through its employee base of some 180,000 staff deployed around the globe and fiscal 2009 net revenues of $21.58 billion, Accenture provides a full lifecycle solution that includes:

- **Management consulting**—customer relationship management, finance and performance management, process and innovation performance, strategy, supply chain management, talent and organization performance

- **Systems integration consulting**—business intelligence services, custom solutions, emerging technology architectures, functional solutions, information management solutions, Microsoft solutions, open source solutions, Oracle solutions, SAP solutions, service oriented architecture, and software as a service

- **Technology consulting**—application renewal, data center technology and operations, enterprise architecture, IT strategy and transformation, network technology, performance engineering, security, and workplace technology and collaboration

- **Outsourcing services**—application outsourcing, infrastructure outsourcing, business process outsourcing, bundled outsourcing, and delivery and operational excellence

Unlike any of the strategy providers we have discussed, Accenture truly is a one-stop shop that not only can develop the requisite strategy to assist its clients in achieving some desired future state but also can design, implement, and host the solutions required for execution. The full-lifecycle solution offered by a firm like Accenture is quite appealing to Fortune 500 clients, as it eliminates the knowledge loss typically realized between the strategy, design, and implementation phases of the consulting lifecycle and yields a consulting partner that is accountable and that has a vested interest in achieving its value proposition and in delivering tangible results.

Delivering High Performance

Through its global delivery model, Accenture is focused on helping its clients achieve their respective mission and vision, and its very recognizable advertisements and tagline, "High Performance. Delivered." clearly articulates its ultimate goal. Helping its clients achieve and sustain high performance and creating sustainable value for their customers, stakeholders, and shareholders is an integral component of every solution that Accenture brings to bear in the marketplace. Accenture also practices what it preaches and is very heavily focused on achieving operational and delivery excellence and setting the standard for what it means to be a high performance business.

Becoming a high performance business is not simply about achieving short-term financial results; according to Accenture's Form 10-K for the fiscal year ended August 31, 2008, it consists of bringing the depth and breadth of Accenture's "expertise in consulting, technology, and outsourcing to help clients perform at the highest levels so they can create sustainable results for their customers, stakeholders, and shareholders."

Accenture does a tremendous job of utilizing its industry and technology expertise to help its clients make forward-thinking decisions regarding footprint expansion and revenue capture in existing markets, new market penetration, and product and service differentiation. In addition, it assists its clients in making the right decisions for all relevant stakeholders including customers, suppliers, employees, and shareholders that will yield long-term, consistent, and profitable growth; in achieving operational excellence; in instituting the right measurement and reward system; in implementing the appropriate organizational and governance structure; and in embracing technology to achieve results.

Combine Accenture's mission to help clients become high performance businesses with a large global presence (serving clients in more than 120 countries, with 44 percent of its revenue coming from the Americas, 46 percent from EMEA, and 10 percent from Asia Pacific); a diverse and talented workforce (almost 180,000 strong), which embodies a strong corporate culture; an innovative and collaborative working environment; extremely strong brand awareness; trusted advisor relationships with its clients; extensive industry and domain expertise; a robust network of alliance partners to augment delivery efforts; quality and repeatable solutions; a reputation for delivering large-scale and complex transformational and outsourcing engagements in a timely, quality, and cost-effective manner that allows clients to achieve and sustain a return on their investment; and a diversified but fully integrated delivery model that brings the right resources and technology to bear at competitive prices, and you have an extremely competitive force to be reckoned with.

In terms of its go-to-market model, Accenture structured its business in fiscal 2009 around five operating groups: Communications & High Tech (22 percent of net revenue), Financial Services (20 percent of net revenue), Products (26 percent of net revenue), Public Service (14 percent of net revenue), and Resources (18 percent of net revenue), which contained seventeen industry groups. Fiscal 2010 operating model changes include a new Health and Public Service operating group as well as a number of new industry groups. This industry focus is a distinct competitive advantage for Accenture, as it yields the ability to develop a strong bank of industry-specific intellectual capital, to develop staff with industry expertise, and to establish quality and repeatable solutions across its client base for similarly situated engagements. When clients are about to embark on a large and complex transformation or outsourcing engagement that will have an overarching impact on the success and viability of their business, they want a proven leader at the helm. With fiscal year 2009 revenues crossing over the $21 billion mark, Accenture is the partner of choice for Fortune Global 500 and Fortune 1000 companies as well as government entities worldwide. The five operating and twenty-two industry group verticals are complemented by three horizontal growth platforms that include management consulting, technology (application outsourcing, infrastructure outsourcing, and systems integration and technology), and business process outsourcing. The growth platforms bring their deep functional expertise and bank of intellectual capital to bear when partnering with the respective operating groups to design and deliver solutions for their clients. The organizational model can be seen in Figure 28.1.

This organizational structure, combined with Accenture's global presence, provides the firm with the ability to develop and deliver battle-tested and industry-specific quality and repeatable solutions in a timely, quality, and cost-effective manner. I believe one of the keys to Accenture's success in the market is that it truly embodies the "one-firm" label that so many consultancies strive to achieve. A key component of successfully delivering against the one-firm model is Accenture's ability to design and deliver solutions in a manner that is commensurate with the nature of the services being provided and competitive with other vendors in the marketplace.

COMMUNICATIONS & HIGH TECH	FINANCIAL SERVICES	PRODUCTS	HEALTH & PUBLIC SERVICE	RESOURCES
Communications	Banking	Automotive	Border management and public safety	Chemicals
Electronics & high tech	Capital markets	Consumer goods & services	Defense	Energy
Media & entertainment	Insurance	Industrial equipment	Health	Natural resources
		Pharmaceuticals and medical products	Human services	Utilities
		Retail	Postal	
		Transportation & travel services	Revenue & customs	

← Growth Platforms →
Business Process Outsourcing
Technology
Management Consulting

Figure 28.1 The Accenture organization model

Pricing and tailoring its solutions accordingly is critical in that Accenture faces intense competition across the consulting lifecycle—from strategy firms that are looking to cross over the strategy and design and implementation boundary, other full lifecycle providers such as IBM, the services divisions of many of the large technology and software providers that augment their products with consulting and systems integration services, small niche service providers that focus upon a particular industry or service offering, and offshore service providers, in India and elsewhere, that offer outsourcing services at competitive price points. All of the firms that fall within this broad competitor set are competing for the same strategy and IT wallet that may face some significant shrinkage given the current economic outlook. As we discussed much earlier in this book, I provided my thoughts on what it takes to successfully sell consulting services to the Fortune 500 client community—quality products, brand awareness, a strong reference base, and a reputation for delivering in a timely, quality, and cost-effective manner. In its fiscal year 2008 Form 10-K, Accenture articulated what it believes to be the principal competitive factors in the industries in which it competes. That list, which expands upon mine, is as follows:

- Skills and capabilities of people

- Innovative service and product offerings

- Ability to add value

- Reputation and client references

- Price

- Scope of services

- Service delivery approach

- Technical and industry expertise

- Quality of services and solutions

- Ability to deliver results in a timely basis

- Availability of appropriate resources

- Global reach and scale

Unlike the major strategy firms that are typically retained for short-term engagements with paper-based deliverable end-products and a limited amount of risk inherent in delivery, Accenture is engaged in a number of large-scale and complex transformational and outsourcing engagements with a significant amount of risk inherent in delivery. As such, its results from operations are subject to a much greater level of delivery and operational risk in a number of areas including:

- Relying upon third-party subcontractors for successful delivery

- The risk profile associated with long-term outsourcing contracts (from which Accenture derives some 40 percent of its revenue)

- Maintaining the integrity of its pricing structure as it relates to premium and commodity-like services

- Maintaining its utilization targets

- Effectively managing the organizational challenges associated with the size and global scale of its operation

- Protecting its most strategic and largest revenue producing clients

- Expanding its delivery footprint in a highly competitive environment

- Negotiating terms and conditions that yield an acceptable level of risk and reward for the company

- Ensuring compliance with internal controls, quality assurance, and risk management guidelines and policies

Let's briefly discuss Accenture's core service offerings and its competitive positioning in the market. While Accenture does have robust management consulting capabilities, it is not recognized in the same vein as the pure-play corporate strategy and operations management providers such as McKinsey, Bain, BCG, or Booz. If you took a random sample of Fortune 500 C-suite executives regarding who is their trusted advisor when it comes to crafting corporate strategy, it is typically one of these four firms. Ask the same group who they want to implement the solutions articulated in that strategy, and Accenture is always at the top of the list.

While Accenture may not have the brand awareness of the high-end strategy firms for delivering pure corporate strategy services, it brings a compelling value proposition to bear when articulating its full-lifecycle delivery capabilities. The typical Fortune 500 procurement executive is prosecuting an agenda that is very heavily focused on mitigating the knowledge loss that occurs during the strategy and implementation provider handoff, holding its preferred vendors accountable for delivering on their value proposition, tying pay to performance, and on achieving timely, quality, and cost-effective delivery. Accenture, through its extensive delivery capabilities, can address each of these areas. Given this dynamic and its management consulting capabilities, Accenture has a unique opportunity to move even farther upstream and to capture a larger share of the corporate strategy wallet.

Accenture is clearly a leader in the IT services (systems integration, technology consulting, and outsourcing) market. I have negotiated master services agreements across all industries within the Fortune 500 client community, and it was almost always a guarantee that the rate structure I was negotiating was being benchmarked against their standard preferred provider for these types of services, which more often than not was Accenture. Given its broad delivery capabilities and reputation for delivering in a timely, quality, and cost-effective manner, Accenture is not at risk of losing this position. Its ability to tailor its service offerings to the rapidly changing technology landscape, maintain the integrity of its rate structure—even when faced with low-cost competitors—and to temper its approach based upon the amount of risk inherent in delivery should reinforce its leadership across this delivery domain.

Accenture has a robust outsourcing business that accounts for roughly 40 percent of its net revenue. Accenture provides business process, application, and infrastructure outsourcing services to its clients through its extensive global delivery network which consists of some 50 delivery centers and 80,000 staff worldwide. Despite its size, scale, and level of maturity in delivering outsourcing services, Accenture's growth and significant footprint expansion in this area comes with significant financial and delivery risk. The typical outsourcing engagement is complex; may require relying upon client or contractor personnel for success; generates lower margins than strategy or IT services engagements, especially during the first year of the contract; and may result in significant financial volatility and exposure upon early termination. Compound that with extremely aggressive client contracting and negotiation processes and extreme price competition, and you are faced with a highly competitive and unpredictable component of the delivery portfolio. Accenture's share of the outsourcing market will most likely continue to grow given the current economic climate, and it will capture additional long-term contracts as companies seek to reduce costs and optimize operational efficiencies. The only operational roadblocks I envision will be maintaining operating margins, executing quality contracts, and effectively managing delivery risk.

Accenture's Pricing Model

From a pricing perspective, Accenture holds a GSA MOBIS Schedule, #GS-10F-0246L, through which it provides the following services to all U.S. government cabinet agencies:

- **Consultation**—strategic, business and action planning, performance management, process and productivity improvement, organizational assessment, and redesign

- **Facilitation**—debriefing and overall planning, defining and refining the agenda, convening and leading large and small group briefings and discussions, use of problem-solving techniques to resolve disputes, recording discussion content and focusing decision making, and providing a draft for the permanent record

- **Surveying**—defining the agenda and planning the survey design, survey development, sampling, pretest/pilot surveying, administering surveys using various types of data collection methods as appropriate, analyses of quantitative and qualitative survey data, database administration, and report production

- **Privatization support services and documentation**—strategic, tactical, and operational planning, initial study planning, comparison of in-house bids to proposed prices, most efficient organization (MEO) management studies, in-house government cost estimates development, performance work statement (PWS) development, and value determination

The Accenture schedule contains a broad range of labor categories, which are fairly prescriptive in terms of years of experience, functional responsibility, and educational requirements. A sample labor category description, for a partner-level resource, is as follows:

BUSINESS FUNCTIONS PARTNER 1

General Experience: A Business Functions Partner 1 possesses at least 12 years of experience in business architecture design implementation, change management efforts, or business process redesign.

Functional Responsibility: A Business Functions Partner has overall accountability for business solution programs. Business functions partners are responsible for product delivery and financial management of client engagements. A business functions partner performs independent quality assurance reviews of program performance and deliverables to ensure that contractual obligations are being met. Business functions partners also are recognized experts in the areas of business process redesign, business architectures, organizational change or specific industries. They lend thought leadership to engagement teams in developing creative solutions to client business problems.

Minimum Education: Bachelor's degree

The rate structure itself contains a large number of labor categories, many of which have multiple cohort levels and contain significantly lower price points than what we have seen for the strategy firms including McKinsey, BCG, and Booz. That variance is a result of the more functional nature of the services being provided and the engagement parameters (team size, staff type and capabilities, leverage model, and duration) associated with the typical Accenture engagement under MOBIS. The rate structure, which ranges from $54.95 for an assistant to $512.65 for a partner, is as seen in Table 28.1.

This rate structure highlights the challenge being faced by providers all across the consulting lifecycle that are seeking to expand their delivery footprint and move either upstream, toward the strategy end of the spectrum, or downstream, toward implementation. A strategy provider that is looking to move slightly downstream beyond its pure strategy domain, will face strong competition from firms like Accenture, and its economic model will

Table 28.1 Accenture GSA MOBIS Schedule Rates

YEAR 7: 4/19/08 THROUGH 4/18/09 MOBIS LABOR CATEGORIES	HOURLY RATE	DAILY RATE
Client financial management assistant	$54.95	$439.60
Executive assistant 1	$54.95	$439.60
Executive assistant 3	$54.95	$439.60
Executive assistant 2	$62.51	$500.08
Business functions analyst 1	$77.46	$619.68
Client financial management analyst 1	$77.80	$622.40
Client financial management analyst 2	$87.91	$703.28
Business functions analyst 2	$88.22	$705.76
Business functions analyst 3	$88.22	$705.76
Client financial management specialist 1	$95.85	$766.80
Business functions analyst 4	$100.61	$804.88
Client financial management specialist 2	$104.36	$834.88
Business functions consultant 1	$106.25	$850.00
Business functions consultant 2	$106.25	$850.00
Business functions consultant 3	$114.53	$916.24
Business functions consultant 4	$131.04	$1,048.32
Business functions manager 1	$146.25	$1,170.00
Client financial management manager	$147.42	$1,179.36
Business functions manager 2	$167.06	$1,336.48
Business functions manager 3	$180.43	$1,443.44
Business functions manager 4	$193.80	$1,550.40
Business functions senior manager 1	$213.85	$1,710.80
Client financial management senior manager	$217.50	$1,740.00
Business functions senior manager 2	$233.90	$1,871.20
Business functions senior manager 3	$274.00	$2,192.00
Client financial management associate partner	$305.57	$2,444.56
Business functions associate partner 1	$313.77	$2,510.16
Business functions associate partner 2	$346.01	$2,768.08
Business functions associate partner 3	$388.95	$3,111.60
Business functions associate partner 4	$430.86	$3,446.88
Business functions partner 1	$512.65	$4,101.20

simply not allow it the luxury of providing staff at competitive price points. Firms like McKinsey, Bain, BCG, and Booz simply don't have functional managers sitting around that they can offer at $180 per hour. So they are constrained from an economic and resource perspective, and unless they develop a new career track with a cost profile to match, they are fairly well confined by the heavy line of demarcation that resides at the end of the strategy engagement. Conversely, a firm like Accenture wants to continue its march upstream and to charge premium prices for the strategy services it is capable of delivering. But the gap from $500 per hour for a partner-level resource at Accenture to $900 per hour for a partner-level resource at McKinsey, Bain, BCG, or Booz, is significant and difficult to traverse. If given the choice, I would prefer the Accenture route, as they can maintain their firm grasp on any downstream work and slowly inch their way upstream and capture a greater share of the strategy consulting wallet. While they may never achieve the $900 or more per hour of the core strategy providers, they can augment that variance with the profit margin they realize from their downstream delivery capability.

From an overall competitive perspective, Accenture is in a very strong position given the diversity of its service offerings in the areas of consulting, technology, and outsourcing, its strong global presence, and its ability to serve as a one-stop shop for its client base. Its brand awareness, trusted advisor relationships with its largest and most strategic accounts, and reputation for delivering in a timely, quality, and cost-effective manner across the strategy, design, and implementation domains will certainly preserve its tenure as a leading provider in the IT services market. To maintain this position, Accenture will also face some significant challenges to meet its growth aspirations; it will need to continue to increase market share within each of its growth platforms; to penetrate emerging markets including Brazil, Russia, India, China, South Korea, and Mexico; and to focus upon achieving delivery and operational excellence in outsourcing and other complex engagements.

Given its strong client relationships and proven downstream delivery capabilities, Accenture should be able to continue to enhance its brand as a premium provider of management consulting services and to expand its share of the corporate strategy wallet. To achieve that objective, Accenture will have to make sure that under no circumstances does it undermine the integrity of its management consulting rate structure by bundling its services and offering premium-priced services at commodity prices. Many full lifecycle providers have a tendency to follow that approach when pursuing highly competitive opportunities. To avoid that trap, Accenture must clearly articulate to its clients that it brings the right staff and expertise to bear based upon the nature of services being provided that are priced in a manner that is competitive with the other brand-name vendors in the marketplace. There can be no exception to this rule; commingling premium and commodity resources and providing them at a blended rate would significantly impact Accenture's ability to expand its management consulting delivery footprint. In addition, the size, scale, risk profile, employee base, and delivery footprint of Accenture's business must be carefully managed to achieve its growth aspirations. But given its strong balance sheet and competitive position, Accenture seems quite well positioned for the challenge. It has a talented staff base in which it invests heavily, has won more awards than I could include in many pages of this text, is not willing to sacrifice quantity for quality, and is focused upon achieving internal operational excellence. Most importantly, Accenture knows how to execute and deliver results for its clients and has met its financial targets and aggressive growth aspirations, even in a very turbulent economy. As Fortune 500 clients embark on an uncertain future and their journey to become high-performance businesses, Accenture seems well positioned to be their preferred partner of choice.

29

IBM

IBM truly embodies the notion of a fully integrated global IT services provider. The past ten years have been witness to a radical shift in global trade, from a country-centric (and U.S.-focused) model to one that is fully integrated and operates beyond geographic boundaries. IBM has been at the forefront of this change by providing hardware, software, systems, and services to its clients to help them embrace technology to evolve their business in line with this fundamental shift in the global economy. Like Accenture, IBM serves as a one-stop shop and then some. If Accenture is the Wal-Mart of management consulting, technology, and outsourcing services, think of IBM as Super Wal-Mart, as they augment those delivery capabilities with a full suite of hardware, software, and financing solutions. Embedded within that delivery suite is IBM's global network of outsourcing and transformation delivery centers that provides maximum client flexibility by leveraging remote and in-country delivery capabilities and that optimizes cost, skills, tools, processes, methodologies, and support.

IBM, maybe more so than any other company, has embraced this global integration by significantly expanding and enhancing its talent base and broadening its delivery footprint across a number of emerging economies that have been more than willing to open their wallet to embrace the change. With some 387,000 employees deployed across 170 countries, IBM has implemented a truly global delivery model (it can easily scale across any geography) through which it tailors the right solutions for its clients by bringing technology and resources to bear in a manner that is commensurate with the services being provided and that is priced competitively with other vendors in the market. Most importantly, IBM focuses upon delivering innovative technologies and solutions that allow its clients to achieve their business objectives. Long gone are the 1990s, when innovation meant successfully implementing a PeopleSoft, Oracle, Siebel, or SAP product suite; today's clients demand innovation across all aspects of their operations and want to embrace cutting edge technology across their organization. IBM is working diligently to bring the right solutions to bear to help its clients achieve their business objectives. With some 4,000 patents received in 2008, it is clear that IBM takes innovation quite seriously. Given 2008 record revenues of $103.6 billion, they appear to be successfully executing upon driving innovation in conjunction with their one-stop-shop delivery strategy.

IBM's Product and Service Diversity

When tailoring solutions for its clients, IBM has a broad range of products and services it can draw upon that converge at the intersection of business strategy and technology. IBM has five major business segments to help it achieve that objective, which include global technology services, global business services, systems and technology, software, and global financing. In 2008, IBM derived 40 percent of its revenue from software, 42 percent from services, and 18 percent from hardware and financing. Where IBM most heavily competes with a firm like Accenture is in the global technology and global services business segments. Their service offerings in these segments include strategic outsourcing services (working with clients to reduce costs and improve productivity and operational efficiency through outsourcing select processes and operations), business transformation outsourcing (business process outsourcing and other offerings that impact the change and operation of business process, applications, and infrastructure), integrated technology services (offerings that help clients access, manage, and support their technology infrastructure and related business processes), maintenance (IT infrastructure support services ranging from product maintenance through solution support), consulting and systems integration (consulting and implementation services for client relationship, financial, and human capital management solutions, business strategy and change), and applications management (application development, management, maintenance, and support services for packaged software as well as for custom and legacy solutions) services.

In addition to its services offerings, IBM rounds out its delivery suite with a broad range of products and support services including servers, storage, microelectronics, engineering and technology services, and retail store solutions on the hardware side as well as a robust suite of middleware and operating system products including WebSphere, Information Management, Tivoli, Lotus, and Rational software, and operating systems. Finally, IBM has a global financing business segment through which it provides short-term inventory and accounts receivable financing to dealers and remarketers of IT products. This consolidated delivery suite provides IBM with the ability to bring to bear for its clients fully integrated and innovative solutions that leverage technology to its fullest advantage.

IBM's ability to expand its delivery footprint within emerging markets has been quite impressive. Operating in some 170 countries, IBM has minimized its systematic risk with such a broad geographic footprint. In 2008, some 65 percent of total revenue was generated outside the United States and revenues for the same period in the BRIC countries (Brazil, Russia, India, and China) increased some 18 percent over the prior year. But what sets IBM apart from the competition has been its definition of an emerging market. While many of the strategy-driven and more technology-driven service providers we have discussed have penetrated the BRIC countries, IBM has taken global expansion to the next level by achieving local currency growth of at least 10 percent in some fifty countries including the Czech Republic, Poland, Malaysia, Singapore, South Africa, Venezuela, and Mexico. Total revenue from this broad group of emerging market countries grew at a rate of more than 10 percent in local currency and composed some 18 percent of total revenue. For the year ended 2008, IBM certainly achieved a broad-based geographic distribution of revenue with some 21 percent of geographic revenue coming from the Asia Pacific region, 37 percent in Europe, Middle East, and Africa, and 42 percent in the Americas.

IBM's evolution since 2000 has certainly well positioned the company for continued success. They had the foresight to see the dramatic shift in the global economy and the mission-critical role that IT and business infrastructure would play in that transformation. It was clear to IBM that meeting the demand associated with that change would require implementing an unprecedented level of global integration into its delivery model. To capitalize upon that fundamental change, IBM completely retooled its business model and delivery sweet-spots by exiting a number of commodity-based businesses like personal computers and hard drives and focusing its expansion efforts on leveraging its strong IT infrastructure capabilities in emerging markets. What amazes me is the ability of an organization of this size and complexity to draw a line in the sand and to successfully evolve its business model. As a result of these changes, IBM has successfully executed upon its vision to provide services under a comprehensive global delivery network (including its supply chain, research labs, software development, and service delivery capabilities) that focuses on quality and repeatable solutions that yield timely, quality, innovative, and cost-effective delivery. This shift has yielded a 22 percent increase in revenue, a 130 percent increase in earnings per share, and a 104 percent increase in free cash flow since 2000. Combine that with some 100 acquisitions, including in July 2002 its $3.5 billion acquisition of PricewaterhouseCoopers' global consulting and technology and technology services business, capital expenditures totaling $60 billion, and some $86 billion returned to shareholders in the form of share repurchases and dividends, and IBM is certainly overachieving from a financial perspective. Its ability to successfully transform its business model has significantly minimized the volatility in its delivery portfolio (some 50 percent of its revenue is generated from recurring revenue streams) and helped it achieve its ambitious out-year growth aspirations.

IBM has extremely strong brand awareness in technology, a lengthy reference base across a broad and diverse group of industries including aerospace and defense, automotive, banking, chemicals and petroleum, computer services, construction, architecture, and engineering, consumer products, education, electronics, energy and utilities, fabrication and assembly, financial markets, government, healthcare, industrial products, insurance, life sciences, media and entertainment, professional services, property and casualty, retail, shipbuilding, telecommunications, travel and transportation, and wholesale distribution and services, and a reputation in the market for delivering its solutions in a timely, quality, and cost-effective manner. Their focus on innovation combined with their deep technology capabilities and product offerings ensures they will play a key role in the critical IT programs undertaken by their clients. Combine that with their broad range of trusted advisor relationships, and you have a clear force to reckon with. That client base numbers in the thousands and includes industry leading companies across all commercial industries. Like its competitors, it has attained trusted advisor status with many of its clients, which helps facilitate footprint expansion and reinforce its position as a full services solution provider that delivers results.

IBM's Pricing Structure

From a pricing perspective, IBM is extremely competitive and will go to extreme measures to capture new opportunities and keep its competitors at bay. They maintain a very lean cost structure with a high leverage ratio that provides them with a significant advantage in the marketplace. They will readily sign up to performance-based contracts that are predicated upon achieving significant cost savings. Unlike many of their competitors, they have a full arsenal of hardware, software, and services at their fingertips that can be used as a distinct competitive advantage to capture new opportunities or to maintain a firmly entrenched position. This portfolio approach allows a company like IBM the ability to provide technology or management consulting services at extremely aggressive prices (at no cost if necessary) for a client that either is currently, or has the possibility of becoming, a large consumer of their hardware and software product service offerings. This makes them a formidable adversary for the pure services firms with which they compete. To add insult to injury, they will make investments in new clients and opportunities if it will help them achieve their growth aspirations. They have mastered the art of pricing based upon the nature of the service being delivered and the amount of risk inherent in delivery.

As we have discussed, one of the key tenets of IBM's global delivery model is innovation and developing quality and repeatable solutions that can be disseminated across its client base. Given that approach, they are not afraid to competitively price a new service offering or solution (even if it may yield a negative short-term financial impact) because they are guaranteed to recover that investment once the service offering or expertise is perfected, as it will be successfully and profitably delivered to a global base of similarly situated clients.

IBM holds a GSA MOBIS Schedule, #GS-23F-7107H, through which it offers consulting (business process reengineering, information technology strategy, business case methodology, customer value management, and change management), facilitation, and survey services to the U.S. federal government. Their schedule contains fairly generic labor categories with a rate structure that ranges from $37 per hour for an interviewer to $338 per hour for a project executive. This rate structure is fairly typical for a consulting firm that is providing transformation services to the major U.S. government cabinet agencies. The current prevailing rates are as seen in Table 29.1.

From a risk management perspective, IBM, like its full services solution provider brethren, faces fairly substantial delivery risk given the complexity of the solutions it brings to bear for its clients. But like Accenture, IBM is not willing to sacrifice quality for quantity and is very heavily focused on continually refining its global delivery model under a "better, faster, and cheaper" approach. The future of the IT services market is unclear given current economic conditions, but given its significant recurring revenue

Table 29.1 IBM GSA MOBIS Rates

LABOR CATEGORIES	GFY 10 HOURLY RATE
Project executive	$338
Functional specialist/subject matter expert	$292
Director	$239
Senior, manager	$193
Manager	$159
Program support	$156
Consultant III	$126
Consultant II	$102
Consultant I	$79
Project assistant	$71
Administrative support	$53
Interviewer	$37

streams (some 50 percent of revenue), its global delivery model and broad geographic footprint, especially in emerging markets, and its diverse industry focus, IBM appears quite capable of weathering the storm. As we discussed, IBM has significantly restructured its operations in recent years, migrating away from commoditized products, and the overwhelmingly majority of its revenue, upward of 90 percent, is derived from software and services, which have held relatively firm during the economic downturn. Moreover, IBM's vast delivery capabilities allow it to develop and disseminate best practices (methodology, approaches, and tools) on a global basis that serve as the foundation for solutions that can be customized based upon the objectives of its client base, whether that be cost cutting, outsourcing, consulting, or systems integration. Finally, IBM has a strong balance sheet containing ample cash for continuing operations, stock buybacks, and acquisitions.

Given its clear financial strength, you might think IBM would kick back, put things on autopilot, and continue driving revenue growth, footprint expansion, and margin enhancement through its global delivery model. But that approach is clearly not within IBM's DNA. IBM is already focusing on its next evolution—the evolution that IBM refers to as a smarter planet—the notion of the infusion of intelligence into the way that the world works. To that end, IBM is focused upon developing sustainable solutions by which the systems that power the world become more intelligent—smarter traffic, smarter power grids, smarter health care, smarter food systems, smarter money, smarter telecommunications, and smarter water. Given IBM's track record in driving innovation and successfully evolving their business model, I sleep better at night knowing they are addressing the most important future needs of not just their clients, but of society as a whole. The opening quote in this book states, "In chaos comes opportunity." In his 2008 letter to IBM shareholders, IBM Chairman, President, and Chief Executive Officer Samuel J. Palmisano eloquently articulates how that approach resonates within IBM given the current economic climate. He states:

> Many companies are reacting to the current global downturn by drastically curtailing spending and investment, even in areas that are important to their future. We are taking a different approach. Of course, we must continue to improve our competitiveness. But

while we maintain discipline and prudence in the near term, we also maintain the discipline to plan for the future. We're not looking back, we're looking ahead. In other words, we will not simply ride out the storm. Rather, we will take a long term view, and go on offense. From cabinet rooms, to board rooms, to kitchen tables around the world, people are eager for change. Such a mandate doesn't come around very often—perhaps once in a generation, or once in a century. It's not something to squander. I and my fellow IBMers have no intention of doing so.

It is this type of approach that will keep IBM firmly entrenched as a leading IT solution provider for many years to come.

30

Deloitte Touche Tohmatsu

Through its staff base in excess of 160,000 and global network of sixty-eight member firms that operate within some 140 countries, Deloitte Touche Tohmatsu provides audit, consulting, management, administration, financial advisory, and tax services to its client base, which includes the world's largest companies as well as public-sector and nonprofit entities. Each of the member firms is a separate legal entity and operates in its respective geography in various forms. Although a significant portion of its staff, some 74,900, is still aligned to its traditional audit business, Deloitte has significant delivery capabilities in the management and administration (21,800 staff), tax (26,900 staff), consulting (29,600 staff), and financial advisory (8,100 staff) practice areas. Deloitte has a diversified global delivery footprint with some 47 percent of revenue generated in the Americas, 41 percent in Europe, the Middle East, and Africa, and 12 percent in Asia Pacific—each region experienced significant growth in 2008 of 12.9 percent, 22.6 percent, and 30.3 percent respectively. The composition of its revenue base and diverse service offerings certainly will serve Deloitte well during the economic crisis, and its enterprise risk and financial advisory services should be in great demand during the economic recovery as companies seek to optimize their business model and mitigate their risk profile.

Deloitte is the only Big Four firm to retain the consulting arm of its business in the wake of the Enron and other accounting scandals that plagued the industry in the 1990s (given the potential conflict of interest between their auditing and consulting lines of business), and that has proven to be a prudent decision. Privately held and managed by its 9,100 partners worldwide, Deloitte has clearly distanced itself from its Big Four brethren KPMG, Pricewaterhouse Coopers, and Ernst & Young, who have now reentered the consulting arena and are looking to aggressively expand their business advisory and consulting capabilities. To maintain its independence and avoid any perceived conflicts of interest, Deloitte does not provide consulting services to its audit clients; despite that limitation, there are ample opportunities where Deloitte can leverage the reach of its member firms and offer its full suite of delivery capabilities. Deloitte took a step to expand its reach with its May 2009 acquisition of Bearing Point's North American Public Services Practice (and some 4,200 consultants) for $350 million. With this acquisition, Deloitte will expand its delivery capabilities across the public sector as well as in a number of other areas including health care, state and local government services, and education.

The Deloitte member firms have certainly capitalized on their strong brand awareness and diverse global delivery capabilities with six consecutive years of double-digit growth (18.6 percent consolidated in their 2008 fiscal year—14.8 percent in audit, 26.6 percent in financial advisory, 22.2 percent in consulting, and 20.4 percent in tax) and total 2008 revenues in excess of $27.4 billion. Deloitte made early stage investments in Brazil, Russia, India, and China, and these investments have yielded significant returns. While Deloitte may not have the corporate strategy brand awareness of a McKinsey, BCG, Bain, or Booz, or the robust outsourcing delivery capability of Accenture or IBM, it brings a unique and compelling value proposition to bear given its diverse delivery capabilities. Unlike many of the more traditional strategy and technology competitors, Deloitte is able to differentiate itself as a consultant focused upon optimizing the business performance of its clients and utilizing its integrated services offerings and expertise in tax, financial management, human resources, strategy, operations management, IT, and multidisciplinary business advisory services to develop customized solutions for its client base. Given its size and scale, Deloitte continues to leverage its value proposition and key strategic differentiators to its advantage.

Deloitte serves a wide variety of industries including consumer business and transportation, energy and resources, financial services, life sciences and health care, manufacturing, public sector, real estate, and telecommunications, media, and technology. Its service offerings are just as diverse and include:

- **Auditing**—auditing services and global IFRS and offerings services

- **Consulting**—enterprise applications, human capital, outsourcing, strategy and operations, and technology integration

- **Enterprise risk**—capital markets, control assurance, corporate responsibility and sustainability services, internal audit, regulatory consulting, and security and privacy services

- **Financial advisory**—corporate finance, forensic and dispute services, mergers and acquisition transaction services, reorganization services, and valuation services

- **Merger and acquisition services**

- **Tax**—global employer services, indirect tax, international tax, merger and acquisition transaction services, research and development credits, tax management consulting, tax publications, tax technology, and transfer pricing

Clearly, Deloitte has strong financial acumen that serves as a common thread across its delivery model, and it has and will continue to use this capability to its advantage in capturing new opportunities and reinforcing its value proposition with current and prospective clients.

Although Deloitte is composed of a network of geographically dispersed member firms, it is very heavily focused on global collaboration and on delivering quality and repeatable solutions to its client base. When faced with a competitive business development or complex delivery opportunity, member firms can draw from their local expertise, or reach out to the global delivery network to assist in the development of innovative and timely, quality, and cost-effective solutions for their clients. When it comes to delivery, Deloitte has developed a number of sweet spots in which they have a robust bank of intellectual capital; an ironclad reference base, including a significant portion of the Fortune 500; battle-tested tools and implementation methodologies, and they are quite fierce competitors in the areas of human capital; the implementation, hosting, and maintenance of enterprise applications (Lawson, Oracle, and SAP); and technology services and integration.

Like many of its competitors, Deloitte has established trusted advisor relationships with its clients and is heavily focused on its client satisfaction metrics. While Deloitte may not be a one-stop shop like IBM or Accenture, it leverages a strong network of partnerships and strategic alliances with companies including Ariba, Cisco, HP, IBM, Lawson, Oracle, Salesforce.com, SAP, and Sun to deliver full lifecycle technology and outsourcing solutions for its clients. There is nothing wrong with this approach, as they lack the resources to develop and deliver solutions in each of the industries and geographies in which they operate, and they mitigate their risk profile by engaging a proven delivery partner and holding them accountable for achieving results. Ultimately, Deloitte focuses on its delivery sweet-spots—strategy consulting, program management, change management, risk management, human capital management, ERP implementations, business optimization, and their strong financial acumen—and minimizes delivery risk by successful leveraging their diverse group of alliance partners.

Deloitte Pricing

From a pricing perspective, Deloitte utilizes a variety of methodologies depending upon the nature of services being provided and the amount of risk inherent in delivery. They will aggressively price new opportunities to capture a new client or to expand their delivery footprint and will utilize value- or performance-based pricing to the extent that objective, measurable, and verifiable measurement criteria can be identified to gauge performance. Deloitte Consulting LLP holds a GSA MOBIS Schedule, #GS-10F-0083L, through which it provides consulting, facilitation, and program integration, as well as project management services. Its rate structure, which is at a fairly significant premium to that of IBM, contains both hourly and daily rates (which are effective until November 2010) for eight labor categories with multiple cohort levels as seen in Table 30.1.

Table 30.1 Deloitte GSA MOBIS Pricing Schedule

LABOR CATEGORY	HOURLY RATE	DAILY RATE
Partner II	$409.77	$3,278.18
Partner I	$394.21	$3,153.70
Director II	$363.09	$2,904.72
Director I	$342.34	$2,738.74
Senior manager II	$326.78	$2,614.25
Senior manager I	$311.22	$2,489.76
Manager II	$300.85	$2,406.77
Manager I	$269.72	$2,157.79
Senior consultant II	$248.98	$1,991.81
Senior consultant I	$217.85	$1,742.83
Consultant II	$181.55	$1,452.36
Consultant I	$155.61	$1,244.88
Business analyst II	$119.30	$954.41
Business analyst I	$103.74	$829.92
Project controller II	$67.43	$539.45
Project controller I	$57.06	$456.46

Deloitte provides fairly detailed labor category descriptions, which contain both a general experience and functional responsibility requirement. A sample labor category description for a Director II-level resource is as follows:

DIRECTOR II

General Experience: A Director II is a senior level position that requires a minimum of 12 years of consulting and/or directly relevant industry experience. Experience includes: executive level management and direction on client engagements, defining engagement strategy, objectives, and scope, including defining engagement deliverables, working experience in project definition and process and systems analysis, creation of competitive strategies, and integration of global solutions. A Director II is proficient in project estimation and resource planning efforts and in resolving global project issues, such as process and technical compatibility, client expectations, and timing. A Director II fosters overall soundness of analytical approach, and is able to suggest alternatives. A Director II manages project resources; champions firm initiatives, and leads developments in new business enterprises through innovation. Other experience includes coordinating multiple projects and team, and assisting clients in achieving desired program results.

Functional Responsibility: A Director II provides strong executive level management and direction. A Director II has served in this position for several years and has extensive industry knowledge and presence. A Director II not only brings a thorough understanding of the client's industry, but also has an extensive tool set of skills to solve the client's problems. This position includes being a leader in strategic, business, and action planning, maintains responsibility for formulating work standards, creating strategic project objectives, and managing client issues and feedback. In addition, the Director II directs client communications and is a senior communication person with client leaders and executives along with the Partner I.

Deloitte Competitive Positioning

Deloitte is well positioned for the future given the diverse delivery capabilities it brings to bear for its client base. Deloitte was the only Big Four accounting firm that did not divest its consulting operations; that is proving to be a prudent decision, as it has positioned itself well ahead of its Big Four brethren that have reentered the market and are playing catch-up. While the corporate strategy and IT wallet will most likely shrink going forward, it is likely that companies will maintain or even increase their investment in enterprise risk and compliance and business advisory services, both of which fall clearly within Deloitte's delivery sweet-spots. Deloitte, unlike some of its competitors, takes a very collaborative approach with its clients and is very heavily focused upon establishing a partnership with its clients that will facilitate successful knowledge transfer and sustainable results. In its GSA Schedule, Deloitte provides some commentary around its relationship agenda as follows:

It is the combination of our collaborative relationships with clients and our programmatic and technical experience that give our clients a true advantage because:

- clients are an integral part of our consulting projects—helping to ensure the effective transfer of knowledge and realization of the recommendations.

- we work with management and project sponsors to help them plan the implementation of their decisions.

- we focus on both the cultural and technical aspects of projects, recognizing that managing change is critical to successful implementation.

It is this focus upon collaboration and its unique service offerings that will continue to allow Deloitte to achieve its growth aspirations even in the face of uncertain economic conditions.

31

HP

Hewlett-Packard (HP) is the world's leading provider of products, technologies, software, and services across a client base that includes individual consumers, small- and medium-sized businesses, large corporations, and education and government entities. In 2008, HP generated some $118 billion in revenue through its expansive delivery suite, which includes personal computing, imaging, and printing products and services; enterprise information technology infrastructure, including storage and server technology and software; and customer services that include technology support and maintenance, consulting, integration, and through its $13.9 billion acquisition of EDS in May 2008, a full suite of application, information technology, and business process outsourcing services that are delivered to commercial clients in the manufacturing, financial services, healthcare, communications, energy, transportation, and consumer and retail industries. HP generates roughly 77 percent of its revenue from products and 23 percent of its revenue from services; I would expect the services component to increase with the EDS acquisition in 2009 and beyond. During fiscal 2008, HP structured its business across seven business segments, which included:

- **Enterprise storage and servers**—pedestal-tower servers, density-optimized rack servers, server blades, storage arrays, storage area networks, storage management software, tape drivers, tape libraries, and optical archival storage

- **HP services**—technology services, consulting and integration, and infrastructure, applications, and business process outsourcing

- **HP software**—enterprise IT management software, information management and business intelligence solutions, and voice and data software platforms

- **Personal systems group**—commercial and consumer personal computers, handheld devices, and digital entertainment equipment

- **Imaging and printing group**—imaging and printing hardware, supplies, and services

- **HP financial services**—leasing, financing, utility programs, asset recovery, and financial asset management services

- **Corporate investments**—HP Labs, business incubation projects, network infrastructure products, and technology licensing

Given the nature of its diverse product suite and global delivery footprint (some 69 percent of fiscal 2008 revenue was derived outside the United States), HP utilizes a broad network of sales, marketing, and distribution partners that includes retailers, resellers, distribution partners, independent distributors, original equipment manufacturers, independent software vendors, and systems integrators. Its diverse product suite certainly comes with a long and distinguished group of competitors that deliver a suite of quality products, command strong brand awareness, and maintain a lengthy reference base of satisfied clients. HP's competitor set across each of its business segments is shown in Table 31.1.

HP Competitive Positioning

With such a broad competitor set, it is critical for HP to articulate its value proposition and competitive differentiators with current and prospective clients. The key differentiators are HP's technology, infrastructure management, industry, and functional expertise; its ability to manage and operate within multivendor environments; its expertise in virtualization and automation; its reputation for collaborating with clients and partners and delivering in a timely, quality, and cost-effective manner; and its broad talent

Table 31.1 HP's Competitor Set

ENTERPRISE STORAGE/ SERVERS	HP SERVICES	HP SOFTWARE
IBM	IBM Global Services	BMC
EMC	Computer Sciences Corp.	CA
Network Appliance	Accenture	IBM
Dell	Fujitsu	
Sun Microsystems	Wipro	
	Infosys	
	Tata	
	Dell	

PERSONAL SYSTEMS SERVICES	IMAGING AND PRINTING	HP FINANCIAL
Dell	Canon	IBM Global Financing
Acer	Lexmark	Banks
Apple	Xerox	
ASUSTeK	Seiko Epson	
Lenovo	Samsung Electronics	
Toshiba	Dell	

base, which has deep expertise in the SAP, Oracle, and Microsoft platforms. Its acquisition of EDS has greatly expanded HP's technology services and outsourcing capabilities, which will allow HP to more effectively compete with IBM on a global basis. But as we all know, writing the big check is the easy part of any acquisition of this size and scale; the true test will be HP's ability to successfully integrate EDS, eliminate redundancies (a headcount reduction of some 25,000 is targeted), restructure operations, capitalize on other synergies between the two businesses, and deliver a fully integrated HP/EDS solution to its clients. I believe this notion of a fully integrated solution and one-stop shop for its large corporate customers (infrastructure technology outsourcing, data center services, workplace services, networking services, managed security, business process outsourcing, CRM and HR outsourcing, and applications outsourcing including development, modernization, and management) will be the key to HP's success in the marketplace. And HP appears to be expanding its one-stop shop footprint given its October 2009 $2.7 billion acquisition of networking-gear maker 3Com Corporation.

While this approach should be readily accepted by HP's large enterprise clients, there may be some challenges with existing EDS clients (and alliance partners) that might prefer a more software and hardware vendor-agnostic approach similar to what is promulgated by IBM. Clearly, HP will have to effectively manage the EDS integration as well as a number of other competitive pressures it faces across its business segments. In its fiscal year 2008 Form 10-K, HP identified the primary criteria by which it competes as follows:

- Technology

- Performance

- Price

- Quality

- Reliability

- Brand

- Reputation

- Distribution

- Range of products and services

- Ease of use of products

- Account relationships

- Customer training

- Service and support

- Security

- Availability of application software

- Internet infrastructure offerings

When you combine this list with the highly competitive and downward pricing pressure being encountered within many of its business segments, it is clear that HP has a tall order to fill if it is to achieve its out-year growth aspirations.

Successfully filling that order, as HP states in its 10-K, will hinge upon targeted growth, operational efficiency, and the strategic deployment of capital. HP will have to make some very critical decisions in the areas of targeted growth and capital deployment as it defines its mission for the future. One of those key decisions will be HP's future vision with regard to its location on the hardware-company versus software-and-services-company continuum. A big part of that vision will be HP's ability to execute upon its cloud computing solution, namely that all of its clients will be running their applications via a software-as-a-service delivery construct, with HP hardware via a cloud that resides right on top of one of HP's data centers. The burning question is: will it attempt to undertake an IBM-like strategy, or be true to its core as a products company and build a robust services business to augment its product offerings? As we discussed previously, IBM successfully migrated away from its lower-margin hardware business and evolved into a software and services company that generated some $46 billion of gross profit (44%) against a revenue base of $104 billion in 2008. Compare and contrast those results with HP, still very much a products company at its core, which generated some $28 billion in gross profit (24%) against a revenue base of $118 billion in 2008.

Ultimately, HP's leadership will drive this result, but this decision will have a significant impact upon its competitive positioning and financial viability in the coming years. Irrespective of this result, HP is in a strong competitive position through which it can offer a comprehensive suite of IT solutions including hardware, software, systems integration, and outsourcing capabilities. Like IBM, HP will be able to have tremendous flexibility in balancing its operating margins across its business segments and offering incentives for existing and prospective clients if they migrate to the complete HP product and services suite; ultimately, this will make HP much more cost competitive when being evaluated against firms like IBM and Accenture.

HP Pricing Strategy

From a pricing perspective, HP does not hold a GSA MOBIS schedule, so a rate structure for consulting and facilitation services is not available. EDS does, however, hold a GSA Information Technology Federal Supply Schedule, GS-35F-0323J, through which it provides maintenance and repair and IT services to all of the major federal agencies. The schedule contains a variety of labor categories that are very heavily IT focused—engineers, database administrators, architects, systems auditors, helpdesk coordinators, telecommunication analysts, and QA specialists—and varies in rate from $35.55 for a support clerk to $191.55 for a senior consultant who holds a top secret security clearance. Setting aside the labor categories that require a security clearance, the highest rate is $169.06 for a strategic program manager. While these rates are significantly less than the prevailing market rates for consulting or facilitation services, they are within the relative range of a typical GSA Information Technology Schedule through which similarly situated services would be delivered. To the extent that HP is pricing a full services solution, it does have a significant level of flexibility, as it can balance margins across business segments, which should hopefully yield a highly competitive and attractive pricing structure, especially for its enterprise clients.

Finally, the successful integration of EDS into HP's culture and operating structure is absolutely mission critical. A key to this effort will be successfully integrating the HP and EDS sales and account management functions into one cohesive organization that can cross-sell the entire suite of services into their largest and most strategic accounts. As the EDS acquisition is still fresh, these questions are yet to be answered. But I believe it is safe to say that HP will be a leading competitor and significant force to be reckoned with for many years to come across the IT services delivery spectrum.

Part 6

Closing the Deal and Staying Relevant

32

Coffee Is for Closers: You Must Close the Deal

As you are most likely able to ascertain from this chapter title, I am a big fan of the movie *Glengarry Glen Ross* and have always adhered to two principles so eloquently stated by Alec Baldwin's character, Blake. They are "coffee is for closers only" and "A-B-C: A-Always, B-Be, C-Closing. Always be closing." It is these two principles that I would always focus on when negotiating master services agreements for both strategy and IT services with Fortune 500 procurement executives. Let's revisit the agenda of the typical Fortune 500 procurement organization. As we discussed, there is not much of a mystery here; specifically, procurement wants:

- To optimize their global consulting spend and share best practices across their organization

- Fewer and more strategic preferred vendors with broad delivery capabilities

- Vendors with "skin in the game"

- Aggressive pricing (OK, as cheap as they can get) with volume and other discounts in exchange for the "preferred" vendor label

- A pricing structure that is commensurate with the nature of services being provided and competitive with their other preferred vendors— separate rate schedules for strategy and IT engagements

- Vendors that deliver best value—timely, quality, and cost-effective delivery

- Competition among vendors for commodity-like services

- An increase in compliance and reduction in maverick spending

- Efficiency gains (reduced cycle time), cost savings, and control over the buying process through the implementation of an e-procurement solution

- A performance management system under which vendors are evaluated across quality, time, and cost parameters and stripped of the "preferred" label if they fail to meet performance standards

- Business and legal terms and conditions that yield an acceptable level of risk and reward

Pricing Concessions and the Economic Climate

Addressing each of these issues with procurement might seem like something that could be accomplished in a few meetings and resolved in a matter of weeks. But I can assure you from my experience that this is absolutely not the case. I have had the good fortune of being the lead negotiator on a number of master agreements that were negotiated and executed in a matter of weeks. I have also had the misfortune of serving as the lead negotiator on master agreement negotiations that have lasted for many months. In almost every instance where the negotiation process dragged out, it was a direct result of price. Sure, there were legal and business terms and conditions that yielded some tenuous discussions, but at the end of the day, reasonable heads prevailed, and we were able to agree upon a set of terms that yielded an acceptable level of risk and reward for both parties to the transaction. But when it comes to price, procurement tends to throw reasonableness out the window in favor of achieving greater discounts. I assure you that procurement will not stop asking for more because they simply feel like they are entitled to do so and because they perceive that they have a strong BATNA. But do they? I urge you to carefully evaluate the relative strength of their BATNA in any such discussions, irrespective of where you might be in the sales or delivery process.

The current economic climate has made Fortune 500 procurement organizations even more aggressive in the negotiation process, looking for significant across the board discounts, irrespective of the brand awareness, reference base, and reputation for timely, quality, and cost-effective delivery of their vendors. In many instances, these requests may come well after the initial agreement has been executed and services delivery has commenced. So in effect, you have to revert back to A-B-C all over again. Procurement will always request an additional discount or concession and expect the vendor to comply in order to preserve the client relationship or to protect their current and future revenue stream.

With these requests, the negotiation process will quickly reach an impasse. When it does, two options will present themselves: you can panic, take the easy ground, and figure out a way to restructure the rate card or deal parameters to give in to the demands of procurement, even if those demands are completely irrational or a direct result of some action completely beyond your control. Alternatively, you can hold your ground, focus on your value proposition, and close the deal. I am not suggesting that you can't consider an alternative pricing structure, but don't just arbitrarily agree to price concessions in isolation; reconsider every component of the transaction that may impact price. If you should provide an additional discount or concession, make sure you get something in return. Be smart: if you simply agree to a price concession, it really begs the question regarding the integrity, and potential overinflation, of the initial price submission. To that end, always be cognizant of the fact that if your client doesn't trust you, then you might as well call it a day and play golf.

I Want the Cadillac

It was always about this time that Alec Baldwin would pop into my head and remind me of another great *Glengarry Glen Ross* quote: "We're adding a little something to this month's sales contest. As you all know, first prize is a Cadillac Eldorado. Anybody want to see second prize? Second prize is a set of steak knives. Third prize is you're fired." I always wanted the Cadillac (and coffee) and was simply unwilling to accept undermining the integrity of my rate structure for purely arbitrary reasons. So my message to you is simply to always be closing—from the initial meeting with procurement, throughout the negotiation process, up until the very minute that the contract is executed. Given the current concession-request-laden environment, continue to reinforce your value proposition throughout delivery; never give the client or procurement the opportunity to question the value you bring to bear in delivery. Constantly reinforcing your value proposition diminishes the merit of any arbitrary concession requests by procurement and renders them with a weak BATNA.

Everyone wants the Cadillac, but remember that Always Be Closing doesn't mean simply giving in to the demands of procurement and sacrificing your value proposition or undermining your rate structure just for the sake of being handed the keys. If you should decide to give additional incentives, concessions, or discounts, then make sure you are getting something in return—a volume commitment, preferred vendor status, access to the C-suite or to certain procurements historically reserved for other competitors, exclusive marketing rights to a particular entity or region, more favorable payment terms, changes in roles, responsibilities, or scope, or the elimination of high-risk terms and conditions. But make sure you get something in return if you pursue this course of action.

When you have given all that you want to give and believe your rates are commensurate with the nature of the services being provided and competitive in relation to other vendors in the market for similarly situated services, then I challenge you to remain calm, hold your ground, focus on your value proposition, make it clear that low price doesn't equal best value, consider alternatives, evaluate the relative BATNA strength of both parties, and be prepared to say "no." It is amazing to me how many seasoned sales and delivery executives enter a state of panic when faced with a request for concession or additional discount and are unable to tell their client "no" and state that their offer is firm and final. Frankly, I believe you may be quite surprised with the results. If you follow an "Always Be Closing" and "OK to Say No" approach to negotiation, you will be well prepared for any Fortune 500 procurement organization.

33

Expanding Your Footprint and Building a Pipeline

It is amazing to me how many firms invest the time and expense (and endure the stress and potentially heated negotiations) associated with attaining preferred vendor status and executing a global master services agreement, but fail to utilize that preferred status to their advantage to enhance brand awareness, market delivery capabilities, and facilitate pipeline development and footprint expansion. As we have discussed, the procurement landscape across Fortune 500 companies is drastically changing; procurement is centralized, more sophisticated, and very influential in the buying process, and clients are streamlining their vendor base, executing master services agreements that will govern delivery on a global basis, and anointing a limited number of preferred vendors across a set of discrete commodity and service lines.

All of this has been done to optimize and leverage global consulting spend and to hold preferred vendors accountable for timely, quality, and cost-effective delivery. While this approach has historically been applicable for commodity items such as paper and coffee, it now extends across the consulting lifecycle from strategy through design, implementation, maintenance, and ongoing operations. While many of the high-level strategy firms have historically been immune to procurement's grasp, that trend is beginning to change as well. The bottom line is that selling professional services to Fortune 500 companies has changed dramatically and will not be reversing course anytime soon. The days of decentralized procurement, multiple engagements with disparate terms and conditions and pricing structures, limited performance management, and purely relationship-based selling are gone forever. The current economic climate has pretty much guaranteed that result.

But all is not lost. The master services agreement is a very valuable weapon to have in your arsenal and can absolutely be utilized to your advantage. It gives you a reason to meet with your clients and stay relevant, even if there are no immediate opportunities on the horizon. As we discussed, the current economic climate has certainly reinforced the notion that Fortune 500 clients expect results and will hold their vendors accountable for achieving the value proposition articulated in their original proposal. One of the methods they are using to achieve this agenda is to seek out a full lifecycle services provider that can deliver a solution from strategy through implementation. Holding a master services agreement with multiple rate cards encompassing strategy (think), design (build), and implementation (run) services will squarely position vendors right in the sightline of this strategy.

The point is that both procurement executives and clients are seeking innovative solutions from new service providers that embody a better, faster, and cheaper approach. Both clients and procurement organizations are looking for alternatives from some of the entrenched providers and stagnant solutions to which they have been subject for many years. This allows you to capitalize upon this opportunity by using the master services agreement and preferred vendor status to your advantage. In effect, it is a free hunting license and communication mechanism, so use it accordingly—walk the halls, talk to procurement and potential buyers, conduct brown-bag sessions, provide sales collateral, promote your capabilities on the procurement intranet website, and participate in other activities that will educate the buying community and facilitate footprint expansion.

A common thread across the Fortune 500 buying community is that they think in line with historical procurement and delivery capabilities—that strategy firms develop strategy, that technology firms design, and that implementation firms implement. But they think this way because they are simply uninformed as to the full depth and breadth of the delivery capabilities of many of their service providers. I can tell you firsthand that they are always looking for options. So to the extent your firm has delivery capabilities that extend beyond your historical delivery sweet-spot within a client and you hold a master services agreement through which those capabilities can be sold, I challenge you to break those barriers, take any necessary steps to cross over the historically impenetrable lines of demarcation, and drive toward footprint expansion.

The path to footprint expansion will not be easy to traverse, but to the extent that you hold a master agreement, have established a trusted advisor relationship with the client, and have delivered in a timely, quality, and cost-effective manner, you should be well positioned for success. So I hope my message is clear; the master services agreement and preferred vendor status are valuable weapons that you must possess in your arsenal to successfully sell professional services to Fortune 500 clients. As the range of this weapon crosses all geographies and industries, use it to your advantage.

34

Remember: Procurement Is Your Friend

Throughout this book, I hope I have made it quite clear that procurement, while considered by many to be the evil empire, can be a valuable ally when you are selling strategy, design, and implementation services to Fortune 500 companies. Irrespective of your brand awareness, trusted advisor relationships, or delivery capabilities, I strongly urge you to build upon existing relationships and to establish new relationships with client procurement organizations, as they can serve as your ally across their buying community.

The current procurement landscape gives them significant influence in the buying process, and it is therefore critical that they understand the depth and breadth of the capabilities that your firm brings to bear as well as your value proposition. At a minimum, such relationships will give your firm insight into the RFP process, will enhance your competitive positioning with new buyers that seek counsel from procurement as to which vendors are best suited to meet their requirements, and will help facilitate footprint expansion.

The bottom line is that procurement must accept your value proposition and believe that you can deliver services in accordance with an engagement profile—staff type and capabilities, duration, leverage model, domain, and industry expertise—that is commensurate with the nature of the services being provided and priced competitively in relation to their other preferred vendors that are capable of delivering similarly situated solutions. Hopefully, they have instituted a performance management process that identifies your firm as one that has a reputation for delivering services in a timely, quality, and cost-effective manner.

Some firms have considered their delivery footprint and brand awareness to be so strong that they can circumvent procurement and continue marketing, selling, and delivering their services across their client community. While this strategy might have been successful five years ago, it is simply no longer a viable approach and will most likely have a detrimental impact on your sales efforts. The current economic climate, extreme downward pricing pressure, and desire for consistency in operations will most likely enhance procurement's power base and level of influence. Given this trend and for all of the reasons I mentioned earlier, I urge you to embrace the concept that procurement can be your friend and ally as you navigate through the Fortune 500 client community. The firms with which I have worked had the foresight to embrace this trend and to invest in building relationships with procurement in the same manner and with the same focus as they would across the client buying community.

As we discussed, the person responsible for building that relationship should not be the delivery partner; it should be someone who understands procurement's agenda, can speak procurement's language, and can be a little less emotional in the negotiation process. I assure you that this approach has yielded footprint expansion, insight into a previously noninclusive RFP process, marketing opportunities, new master services agreements with preferred vendor status, introductions to new buyers, and most importantly, the generation of net new tactical revenue. So when you are developing account plans and strategy for next year, remember that procurement is your friend, include them in your relationship map, and engage them accordingly.

35

Where Do
We Go from Here?

As I thought about the content for the conclusion of this book, I considered a number of options. I could provide a detailed summary and recap of everything we discussed, filled with some quotes and anecdotes, but I wanted to give you something practical that you could utilize long after you flipped the last page of this book. In that spirit I have decided to provide you with a list of my rules for the road—a set of guiding principles you can use in your efforts to sell professional services, to negotiate master services agreements, and to build relationships with procurement organizations across the Fortune 500 client community. These rules apply irrespective of the state of the consulting market and the broader economy. I sincerely hope these guidelines help you negotiate more effectively, achieve your sales objectives, and deliver your services in a timely, quality, and cost-effective manner. They are as follows:

1. In chaos comes opportunity.

2. Successfully selling any product or service requires brand awareness, quality products and services, and a reference base that will speak to your ability to deliver a similarly situated solution in a timely, quality, and cost-effective manner.

3. Carefully pick your entry points and delivery sweet-spots in the consulting lifecycle; proceed with caution if you intend to cross over the strategy, design, and implementation or public and private sector domains.

4. Know the competitor set within the area of the lifecycle in which you intend to focus. Specifically, develop an understanding of their value proposition, pricing structure, industry focus, relationships, and those areas where they are deeply entrenched within a particular client or industry.

5. Know the industry in which you intend to focus. Specifically, bring staff to bear who have industry-specific expertise and who can speak the client's language.

6. Bring references or go home. Unless you can provide references where you have delivered a similarly situated solution, don't expect an easy road to success.

7. Avoid being commoditized. Carefully articulate your value proposition and the distinct advantages that differentiate you from the competition. Once procurement or anyone within the buying community renders the services you are providing to be commodities, they will focus very heavily on price and migrate to the low-cost provider.

8. If you lack brand awareness, size, or a reference base, learn to crawl before you walk. Consider developing or leveraging a relationship with a larger or more entrenched industry-focused provider through teaming agreements, alliances, or joint royalty and marketing agreements.

9. If you intend to deliver services at different entry points across the consulting lifecycle and across the public and private sector domain, it is absolutely critical to differentiate the engagement parameters, staff type and capabilities, and pricing structure associated with each entry point and domain in which you intend to focus. If you only remember one rule, this should be the one. Never undermine the integrity of your rate structure (providing premium services for commodity prices), and never commingle staff across the various phases (allowing premium service staff to deliver commodity services and vice versa) of the lifecycle in which you focus.

10. Propose a rate structure that is commensurate with the nature of the services being provided and that is priced competitively with other vendors in the marketplace. If you fail to adhere to this approach, you will not succeed. Remember that strategy rates will most likely be benchmarked against McKinsey, Bain, BCG, and Booz and that design and implementation rates will most likely be benchmarked against Accenture, IBM, and Deloitte.

11. It is very difficult and costly to unseat a firmly entrenched competitor that is delivering in a timely, quality, and cost-competitive manner. It may be more prudent to focus your sales efforts on other functional areas, geographies, or components of the wallet when faced with this dynamic.

12. Build strong relationships with Fortune 500 procurement organizations, as they heavily influence the buying community and can mean the difference between success and failure. It is their perception of brand awareness, delivery capabilities, and reputation for quality that will drive your perception within their buying community.

13. Temper your negotiation and pricing approach based upon the amount of risk inherent in delivery.

14. Temper your negotiation and pricing approach based upon the geographic region in which you are engaged.

15. Temper your negotiation and pricing approach based upon the individual who is sitting across from you at the negotiation table. Always remember the "Harley Principle." Better yet, go out and buy a Harley, and always make sure to identify with the individual with whom you are engaged.

16. Remember that conflicts are created, conducted, and sustained by human beings and can be resolved by human beings.

17. Insist upon multiple rate cards—at a minimum one for strategy and one for IT-related services. There can be no exceptions to this rule.

18. Clearly articulate the different engagement parameters and the ultimate client (C-suite or otherwise), engagement type, team size and project duration, staff type and capabilities, and service line (strategy, human resources, IT, finance, etc.) associated with each rate card, and agree to work with the client to identify the appropriate card for each new opportunity.

19. *Never*, under any circumstance, commingle resources from one rate card with the other. If you commingle resources, you will completely undermine the integrity of the differentiated pricing structure and lose credibility and trust with the client. This is a problem from which you will not be able to recover.

20. To the extent that procurement is benchmarking your rates, make sure you are being evaluated against similarly situated vendors delivering similarly situated services. Work diligently with procurement on this issue.

21. Be clear regarding the firmness of the rates contained in the master agreement. Many procurement organizations encourage their buyers to consider the rate card to be merely a departure point for additional price concessions. This will clearly impact your pricing and negotiation approach.

22. Carefully review client-mandated labor category descriptions, seek relief where appropriate, and map your internal labor categories as aggressively as possible.

23. Where labor category descriptions are purely qualitative in nature (and assuming you have qualified staff), utilize upward slotting mobility to your advantage.

24. Where labor categories are not client mandated, keep the structure simple and straightforward. Fewer categories allow for much greater flexibility in the delivery process. In addition, provide labor category descriptions that are skills based and not tied to years of experience, degrees, or certifications.

25. Think carefully about the composition of the typical team you will deploy during the period of performance, and structure any specific labor category discounts accordingly.

26. Express rates in a daily, weekly, or team-based structure—shift the emphasis from the hourly rate to doing whatever it takes to deliver results.

27. Offer volume discounts where appropriate based upon a set of pre-defined contracting volume materiality thresholds, based upon the duration of the engagement, or based upon the size of the team. Offer the discount as a credit against future work (rather than as a cash rebate) to ensure a long-term pipeline with the client. In any event, keep the discounting scheme as simple as possible.

28. Make sure to include a rate escalation factor, as it will serve as the only price increase you will receive during the term of the master agreement.

29. Provide a rate card structure that serves all contemplated delivery geographies—provide rates in local currency that are commensurate with the cost profile in that country or region.

30. Agree upon the prevailing rate card (home location versus location where services are being delivered) for resources that will be crossing geographic boundaries for service delivery.

31. Agree upon a policy for rate increases and labor category re-slotting resulting from staff promotions during the course of the engagement.

32. Watch *Glengarry Glen Ross* and remember "Coffee is for closers only" and "A-B-C: A-Always, B-Be, C-Closing. Always be closing."

33. When negotiating terms and conditions, rate structures, or requests for additional discounts or concessions, carefully evaluate the relative strength of each party's BATNA, irrespective of where you might be in the sales or delivery process.

34. Given the current concession-request-laden environment, continue to reinforce your value proposition throughout delivery; never give the client or procurement the opportunity to question the value you bring to bear in delivery. Constantly reinforcing your value proposition diminishes the merit of any arbitrary concession requests by procurement and renders them with a weak BATNA.

35. If you should decide to give additional incentives, concessions, or discounts, make sure you are getting something substantive in return.

36. When you have given all that you want to give and believe your rates are commensurate with the nature of the services being provided and competitive in relation to other vendors in the market for similarly situated services, remain calm, hold your ground, focus on your value proposition, make it clear that low price doesn't equal best value, consider alternatives, evaluate the relative BATNA strength of both parties, and be prepared to say "no."

37. It is OK to tell the client "no" and to state that your offer is firm and final.

38. The master services agreement and preferred vendor status are valuable weapons that you must possess in your arsenal to successfully sell professional services across the Fortune 500 client community. As the comprehensive use of master services agreements crosses all geographies and industries, use it to your advantage.

39. Procurement is your friend.

40. In accordance with Rule #39, build upon existing relationships and establish new relationships with client procurement organizations, as they can serve as your ally across their buying community.

41. Obtain a clear understanding of the model and underlying performance metrics that procurement will utilize to gauge the effectiveness of their consultants.

42. Take the time and make the necessary investments to build and sustain long-term and trusted advisor relationships with your clients.

43. Remember that relationships matter, but it is the deal that counts.

44. Make every attempt to keep your competitive arousal in check when negotiating terms and conditions and rate cards. Focus on understanding the opposing party versus seeking to be understood.

45. The primary reason projects fail is scope creep. Develop statements of work that are narrowly tailored and free from ambiguity, and strictly adhere to a well-documented change order process for any deviations from them.

46. When it comes to acceptance criteria, you need to know only three words—*objective*, *measurable*, and *verifiable*.

47. When negotiating terms and conditions, remember that you should never absorb a particular risk if you are not best able to control the events that may lead to its occurrence.

48. Make sure you understand the top ten most frequently negotiated terms and conditions (published annually by the International Association for Contract and Commercial Management) and the relative range of risk from the perspective of both the consultant and the client. Where possible, focus on terms that promote collaboration and success rather than those that support the allocation of blame and failure.

49. Don't get engaged in sport discounting. Remember that you are no more likely to win the deal with a nominal discount than with a mid-sized discount. It takes zero negotiation skill to provide a client with what you believe to be a competitive price for your services if you only intend to discount it by 30 percent two weeks later in the negotiation process. All you are doing is undermining the integrity of your original proposal and eroding any trust you have built with the client.

50. When considering the rate structure for a long-term master agreement, think carefully about the types of opportunities in which you will be engaged, the team size and leverage model that will be required for delivery, and the other preferred vendors with whom you will be competing for opportunities.

51. When evaluating strategy rates, calculate the variance to standard across each labor category, and determine the viability of the potential rate card given the opportunities and leverage model against which you intend to deploy during the term of the master agreement.

52. When evaluating design and implementation rates, carefully review the resources, and their fully loaded cost rates, contained in the labor pool from which you will draw during the course of delivery. Carefully determine at what percentile you can draw a line and still deliver in a timely, quality, and profitable manner during the term of the agreement.

53. The use of master services and frame agreements has become the cornerstone of the sourcing strategy being implemented across all industries within the Fortune 500 client community. Given this dynamic, it is critical to hold master services agreements with all strategic clients, to build relationships with procurement executives that may influence the buying process, and to deliver in a manner that will result in the preservation of the "preferred" vendor label.

54. Be smart: if you simply agree to a price concession, it really begs the question regarding the integrity, and potential overinflation, of the initial price submission. Let us not forget the following principle: if your client doesn't trust you, then you might as well call it a day and play golf.

55. Know when to hold the line, say "no," and tell procurement that your rate structure and proposal are firm. This rule is becoming increasingly difficult given the current economic climate in which it is not uncommon for Fortune 500 clients to come back to every master agreement holder and request an additional across the board discount to all rates contained within the master agreement. If you are faced with this issue, I would suggest going back to the top of this list and pursuing strategies that may result in a cost reduction to the client that do not have a corresponding detrimental impact on the financial viability of the rate card or on the viability and likelihood of success of the solutions you will bring to bear during delivery. If you decide to offer an additional discount or incentive, make sure that you are getting something in return.

With these rules in your hand, I will look forward to seeing you in the market.

Index

ABOUT THE AUTHOR

Gary S. Luefschuetz is an attorney, certified public accountant, and operations and finance executive with extensive general management, operations, pricing, capture, negotiation, contract management, procurement and strategic sourcing, quality assurance, and risk management experience in the software and professional services industries at companies that include Accenture, Booz Allen Hamilton, Unisys, and PeopleSoft. He is a seasoned negotiator with extensive experience negotiating professional services and technology agreements across the consulting lifecycle within the public sector and across all commercial industries.

Mr. Luefschuetz has a proven track record of building trusted advisor relationships with finance and procurement executives across the Fortune 500 client community and negotiating master services agreements that encompass the delivery of management consulting, systems integration, and technology consulting services. Throughout his career, Mr. Luefschuetz has served in an advisory and board member capacity for a variety of technology companies and in conjunction with Thomson West Books published *The Art & Science of Negotiating Professional Services Agreements*. Mr. Luefschuetz received a bachelor of science in management degree from Tulane University, a master of business administration degree from The American University Kogod College of Business, and is a magna cum laude graduate of The American University Washington College of Law. Mr. Luefschuetz is admitted to the Bar in Maryland and the District of Columbia.